CONFLICTED AMERICAN LANDSCAPES

CONFLICTED AMERICAN LANDSCAPES

DAVID E. NYE

The MIT Press
Cambridge, Massachusetts
London, England

© 2021 Massachusetts Institute of Technology

All rights reserved. No part of this book may be reproduced in any form by any electronic or mechanical means (including photocopying, recording, or information storage and retrieval) without permission in writing from the publisher.

This book was set in Bembo Book MT Pro by New Best-set Typesetters Ltd. Printed and bound in the United States of America.

Library of Congress Cataloging-in-Publication Data

Names: Nye, David E., 1946- author.
Title: Conflicted American landscapes / David E. Nye.
Description: Cambridge, Massachusetts : The MIT Press, 2021. | Includes bibliographical references and index.
Identifiers: LCCN 2020021795 | ISBN 9780262542081 (paperback)
Subjects: LCSH: Landscape assessment. | Landscape protection. | Landscape assessment—Southwest, New. | Environmental policy—Southwest, New. | Nature conservation—Southwest, New. | National parks and reserves—Southwest, New.
Classification: LCC GF91.U6 N94 2021 | DDC 304.20979—dc23
LC record available at https://lccn.loc.gov/2020021795

10 9 8 7 6 5 4 3 2 1

Dedicated to my friends for more than half a century:
Elizabeth and Douglas Lewis

and

Janet and Lee Woolman

CONTENTS

ACKNOWLEDGMENTS ix

1 THE PROBLEM 1
2 THE ONCE-DOMINANT AMERICAN DISCOURSE ON NATURE 9
3 DETROIT'S RIVER ROUGE: THE LIMITS OF UTILITARIANISM 29
4 NATURAL BRIDGES: CONFLICTS OF MEANING 47
5 DISCOVERING THE COLORADO RIVER: BEYOND USE VALUE 67
6 GRAND CANYON, 1870–1940: SUBLIME GEOLOGY 87
7 SKYSCRAPER AND SKYLINE: UTILITARIAN SUBLIME 107
8 NUCLEAR ANTI-LANDSCAPES 127
9 GRAND CANYON SINCE 1945: EPHEMERAL ANTHROPOCENE 151
10 CONFLICTED LANDSCAPES 171
11 PRAGMATIC SOLUTIONS 191

NOTES 203
BIBLIOGRAPHY 231
INDEX 257

ACKNOWLEDGMENTS

The impulse that led to this book came from a year at the now closed Center for Man and Nature at the University of Southern Denmark. Its many conferences and guest speakers realigned my research trajectory to focus more on environmental issues. Chapters 4 and 5 began as talks at that center. Other chapters were presented as lectures or papers, and for these opportunities I thank Nottingham University, Mainz University, the University of Oslo, the University of Amsterdam, the Society for the History of Technology, the European American Studies Association, and the Nordic Association of American Studies.

I have learned from other scholars for decades. Debts to individuals are so numerous I find it impossible to compile a comprehensive list. But this list begins with Leo Marx, whom I studied with half a century ago at Amherst College and have since cherished as a friend and colleague. I have benefitted greatly from conversations over the years with Klaus Benesch, Mick Gidley, Richard Hirsh, Ronald Martin, Miles Orvell, Dale Carter, Ronald Johnson, Jeffrey Meikle, Rob Kroes, Lawrence Buell, Lindy Biggs, David Lowenthal, Svend Erik Larsen, Marty Melosi, Cecelia Tichi, Merritt Roe Smith, Robert Emmett, Anne Mørk, Barbara Allen, Steven Hartman, Mark Luccarelli, Thomas Zeller, the late Hal Rothman, and the late Stuart Kidd. I have also learned from lectures or papers given by William Cronon, Jacob Wamberg, Christopher Bailey, Stephen Mosley, Pia Maria Ahlback, Peter Goin, and Elizabeth Raymond.

Libraries were essential to this project, notably the University of Minnesota's Wilson Library; the British Library, London; the Brotherton Library, Leeds University; Cambridge University Library; Boston Public Library; New York Public Library; Minneapolis Public Library; Grand Canyon Visitor Center Library; the University of Southern Denmark's library; the libraries of the Massachusetts Institute of Technology; and the archives held at The Henry Ford in Dearborn.

Readers familiar with my *American Technological Sublime* (1994) or *America as Second Creation* (2003) will see that this book explores topics that are adjacent to those works. This has required a little repetition to introduce new readers to concepts such as the geometrical sublime and second creation narratives. Half of the chapters appeared as articles in Germany, Britain, or the United States, as listed below. These have been extensively revised, including additional primary sources.

Chapter 3: "Narrating the Contested Space of Detroit's River Rouge." *Zeitschrift für Anglistik und Amerikanistik* 64, no. 1 (November 2015): 27–42.

Chapter 5: "Remaking a 'Natural Menace': Engineering the Colorado River." In *Technologies of Landscape: from Reaping to Recycling*, edited by David E. Nye, 97–116. Amherst: University of Massachusetts Press, 1999.

Chapter 6: "Visualizing Eternity: Photographic Constructions of the Grand Canyon." In *Picturing Place: Photography and the Geographical Imagination*, edited by Joan M. Schwartz and James R. Ryan, 74–95. London: I. B. Taurus, 2003.

Chapter 7: "The Sublime and the Skyline." In *The American Skyscraper: Cultural Histories*, edited by Roberta Moudry, 255–270. Cambridge: Cambridge University Press, 2005.

Chapter 9: "De-Realizing the Grand Canyon." In *Emotion in Postmodernism*, edited by Gerhard Hoffmann and Alfred Hornung, 75–94. Heidelberg: Universitätsverlag C. Winter, 1997.

1

THE PROBLEM

The lands of the United States are riven with conflicts over science, religion, identity, and politics. Some of these disputes seem beyond compromise. Millions of creationists contend that the biblical flood described in the Book of Genesis carved American landscapes fewer than ten thousand years ago, a view completely at odds with the science of geology. Millions of environmentalists are furious with fracking by gas and oil companies. In western states, millions contend that the government controls too much land and throttles free enterprise. There are arguments over dams and water rights, Native American demands for protection of sacred places, lawsuits about where to put nuclear waste, protests against mines and pipelines, demonstrations both for and against new national monuments, conflicts between utilities and the Environmental Protection Agency, and scientific warnings about global warming, pesticide use, and species extinction. Americans invented the idea of national parks. They sing of pastoral landscapes—"amber waves of grain" and the "fruited plain"—and of sublime "purple mountain majesties." They identify their nation with nature but disagree about when and how nature emerged, about how to use natural resources, and about which lands are sacrosanct.

A book about this crisis requires an interdisciplinary definition of landscape that combines aesthetics, geography, and cultural history, one that recognizes that every landscape is inseparable from the technologies of agriculture, energy, transportation, and construction. The cultural geographer J. B. Jackson usefully defined "landscape" as a "composition of manmade or man-modified spaces to serve as infrastructure or background for our collective existence."[1] This definition places human beings inside the frame rather than looking at a scene from outside. It situates mankind in an evolving ecology along with plants, insects, birds, fish, and animals, and it correctly presents landscape as being always already a man-modified place. A landscape is conflicted when several groups want different "modified spaces" in the same location. Some want to develop and profit from sites that others want to preserve. An agricultural community like the Amish may come into conflict with expanding suburbia. Mining corporations battle environmentalists who want an ore-rich area to be a bird sanctuary. The Bureau of Reclamation may plan to flood part of a national monument. In some cases, a conflicted landscape may be degraded until it loses symbolic value or even until it can no longer support many life forms. It can become a fatal environment, an "anti-landscape."

Many of the conflicted landscapes examined in this book are in the Southwest. Yet this is not a history or cultural geography of that region.[2] Rather, it explores how inconsistent conceptions of nature lead to conflict. The argument is not regional but national, and it includes chapters on Detroit's River Rouge, the creation of skyscraper cities, and the mines and processing sites of the nuclear industry. Previous scholars have analyzed how White Americans idealized nature in speeches, literature, painting, photography, and architecture.[3] They noted that a majority of Americans prefer suburbs or the countryside to the metropolis,[4] and discussed why they have made national parks, monuments, and wilderness areas shrines of national identity.[5] Every country defines itself in part through landscapes; Americans invested much of their national identity in sites such as the Grand Canyon, Yosemite, and Yellowstone.[6] Unlike the Native Americans who can point to ancestral graves, ruins, petroglyphs, and earth mounds over a thousand years old, immigrant Americans, whether White, Black, Hispanic, or Asian, had no ancient North American heritage. The British had Stonehenge, Roman ruins, ancient houses, palaces, royalty, and rich local traditions, but in 1776, Americans lacked such symbolic sites and institutions. Instead, they identified their new country with the natural world that combined three conflicting conceptions of nature: utilitarian, pastoral, and primitive.[7] These competed with one another to some degree, but Americans became adept at alternating between these concepts depending upon where they found themselves. When looking at a city or factory, the utilitarian view seemed appropriate. In rural America, the pastoral ideology took precedence. And were the same person to travel to a remote mountain, the primitive aesthetic became dominant. By the middle of the nineteenth century, Americans had not one but three contradictory conceptions of nature. The primitive aesthetic celebrated the natural sublime and wilderness areas. The pastoral aesthetic lauded the fusion of nature and culture, notably in gardens, city parks, family farms, ornamental landscapes, and state and national parks. The pastoral was the middle landscape between raw wilderness and the heavily populated, built-up zones. In the utilitarian view, land was real estate that ought to be fully developed, and the most impressive improvements were appreciated in terms of the technological sublime. Each aesthetic still has institutional affiliations. The Sierra Club, Friends of the Earth, and other environmental groups focus on protecting wilderness. The National Park Service (NPS), local communities, and conservationists promote and protect pastoral landscapes. Others champion utilitarian development, including real estate developers, mining interests, chambers of commerce, the Bureau of Reclamation, and the Army Corps of Engineers. These three conceptions of nature long defined a discourse, in which most Americans slipped back and forth between contradictory ways of thinking, depending on location and circumstance.

This dominant discourse marginalized three other understandings of nature that also play a role in defining the national landscape, particularly after 1970. First, some Christians hold the creationist view that the world is no more than ten thousand years old. According to a 2013 Pew Research Center poll, one third of all Americans are creationists, who believe that human beings have always existed in their present form. An equal number, 32 percent, believe in scientific evolution, 24 percent believe a supreme being has guided evolution, and the rest are undecided.[8] One third of Americans think a great flood like that described in the Old Testament created the Grand Canyon.[9] As one geologist summarized their position, "Young-Earth creationists believe the world is fewer than 10,000 years old and that Noah's Flood remodeled it into the topography we know today in one fell swoop a few thousand years ago. . . . [However] the geological case for a global flood that creationists offer as an alternative to evolution was discredited before Darwin set foot aboard The Beagle."[10] Young earth creationists see impressive natural sites, such as Niagara Falls and Yosemite, as the Creator's handiwork. Most creationists are also "premillennialists, believing that Jesus will come soon and reign over the world before the Last Judgment."[11] For them, not only is the Earth's history brief, but it will soon end. In terms of political affiliation, a Gallup poll found that 60 percent of Republicans are either creationists or believe in "intelligent design," compared to the 38 percent of Democrats and 40 percent of Independents holding such views.[12] In recent decades, the number of creationists has increased, notably in the South and Southwest.[13]

A second challenge to the dominant conceptions of nature comes from Native Americans. In Utah, petroglyphs incised on "Newspaper Rock" include several made after the Spanish invasion brought horses to the New World. One shows a rider on horseback hunting a deer with bow and arrow (see figure 1.1). Before this image could be carved, Native Americans had to acquire Spanish horses, learn to ride them, and begin to hunt in a new way, which had occurred by the middle of the seventeenth century.[14] Newspaper Rock shows that Native American cultures were not static but readily

Figure 1.1 Carol M. Highsmith (1946–), *Portion of Newspaper Rock, Utah*, c. 2005. *Source:* Library of Congress.

adopted new tools and animals. Such images are also a reminder that since Europeans invaded North America, it has been a conflicted landscape. The conflict was not only between invaders and natives but between tribes who became more mobile once they could travel on horseback.

From the Boston Tea Party to the present, White Americans have at times appropriated tribal symbols and native identities.[15] I have endeavored to not make that mistake. I cannot decipher most of Newspaper Rock, nor can I speak for any tribe, much less for all Native Americans. Some Navajo did not want a large coal mine on their reservation, but others worked in that mine or the power station it fueled. Likewise, some Navajo want to develop tourism near the Grand Canyon, but others do not. Tribes are hardly homogeneous, yet when defining American landscapes native voices need to be heard along with those of government officials, tourists, environmentalists, engineers, corporations, and scholars. In this work I will cite individual Native Americans who reject White conceptions of nature.[16] There are tribal differences, but they share some fundamental concepts. They believe that human beings are part of a world that is alive and regard other species as their relatives.[17] As a native Hawaiian declared, "Hawaiians traditionally have viewed the entire world as being alive in the same way that humans are alive. . . . Hawaiians also viewed the land, the sky, the sea, and all the other species of nature preceding them as family."[18] One finds similar views articulated by Black Elk, a Sioux holy man, or Louise Erdrich, a contemporary Ojibwe novelist.[19] Margaret Saluskin, a Yakama, put it this way: "Salmon was presented to me and my family as our brother. The same with the deer. And our sisters are the roots and berries. And you should treat them as such. Their life to you is just as valuable as another person's would be."[20] Likewise, the landscape is inseparable from identity. An elder from Taos Pueblo declared: "The story of my people and the story of this place are one single story."[21] As these statements suggest, many Native Americans refuse to separate nature and culture, and places have transcendent meaning. Belden C Lane observed that a Navajo "sees more than the mesas, buttes, dry canyons, and twisted riverbeds observed by the casual seer. He recognizes as well another geography of transcendence that exists in, with, and under the painted desert itself."[22]

Americans whose ancestors arrived after 1492 can never assert, like Native Americans, an ancient birthright to the land or a kinship with its fauna and flora. European Americans began as outsiders, as expressed in

Robert Frost's poem "The Gift Outright," which he read aloud in 1961 at John F. Kennedy's inauguration. It begins, "The land was ours before we were the land's." Frost's "we" refers only to Europeans, who, he explains, "were England's, still colonials." The rest of the poem suggests that colonists could only overcome their separation from the new world by giving themselves to the land. This "deed of gift" required "many deeds of war." Native Americans, excluded from Frost's "we," can only read this as a reference to the wars against them.

In reply to Frost, Heid E. Erdrich, an Ojibwe, wrote "The Theft Outright."[23] Because Native Americans believe they emerged out of the earth, the poem begins, "We were the land's before we were." In contrast to the alienation that White immigrants had to overcome, the Native American feels, "We were the land before we were a people." After the European invasion and conquest, Native Americans are "possessed by what we no longer possess." Frost's phrase "deed of gift"—a legal term—is then transformed into a series of illegal actions: "the deed of theft was many deeds and leases and claim stakes and tenure disputes and moved plat markers stolen still today." Standing on the podium at John F. Kennedy's inauguration, Frost evoked the triumphant mythology of Manifest Destiny, speaking of "the land vaguely realizing westward, / But still unstoried, artless, unenhanced." Erdrich rejects the idea that Native America was incomplete, awaiting White people to provide it with stories, art, and culture: "The land, not the least vaguely, realizing in all four directions, / still storied, art-filled, fully enhanced."

Native Americans challenge Euro-American conceptions of history and nature. They also suggest alternatives. As Winona LaDuke argues, there is a "relationship between the loss of cultural diversity and the loss of biodiversity." Where Native Americans reside on their ancestral lands, "there is also a corresponding enclave of biodiversity."[24] Far from being rewarded for preserving their fellow species, however, tribal lands have often been mined, drilled for oil and gas, clear-cut for lumber, polluted by toxic waste, or expropriated for dams, military bases, and atomic tests. Places that Native Americans hold sacred have repeatedly been desecrated. The crisis of conflicted landscapes is nowhere more extreme than on tribal lands.

The last of the six conceptions of nature, in stark contrast to that of most Native Americans, is an extreme form of utilitarianism shared by extractive industries and the military. Severe land exploitation has produced sacrifice zones, or fatal environments that human beings cannot inhabit, notably places damaged by mining or expropriated by the military. For example, corporations in Picher, Oklahoma, mined zinc and lead for the military. They left behind 170 million tons of mine tailings that cover 7,000 acres and leach toxic substances into the ground and water.[25] Some residents moved away; later the government evacuated the rest, and Picher became a ghost town.[26] The military also stimulated demand for plutonium to be used in reactors and atomic weapons, creating radioactive waste. Wherever it was stored became an anti-landscape too dangerous for human beings to inhabit. Other anti-landscapes include ordnance depots, missile test ranges, and desert warfare training sites. Such fatal environments can be found in all parts of the country. Children who lived on a thirty-square mile Army base in Ohio went exploring and found "dumps and man-made deserts, ponds once used for hatching fish and now smothered in oil, machine guns rusting in weeds, clicking signal boxes," and a "field crammed with the ratty hulks of World War II Flying Fortresses."[27] Military bases cover more land in the Southwest than national parks and wilderness areas. The Goldwater Range, a test site for missiles and simulated battle in Arizona's Sonoran Desert, is as large as the state of Connecticut. Those who live on or near such bases are primarily a transient population being trained as pilots, technicians, or soldiers who do not view military spaces as landscapes in Jackson's sense. They are not a nurturing infrastructure that supports collective existence. They are fatal environments that contain chemicals, bomb fragments, and radioactive materials, even if their buffer zones may have the unintended benefit of protecting endangered species.

One cannot harmonize these six conceptions of nature (wilderness, pastoral, utilitarian, fundamentalist Christian, Native American, sacrifice zones) to create a compromise; they are divergent ideas that lead to conflicted landscapes. Here are some sample controversies: Can uranium mines be permitted on the edge of a national park or a wilderness? Should hydroelectric dam waters be permitted to flood a national monument? Should creationists be allowed to do geologic research inside the Grand Canyon? Can the military practice low-level flight over a wilderness? Is atomic testing safe for those living nearby? Should strip mining be permitted on Native American burial grounds? Historically, the official American answer to these questions has been "Yes." Should Native Americans control what they regard as a sacred site inside a national monument? May Christians build a church inside a national park? Should land taken from Native Americans for military use be returned to them? So far, the answer to these questions usually has been "No." Other questions are too complicated for a yes or no answer, such as: How can mass-production be reinvented to minimize waste and maximize recycling? What should Americans do with their tons of nuclear waste? How can national parks cope with millions of visitors?

The next chapter examines the three conceptions of utilitarianism, wilderness, and pastoralism that long defined the American discourse on nature. Subsequent chapters explain how a combination of pastoralism and utilitarianism was long dominant, but proved inadequate to comprehend natural bridges and other unusual formations such as the Grand Canyon, which explorers perceived as a "profitless locality" but later generations made a national icon. The invention of skyscraper cities occurred simultaneously with the establishment of the national parks, which offered rejuvenation to exhausted metropolitans. To millions of Americans, both the natural sublime of mountains and canyons and the technological sublime of the skyscraper city seemed quintessentially American. However, after 1945 new military uses of space destabilized these perceptions. It proved difficult to incorporate atomic weapons and nuclear waste into either wilderness or utilitarian visions of the beneficent conquest of nature. The contradictions in American conceptions of nature became ever more evident, and by the 1990s the consensus between the major political parties about national parks, monuments, and wilderness was breaking down. After 2000, most Democrats believed global warming, species extinction, and pollution were an inconvenient truth; most Republicans argued these problems were exaggerated or called them "fake news." Today, the world's environmental crisis has become intertwined with America's conflicted landscapes.

2

THE ONCE-DOMINANT AMERICAN DISCOURSE ON NATURE

Americans long identified themselves with nature, and contemporary conflicts in how they perceive it register a crisis in this national self-definition. After their Revolution, Americans developed a discourse that combined three ideas of nature: wilderness, pastoralism, and utilitarianism. That discourse embraced both growth and preservation. In the nineteenth century, as the nation expanded rapidly and transformed forests and prairies into farmland, bipartisan majorities agreed to preserve some unique sites as national parks. In the 1900s, they further agreed to set aside national monuments, and in the 1960s a broad spectrum of politicians, from Barry Goldwater and George Romney in the Republican Party to Jack Kennedy and Lyndon Johnson in the Democratic Party, agreed to set aside wilderness areas. Goldwater was a patron of the Grand Canyon in his home state of Arizona, and long before it was fashionable he made Colorado River rafting trips.

After 1970, as both tourism and population increased, politicians were pressured to choose either preservation or development, and the bipartisan national discourse on nature began to break down. How many national parks, monuments, and wilderness areas should there be? How many square miles needed to be set aside? These were not abstract problems but political issues. Designation of a monument or park prevented mining, logging, or dam building, even as it stimulated tourism. Designation of a wilderness area forever prohibited development (such as road building) or use (such as extraction of oil and gas), but it increased the value of adjacent land. Homes on the wilderness border were guaranteed solitude, minimal pollution, and prestige. A wilderness area stimulated tourism and encouraged pockets of intensive investment.

The effect of federal recognition could become what Hal Rothman has called a "devil's bargain," in which people lose control of their community due to a combination of federal restrictions and the invasion of chains of restaurants and motels and other tourist-focused businesses.[1] Land values rise as wealthy outsiders build second homes. High-end stores and services open to meet their needs. Ranchers, farmers, and other long-term residents may find their community changed beyond recognition. The borders between ordinary real estate and federal parks and wilderness become borders between different systems of meaning. On one side of the line, commercial development increases. On the other side, environmental laws prevent change. As tourism expands and local populations grow, tensions increase between these two land systems.

The tension between wilderness and utilitarianism remains a central issue. Those who value the primitive place the highest value on wild nature. Its apotheosis is unsubdued wilderness; its aesthetic is the natural sublime, especially what Immanuel Kant termed the "mathematical sublime," or the encounter with an object so great that the mind has difficulty comprehending it. This emotion is typically experienced in the presence of a vast natural scene. Two famous examples are William Wordsworth seeing the Swiss Alps for the first time and John Muir's description of the Grand Canyon. Muir wrote of "the impression of wild, primeval beauty and power one receives in merely gazing from its brink. The view down the gulf of color and over the rim of its wonderful wall, more than any other view I know, leads us to think of our earth as a star with stars swimming in light, every radiant spire pointing the way to the heavens."[2]

The first European settlers in North America tended to fear wild lands, but by the nineteenth century Americans had become enthusiastic about the natural sublime.[3] They lionized frontiersmen such as Daniel Boone as the ideal Americans,[4] and they journeyed to see Niagara Falls, the Hudson River Valley, and other spectacular places.[5] The painter Thomas Cole spoke for many of his contemporaries in an article in *American Monthly Magazine*, where he declared: "Niagara! that wonder of the world!—where the sublime and beautiful are bound together in an indissoluble chain. In gazing on it we feel as though a great void had been filled in our minds—our conceptions expand—we become a part of what we behold! At our feet the floods of a thousand rivers are poured out—the contents of vast inland seas. In its volume we conceive immensity; in its course, everlasting duration; in its impetuosity, uncontrollable power. These are the elements of its sublimity."[6] Americans began to protect unique natural sites, starting with Yosemite in 1864 and Yellowstone in 1872, creating a system of national parks shielded from commercial development. Each site was gradually organized into a series of vantage points and trails through stunning scenery.

A century later, some mountain areas and forest lands held by Native American tribes, the states, and the federal government remained largely unexploited. When the Wilderness Act was passed in 1964, some of these lands were designated as wilderness, and millions of acres were added in subsequent decades. For example, in 1974 Richard Nixon added almost six million acres of wilderness, nearly doubling its extent.[7] Wilderness seemed to be outside culture, a nature without human beings that visitors could only experience through patient self-effacement. Wilderness implied civilization as its opposite, with a range of modified landscapes in between.

By 2016 the federal government presided over 765 wilderness areas, covering 110 million acres, or 171,875 square miles, an area larger than Germany, the Netherlands, and Belgium combined. Wilderness areas controlled by states and Native American tribes are smaller but still extensive. In addition, land trusts and nature conservancies have acquired and protected tracts of land. Those who embrace the primitive vision are likely to be members of organizations such as the Sierra Club; the Massachusetts Audubon Society, which maintains twenty wildlife sanctuaries; or the Blue Ridge Land Conservancy, which protects twenty-eight square miles in Virginia. These institutions reject the utilitarian assumption that all space should be treated as real estate.

Wilderness is usually defined as the condition of nature before human beings appeared. Soon after the Native Americans arrived in North America, the megafauna disappeared, notably the mammoth, saber-toothed tiger, giant sloth, giant beaver, camel, and American horse. Because these robust and mobile species vanished during a short time, some scientists have concluded that hunters exterminated them. Alston Chase argued that wilderness disappeared ten thousand years ago when Native Americans exterminated these species, and "left behind a fragile and empty ecosystem, with many vacant niches."[8] Paleontologist Paul S. Martin asked, "Was late Pleistocene extinction so effective in upsetting the ecosystem that our National Parks, wilderness areas, and wild lands are an illusion?"[9] Other scholars contend that climate change played a central role as the glaciers retreated, but the sudden extinction itself is not questioned.[10]

At the moment of European discovery, the Americas were not a wilderness. Millions of people lived from Patagonia to Labrador and Alaska, including deserts and mountains once thought untouched.[11] Europeans brought with them invasive diseases, plants, animals, and birds that eliminated any vestige of wilderness. When Americans began to set aside parks and wilderness areas, these were cultural inventions. Early explorers of Yellowstone had the fantasy that it was a wilderness, but as Mark David Spence notes, "it had been shaped by thousands of years of human use" since the end of the last Ice Age.[12] Native Americans had trapped and hunted extensively, at times using fire to drive game. To make Yosemite and Yellowstone seem authentically pristine, the government forcibly removed Native Americans. A century later, guidebooks asserted that most of Yellowstone had been uninhabited in 1872 and that it still remained basically untouched.[13] The Grand Canyon, in contrast, became a national park after the establishment of Native American reservations there, and they were not evicted, although several attempts were made.[14]

The high value Americans place on wilderness assumes a dichotomy between nature and culture. Wilderness legislation advocates in the 1960s were fond of repeating Thoreau's statement that "in wildness is the preservation of the world."[15] As William Cronon has noted, for many environmentalists the mountains and deserts serve as cathedrals, and "wilderness presents itself as the best antidote to our human selves, a refuge we must somehow recover if we hope to save the planet."[16] Cronon argued that wilderness was a beguiling cultural production, where "we see the reflection of our own unexamined longings and desires." Americans combined the sublime with romantic individualism and imagined the western frontier as the site of regeneration.[17] As Cronon summarized, "wilderness represents a flight from history. Seen as the original garden, it is a place outside of time, from which human beings had to be ejected before the fallen world of history could properly begin. Seen as the frontier, it is a savage world at the dawn of civilization. . . . Seen as the sacred sublime, it is the home of a God who transcends history."[18] Such an idealized, pristine Nature can only flourish if human beings are absent.

Official wilderness areas can be compromised in practice. In 1989, the U.S. General Accounting Office (GAO) discovered problems during visits to ten wilderness sites. They concluded that many visitors did not have a "primitive recreational experience." Some problems were caused by the government itself, such as low-level Air Force training flights over the Pecos Wilderness. A more widespread problem was that service sites were more extensive "than needed to administer the wilderness or provide for recreational opportunities."[19] Some of the wilderness areas that the GAO studied had as many as sixteen structures including a mess hall, bunkhouse, blacksmith shop, barn, and visitor center. Where new roads and parking lots improved access to wilderness, the public caused problems, including accidental introduction of exotic weeds by pack animals, and "erosion, litter, loss of vegetation, and damage by horses." Further deterioration came from offsite noise, acid rain, and air and water pollution. The GAO also discovered seventy-four sites where marijuana had been planted secretly. Damage assessment was difficult, however, because no one had "inventoried the wilderness" and there was no baseline to measure against.[20] The GAO called for better inventories and more funding for trail maintenance, campsite cleanup, public education, and training of the already large corps of volunteers.[21] Assuming these proposals were implemented, however, what kind of wilderness needs administration, inventories, maintenance, education programs, and marijuana control?

Like the concepts of wilderness and the sublime, the utilitarian understanding of nature is rooted in philosophy, notably the work of John Locke. He argued in his *Second Treatise on Civil Government* that farmland only became valuable when linked to a market. Isolated land that had "no hopes of commerce with other parts of the world," Locke said, "would not be worth the enclosing." When he wrote in 1690, this was the case with "the inland parts of America," which remained valueless because crops raised there could not be sold. As Leo Marx noted, "Land in North America, according to Locke, is destined to remain worthless until it acquires the status of a commodity in a market or capitalist economy."[22] The duty of government, therefore, was to transform land into a commodity. This duty was undertaken even before the American Constitution was written, immediately after the Revolution. In 1785, the government established the National Land Ordinance, which imposed a rectilinear grid on the entire United States west of the original thirteen colonies.[23] Once surveyed, land could be purchased for the same price per acre regardless of its condition. Land became a commodity, and its value increased as transportation knitted the nation together. Marx emphasized that this utilitarian view of nature remains "the dominant version of the American ideology of space," in which nature is "the white on the map, empty space, untapped resources" that ought to be "discovered, subdued, and settled—made useful—by arriving Europeans."[24] In this view, raw nature has little value until it is redefined as property and becomes part of a market economy. As expressed in the surveyor's grid pattern, nature is a blank slate that human beings transform. The more complete the transformation and the more human beings dominate and control nature, the higher its economic and social value. Marshes can be drained and filled in to create agricultural land (as was done in parts of Indiana) or to create urban real estate (as was done in Boston). A river that is difficult to navigate can be damned, making it useful for transportation, generating electrical power, and stimulating local industry, as was the case with the Tennessee Valley Authority. A square of Arizona desert can be irrigated, making possible high-density settlement in an otherwise unpopulated area (figure 2.1).

This is not an ideology of half-measures but rather one of radical intervention. A young journalist in Pennsylvania once told a visiting Englishman

Figure 2.1   Carol M. Highsmith (1946–), *Portion of Scottsdale, Arizona, Aerial View*, March 2018. *Source:* Library of Congress.

that Americans "have the faith to smash up the beauty of Nature in the hope of getting something better. It would be a beautiful world entirely if there were no such thing as man. Nature's beauty has no need of us. But we happen to be here. We have something in us that Nature could never think of. [The city of] Scranton expresses man's passion more truly than the virginal beauty of the Allegheny mountains or the valley of the young Susquehanna."[25] This utilitarian vision was embodied in narratives of transformation.[26] Whether a story about using an ax to open up the forest to farming, about diverting a stream to drive a grist mill, about building a railroad to open the American West for settlement, or about building an irrigation system to make the desert bloom, in each case, a transformation of the environment was narrated as a development that occurred automatically whenever a particular technology was introduced. Build a sawmill, the argument went, and the forest will be cleared away. Build a railroad, and settlers will people the countryside. Such narratives assume a partnership with the land. Forests were chopped down, rivers dammed, mines opened, and factories built to release powers latent within nature. Development did not destroy the land but gave it full expression. Settlers completed patterns sketched out in the "raw" nature of first creation, which awaited fulfillment. In the second creation narrative Americans did not violate nature but improved it, and by doing so realized their national destiny. In such stories, the river wanted to turn a waterwheel rather than run uselessly to the sea, the prairie yearned for the plow, so it could be productive, and the desert thirsted for water. President Theodore Roosevelt declared in his first message to Congress, "The western half of the United States would sustain a population greater than that of our whole country today, if the waters that now run waste were saved and used for irrigation."[27] Implicit in such texts was the message that the waters wanted to be put to use. Each site had a higher purpose that Americans needed to discover and realize in partnership with the land. As one advocate for irrigation put it, "The man who works intelligently in creating his irrigated farm with the raw materials of land and water, knows that in this smaller sphere he is engaged in finishing the world. He feels himself to be an instrument in the process of evolution."[28]

Second creation narratives have a characteristic structure, in which a group or individual enters an undeveloped region, bringing one or more new technologies. Using them, they begin to transform the region. They prosper, and more settlers arrive. Land values increase, and some settlers become wealthy, as the first creation is replaced (and improved) by a second creation. Then the process begins again elsewhere, as some residents depart for another empty region. In this technological creation story, railways, mines, mills, and factories plant the seeds of new communities and drive their growth. The narrative of the mill village or mining town is a secular tale of success through hard work, quite unlike the religious story of the city on a hill. The center of value is not a church but a mill, railway, irrigation ditch, mine, or factory that is a natural outgrowth of its location.

Second creation stories assume constant movement into new regions. As Marx notes, "The nation's overall direction in its treatment of space has been set by the dominant progressive [utilitarian] ideology and its associated tenets: the maximizing of economic growth, trust in the operation of the market, the commodification of land, and the individualist ideal of 'success' marked by upward social mobility and the ownership of a single-family, detached home."[29] During the twentieth century these values were forcibly at work, notably in the Southwest. Utah expanded from 277,000 inhabitants in 1900 to 3 million people in 2010. During the same years, Arizona grew from 123,000 to 6.8 million, Nevada from 43,000 to 2.9 million, and Los Angeles from 102,000 to 13.2 million.[30] Migration accounts for much of the growth. Tocqueville noted already in the 1830s that Americans were restlessly moving. "In the United States a man builds a house in which to spend his old age, and he sells it before the roof is on. . . . He settles in one place, which he soon afterwards leaves to carry his changeable longings elsewhere."[31] Generations later, the U.S. Census reported that the average American moved more than eleven times during a lifetime,[32] more than twice as often as Europeans. The average British person moved five times in a lifetime; people in the Netherlands, France, and Germany four times; and Spaniards only twice. As Lane observes, "Americans are fascinated by *space*, but their attachment to particular *places* may often be negligible." Most space remains utilitarian, with only a small number of sites set aside as transcendent places of national identity.[33]

Continual geographical movement undermined close identification with any one place and encouraged the standardization of landscape. The uniformity of American cultural geography was well established by 1919, when the British ambassador Lord Bryce observed that American cities differed only in the proportions that were wood or brick. "In all else they are alike, both great and small. In all, the same wide streets, crossing at right angles, ill paved but planted along the sidewalks with maple trees. . . . In all, the same shops, arranged on the same plan . . . the same large hotels with seedy men hovering about in the cheerless entrance hall, the same streetcars. . . . Their monotony haunts one like a nightmare."[34] Bryce noted a few exceptions to this generalization, and all were colonial cities founded before the grid system was imposed, including Boston, New York, and New Orleans. Since Bryce's time, the American landscape has become even more homogeneous. Local restaurants, motels, and stores have been replaced by chains like McDonald's, Marriott, and Walmart. Suburban neighborhoods often begin as similar or identical houses, which owners modify to become somewhat distinctive within zoning constraints. Highways must adhere to uniform standards to qualify for federal funding. The traveler to a unique national park drives an interstate highway whose dimensions, contours, and signage replicate other interstates. Only a fraction of the tourists can find a room inside the park, and the rest stay at the motel chains outside its gates. Moving through this uniform landscape, the restless American often lacks a strong identification with his or her temporary place and takes little responsibility for it. Instead, Americans identify with a few unique locations, such as Yosemite or the Grand Canyon. Elsewhere, the utilitarian view of nature remains dominant.

This functionalist ideology also had its sublime aesthetics. At the apex of this system, the gridded landscape was projected outward, in transcontinental railroads, and upward, in buildings that thrust into the sky. Spectacular developments were appreciated as works of the technological sublime. This aesthetic developed in tandem with the growth of the country and was first applied to the nation's canals, railroads, railroad stations, bridges, and dams. Toward the end of the nineteenth century it expanded to include factories, skyscrapers, and airplanes, all of which were considered sublime.[35] This was not simply a matter of substituting machines and architecture for mountains. The natural sublime of the mountains evoked God, but railroads, skyscrapers, and rockets to the moon were built by human beings. People might be awed by either the natural or the technological sublime, but gazing at Yosemite or the Grand Canyon seemed an escape from history into a timeless nature, while the view from a speeding railroad or from the top of a skyscraper suggested acceleration into the future. The natural sublime revealed human insignificance compared to nature's power and immensity; the technological sublime demonstrated the power of human reasoning and the conquest of nature.

Utilitarian nature had just as weak a foundation as wilderness, for its underlying assumptions were mistaken.[36] The division of land into squares was impossible in practice, because the earth is not flat, and the actual boundaries could only be trapezoids that approximated the perfect squares called for. This approximation worked well enough where land was relatively flat and of similar quality. But the grid was imposed on mountains, deserts, lakes, swamps, stony ground, and even rivers. The grid system also imposed a system of roads that ran strictly north-south or east-west. Better roads would have respected the contours of the land. Moreover, the size of lots standardized in Jefferson's day assumed as its basic unit the single-family farm located on 160 acres of fertile land with adequate rainfall. But in the West, the land and climate were no longer like upstate New York or rural Virginia. Beyond the 100th meridian it was arid.[37]

Nor was this the worst flaw of the utilitarian vision. It also assumed the long-term abundance of land and natural resources. North America seemed so large in 1785 that the land appeared inexhaustible.[38] Yet the land available for homesteading lasted only a century, when it became clear that the United States would not remain a nation of farmers. Furthermore, the technologies of the mill, railroad, and irrigation did not benefit social classes equally, nor did they automatically raise living standards for all.[39] Finally, the utilitarian vision mistakenly assumed that nature could absorb industrialization's pollution and waste. Aside from the internal contradictions in this vision, Native Americans resisted it. To them, North America is neither wilderness nor abstract space to be carved up and sold for personal gain. The Anglo-American tradition is secular and legalistic, while Native Americans often understand the land in religious terms.

Between the extremes defined by wilderness and utilitarian aesthetics is the middle ground of the pastoral. Instead of unbridled development focused in cities, this landscape results when development is intentionally limited and fused with nature. When Jefferson advocated the national grid, he envisioned a decentralized, pastoral landscape inhabited by independent farmers. Jefferson did not want an urban society, and many of his contemporaries shared that view. They admired paintings of sublime landscapes by Thomas Cole and other Hudson River School artists.[40] They built houses encompassed by shrubs, vines, and shade trees, expressing a romantic conception of nature popularized by landscape designers and architects such as Andrew Jackson Downing.[41] They created new kinds of cemeteries that were beautifully landscaped.[42] The pastoral was also embodied in small towns, such as Concord, Massachusetts, where Ralph Waldo Emerson wrote his widely read essays, and where Thoreau built his simple house on the outskirts of town at Walden Pond.

Some painters, notably Cole, depicted the sublime wilderness in contrast to pastoral landscape. A notable example is *View from Mount Holyoke, Northampton, Massachusetts, after a Thunderstorm—The Oxbow* (1836), which depicts a nearly circular bend in the Connecticut River[43] (see figure 2.2). Cole positioned himself and the viewer in untamed, wild nature at the top of Mt. Holyoke, looking down at a pastoral valley dotted with farms. Some distant hillsides were also being stripped of trees. The scene dramatizes how rapidly civilization was clearing the land, creating fruitful fields but eliminating the pristine and the sublime. Gordon Sayre notes that the painting "neatly captures how the American landscape was changing from forest to field agriculture without passing through pastoralism," in its classical definition as a historical period between hunting and agriculture,

Figure 2.2 Thomas Cole (1801–1848), *View from Mount Holyoke, Northampton, Massachusetts, after a Thunderstorm—The Oxbow*, 1836. *Source:* The Met Fifth Avenue.

when migrating herds dominated the landscape.[44] There were scarcely any shepherds in America, however, and Cole worried about the sudden conquest of nature: "the ravages of the axe are daily increasing—the most noble scenes are made desolate, and oftentimes with a wantonness and barbarism scarcely credible in a civilized nation."[45]

To preserve something like a pastoral condition, Americans set aside state and national forests and created parks. In the 1850s, the nation's leading landscape architect Frederick Law Olmsted, who created Central Park in New York City, was employed to landscape the forty-mile carriage road into the Yosemite Valley. His design included turnouts and scenic outlooks. Olmsted understood Yosemite as a pleasing contrast between the winding Merced River on the valley floor and the sublime mountains. He wrote: "We are camped near the middle of the chasm on the bank of the Merced, which is here a stream meandering through a meadow . . . like the Avon at Stratford—a trout stream with rushes & ferns, willows and poplars. The walls of the chasm are a quarter of a mile distant, each side—nearly a mile in height–half a mile of perpendicular or overhanging rock in some places. Of course, it is awfully grand, but it is not frightful or fearful. It is sublimely beautiful, much more beautiful than I had supposed."[46] Towering over the "sweet and peaceful" meadowland, the sheer rock walls made a breathtaking contrast that Olmsted's landscaping emphasized.[47] By 1870 Yosemite had well-maintained trails and hotels, and national parks that were established later developed the same way (see figure 2.3). The national parks were designed as meeting points between pastoral and wild nature. Park buildings were rustic and hotel exteriors emphasized fieldstone and rough-hewn logs. Inside they featured large fireplaces, and decorated walls with Indian blankets, native handicrafts, mounted animal heads, and photographs of local landscapes.[48] They encouraged informal attire, but they were not Spartan. The hotels offered private bedrooms, telephones, electric lighting, hot and cold running water, steam heat, hot meals, and other luxuries.

Only a few hundred people a year came to Yosemite in the 1850s, but millions did a century later, and demand grew for solitude in undeveloped wilderness. After years of hearings, in 1964 Congress passed legislation to create wilderness areas that were to have no roads, hotels, or other human constructions, and hikers were expected to leave nothing behind.[49] The national parks provided hotels, trails, and lookouts as a pastoral foreground

Figure 2.3 John P. Soule (1828–1904), "Sentinel Rock (3,270 feet high) and Hutchings' Hotel" by the Merced River, Yosemite Valley, 1870. *Source:* Library of Congress.

juxtaposed with a vast background of wild nature; wilderness dispensed with this foreground.

Many Americans understand both national parks and wilderness areas as places where citizens transcend ordinary life through an intense encounter with wild nature that is seen as being outside of culture and yet quintessentially American. A symbol is by definition a social construction, and a "natural symbol" would seem to be a contradiction in terms. How can a natural site embody cultural meaning? The Natural Bridge of Virginia, Rainbow Natural Bridge in Utah, and Niagara Falls all existed long before any human beings—Native or European—arrived in North America. Yet these sites were appropriated as part of the national identity and preserved so that future generations might return to the moment when Europeans first arrived in North America. When designating several wilderness areas in 1984, President Ronald Reagan declared that they must remain "just as they are" so that "generations hence, parents will take their children to these woods to show them how the land must have looked to the first Pilgrims and pioneers."[50] Yet no one today has the same mental organization as a seventeenth-century Calvinist, who viewed wild nature as a threatening environment that needed to be subjugated.[51] Only 200 years later did many Americans seek either the sublime or the transcendental in nature.

Moreover, no place in the United States looks as it did in 1620. Future Americans will know that they live in the Anthropocene, where humanity leaves its mark in the geological record. They may see the national parks and wilderness areas as places where Native Americans were evicted, and as environments affected by species extinction, pollution, acid rain, and invasive species.

Lawrence Buell argues that "pastoral's internal contradictions, inherent from antiquity, have intensified since classicism began to break down in the post-Renaissance." To the extent that pastoral writing identified the nation with landscape it could become a "highly selective ideological construct."[52] Yet pastoralism also has what he terms "constructive potential," for it increases environmental awareness, undermines the assumption that human beings are the only species that have rights, and upends ideological hierarchies, such as civilized/barbarian/savage. Pastoralism can point toward either "green development" or preservation, either growth or stasis. It can take the form of a White "settler pastoral" in accounts of homesteading the West, but it can also support a counterhegemonic narrative of Native American resistance to White culture.[53]

The federal government plays multiple roles that both uphold and undermine each of the three ideologies of nature. Some of its agencies are charged with protecting wilderness areas, while others seek to stimulate economic development, including grazing, agriculture, mining, road building, logging, dam construction, and tourism. The Environmental Protection Agency (EPA) may dispute with the Bureau of Mines over pollution standards or with the Department of Agriculture over the intensity of pesticide use. The NPS is expected to both preserve and develop the same sites. Grand Canyon National Park contains wilderness areas but also roads, hotels, campgrounds, a general store, and a railroad depot. Complicating matters further, Native Americans inhabit some portions of the Grand Canyon, and they also must decide how to balance tourism and protection of the environment. The Bureau of Indian Affairs (BIA) in theory is to protect tribal interests but in practice may lease lands to mining companies or to the Department of Defense, causing serious ecological damage. As Mark Harvey notes, "Earlier in the twentieth century federal conservation agencies like the Bureau of Reclamation, Forest Service, and Bureau of Land Management" became "deeply enmeshed in the economy of western states, setting the stage for a series of sharp conflicts with preservationists who became substantially stronger in the postwar years."[54] In short, the national government plays contradictory roles.

American debates about the dangers of development have recurred for more than two centuries.[55] On the utilitarian side, the second creation narrative explained the nation's history in terms of the technological improvements. Americans developed a new form of the axe and used it to remove millions of acres of forest and create farms. They dug canals, built railroads, mastered rivers, and irrigated the desert. But counternarratives interpreted these actions not as a triumphant second creation but rather as the despoliation of habitat, as the eviction of Native Americans, as environmental pollution, and as the exploitation of labor. The utilitarian narrative presented a lumber mill as the kernel of a new community, but counternarratives argued that the mill blocked fish migration, flooded valuable land, and encouraged deforestation of the watershed. The utilitarian narrative depicted an unfinished new world that awaited technological fulfillment; the counternarratives interpreted the same events as stories of exploitation and destruction. These warring narratives concerned the majority of the land.

National parks and monuments have been removed from the property market, and therefore they remain outside these narratives, existing as a secular form of sacred space. They do not need a second creation, because they are inherently exemplary, and Americans make pilgrimages to affirm patriotic identification with them.[56] Yet business interests have not always accepted this understanding of the national parks and monuments. If Yosemite was preserved, in 1913 Woodrow Wilson signed the bill that doomed the nearby Hetch Hetchy Valley to inundation. A century later, those who drill for oil and natural gas or mine coal, uranium, copper, and other metals continue to lobby for access to federal lands, including national parks and monuments.

There are inherent problems in defining natural sites as cultural symbols. At the outset, each already had a meaning and a use in one or more Native American cultures. For example, both the Hopi and Navajo protested the development of a ski resort on the San Francisco Peaks, which they regard as sacred space. The Hopi believe the mountain was created by two of their gods. It has a prominent place in their rituals, and on a daily basis they read it as "a combination of clock, barometer, and calendar." Because it is located within the Coconino National Forest, however, the

San Francisco Peaks could be developed. That process began in the 1930s when the Civilian Conservation Corps built a road and a ski lodge on the mountain (figure 2.4). Twenty years later, lift cables were added and more skiers came. Both tribes protested these developments. The Navajo believe, "This peak was made by holy people in the beginning."[57] However, the federal courts judged that the tribes had not proven the San Francisco Peaks were "indispensable to their religious practices."[58] The ski resort expanded, and it began to make artificial snow from recycled sewage water.[59] In all parts of the United States White Americans forced developments opposed by Native Americans. Often, they expelled tribes, developed their land, and in the process erased original names and the stories that explained these sites.

The San Francisco Peaks, like many examples in this book, are in the Southwest, which D. W. Meinig defined as the area between El Paso, Texas, and the border with California, encompassing all of New Mexico and Arizona, and the southern portions of Colorado, Utah, and Nevada.[60] The region includes the lower Colorado River and the northern portions of the Rio Grande. The word "landscape" is especially appropriate here, and not only in the conventional sense of the term, as an attractive view. Tourists in this region see the mountains, deserts, and canyons as a series of striking tableaux, but they also need to find food, potable water, and shelter for the night. In other words, they live within a landscape as Jackson defined it, "A composition of man-made or man-modified spaces to serve as infrastructure or background for our collective existence."[61] This landscape includes not only scenery but also roads, farms, gas stations, and other practical arrangements. All landscapes are socially constructed. People have left their mark on the land, both intentionally and inadvertently. Native Americans hunted and farmed. Hispanic Americans introduced new domestic animals and crops. They brought to New Mexico the agricultural methods codified in *Agricultura General* by Alonso de Herrera (1470–1539), such as terracing irrigated land to avoid erosion. Herrera's work was reprinted and translated into Latin, French, and Italian. It provided detailed information on every aspect of agriculture, and contemporary New Mexico farmers who preserve traditional cultivation methods recognize it as one source of their practices, which also include Native American plants and farming techniques. The result is a permaculture quite unlike the monoculture brought by Anglo-Americans to the Southwest. In permaculture trees and plants

Figure 2.4 "San Francisco Peaks, first snow, November 2017." Both the Hopi and the Navajo consider the peaks a sacred site, and they sought to prevent creation of the Snow Bowl Ski Resort, whose trails scar the mountainside. *Source:* United States Forest Service.

are the skillfully distributed on terraced land so that the water is used to the maximum with a minimum of erosion. Herrera advised, for example, which plants could be placed on the periphery because they could manage on less water in a drought, and which trees could function as a screen to lower temperatures and slow water evaporation for plants placed behind them. Herrera did not advise annually plowing up large areas and replanting with the same crop. In contrast, Anglo-Americans superimposed the rectilinear landscape of the national grid, which defined the location of mines, roads, towns, dams, canals, and irrigation ditches, and they introduced industrial farming based on monoculture[62] (figure 5.3).

As the differences between Native American, Spanish, and Anglo-American agriculture suggest, the word "landscape" is also a verb, referring to the active process of changing the appearance of the world. Landscaping occurs continually, often not as a meticulously planned activity but as a concatenation of many choices, ranging from state laws to decorative whims of property owners who introduce new plants. Furthermore, there is no innocent eye looking at landscape; it is always seen through the lens of the prevailing visual culture. Visual conventions shape perceptions that in modern societies emerged from painting and photography and were adopted by film, television, and advertising. Landscape is not natural, but cultural. It is not merely something seen, rather it is the infrastructure of existence. Landscape is a shared creation and a collective responsibility.

The following chapters focus on conflicts between different "man-made or man-modified spaces" in the Southwest, including Native American reservations, military bases, cities, wilderness areas, national parks, and mines. Many sites embody the utilitarian conception of the land, including dams, irrigation canals, and swatches of irrigated land. The national parks and monuments, including Zion National Park and the Grand Canyon, facilitate tourism yet seek to protect their unique environments. In contrast, wilderness areas are expected to remain undeveloped, and their visitors are not to leave a trace. Other landscapes are off limits to civilians, notably the three-million-acre Nellis Air Force Base where American and NATO pilots are trained. Even less accessible is the 1,350-square-mile Nevada Test Site, fifty-six miles north of Las Vegas, where nuclear bombs have been exploded since 1950.[63] The Southwest's landscapes exemplify all six conceptions of nature discussed in the introduction. The conflicts between them have created many anomalies, including marijuana planted illegally in the wilderness, endangered species flourishing inside an atomic test site, a warm brown river made cold and blue after sitting behind a dam, artificial snow made of sewage water on mountains sacred to Native Americans, invasive plants covering a riverbank, smog blurring a sublime view, skyscrapers in the desert, dams with little water, and radioactive waste buried under monuments built to last ten thousand years.

As the next chapter shows, in contrast to the Southwest, the eastern United States has more nearly erased Native American cultures. In Michigan, utilitarian and pastoral conceptions of nature replaced Native American and French landscapes.

3

DETROIT'S RIVER ROUGE: THE LIMITS OF UTILITARIANISM

The River Rouge in Michigan was the kind of stream European settlers in North America felt they understood. Winding through forests, it slowly made its way to the Detroit River. Part of the Great Lakes watershed, with a basin of 467 square miles, it was a useful stream for explorers, trappers, hunters, or travelers. Unlike the unruly Colorado River in its deep gorge, which impeded Spanish development of the Southwest, the Rouge could be navigated to reach forests and fertile lands upriver. It suited many kinds of land use, and the river was continually reshaped. It fit the central premise of second creation stories that narrate the history of the United States as the transformation of empty space. As Tocqueville observed in the 1830s: "The Anglo-American . . . fells the forests and drains the marshes; lakes as large as seas and huge rivers resist its triumphant march in vain. The wilds become villages, and the villages towns. The American, the daily witness of such wonders, does not see anything astonishing in all this. This incredible destruction, this even more surprising growth, seems to him the usual progress of things in this world. He gets accustomed to it as to the unalterable order of nature."[1]

In settler accounts, one repeatedly finds this contrast between wild space and its transformation. Such stories erase previous inhabitants and species and ignore a place's earlier meanings and uses. Americans did not transform abstract space into place. Rather, they erased vestiges of the past to create the illusion of empty space, ready for a new beginning.[2] The River Rouge in Michigan has had several new beginnings since the early seventeenth century when it was still a homeland to Native Americans.

The dominant view in American history long was that the first inhabitants had scarcely touched the land, which remained largely wilderness until it came into European hands. Americans conceived the continent as raw and unfinished nature that awaited second creation.[3] History was understood as the movement from wilderness to civilization, from raw to refined, from birch bark canoe to railroad, from village to skyscraper city. Many factory cities emerged quickly once a river's water power had been harnessed, including Columbus, Georgia; Lowell, Massachusetts; Rochester, New York; and Minneapolis, Minnesota.[4] Later, industrial centers were based on access to coal, iron ore, and other raw materials, and they were often located where railways met waterways. The River Rouge's changing uses and conflicted meanings since colonial times provide a microcosm of North American history, from Native Americans to French fur traders to British imperialists to American revolutionaries and then to economic development from small industries to the world's largest automobile factory to a polluted Superfund site that required environmental restoration.

The River Rouge is only 125 miles long, much smaller than the Mississippi, St. Lawrence, or Colorado rivers. It emerged at the end of the last Ice Age and drains southeast Michigan into the Detroit River. Much of the low-lying area near its mouth was once marshland where Native Americans hunted and fished. On its banks in c. 1000 AD the Mound Builders constructed "elaborate enclosures, embankments and mounds . . . apparently for religious purposes." Along the Mississippi and Ohio rivers they built many mounds including large complexes near present-day St. Louis, Missouri, and Marietta, Ohio. In Wisconsin alone, they constructed more than fifteen thousand earthworks "clustered along lakes, beside rivers, and on hilltops, often arranged in complex patterns that harmoniously, even artfully, blended with the natural topography."[5] They often built at strategic locations that Europeans later developed, destroying much archeological evidence. The mounds were situated with considerable precision, including "large squares, circles and regular polygons" that required a knowledge of surveying. Several were along the River Rouge near Ft. Wayne. The largest "near the mouth of River Rouge, at Delray" was "700 to 800 feet long, 400 feet wide and possibly 40 feet in height; not all of which, however, was artificial." Standing on "top of the mound gave a commanding view of the river and may have originally carried some form of structure."[6] It was a burial site oriented to the sun and moon. Recent mathematical analysis of a mound complex in Ohio shows that they were laid out to observe "the 18.6-year moon cycle, which suggests a well-planned observation program."[7] Burial mounds linked heaven and earth, the dead and the living, the sacred and the profane.[8] This Mound Builder culture collapsed about 1200 AD.

Centuries later, European arrival and expansion drove other Native Americans westward, including the Hurons, who resettled in the River Rouge area and allied themselves with the French. Waterways were the main pathways through the region, and early settlers located in navigable areas. Etienne Brule came in 1618, followed by Jean Nicolet in 1634 and Father Jacques Marquette in 1668. Detroit was founded in July 1701 by Antoine Cadillac, who arrived with fifty soldiers and fifty artisans and traders.[9] The French erased many place names and invented new ones, including the River Rouge. Because they focused on the fur trade, the French did not seek so much to replace the Native Americans as to yoke them to the market and focus their energies on trapping. From the perspective of trading companies in Montreal and Quebec, the River Rouge was a watershed abundant in beaver, and it was best not disturbed by too many settlers. The fur trade was immensely profitable. "It was not unusual for a merchant to make a profit of one thousand percent on the trade goods to be exchanged for furs" and for the furs to appreciate another thousand percent by the time they were sold in Europe.[10] The fur trade reduced the available game, set one Native American tribe against another, and made them dependent on traders for weapons, needles, blankets, traps, and metal tools. At first a trading post, Detroit gradually became a French town, as several thousand colonists "located in the vicinity of Fort Detroit during the eighteenth century," and the dominant local language remained French until the end of that century.[11]

The British and Americans were more aggressive than the French and emphasized "expulsion of the native population from the colonized area and the creation of a frontier of separation between the two peoples."[12] They transformed the landscape from one supporting Native American cultures to one based on European agriculture. French imperialism was a more "benign articulation of the two peoples at a point of exchange. Each group operated largely within a separate territory, but bound together in an encompassing economic system, as in Canada."[13] Accordingly, the French at first had a small presence in the Detroit area. Their long rectangular lots usually bordered a river or stream, with a short side about 375 feet wide at the water's edge and running back 3,700 feet or more. On a map, these land holdings are almost as uniform as the white keys on a piano, affording each settler direct access to navigable water. By 1760 French settlements stretched for twenty miles along the shores of the Detroit River, but few lived on the River Rouge.[14]

Colonization increased after the defeat of Chief Pontiac in 1763 and the British victory in the French and Indian War.[15] Yet British Detroit remained a major trading post for Native Americans. In 1781, a party of Whites traveling from Ohio to Michigan observed, "We met today, as indeed every day as far as Detroit, a multitude of Indians of various nations, who were all bringing from Detroit horse loads of wares and gifts, and in such number that one would think they must have emptied all Detroit."[16] As American settlers began to push out the Native Americans, they imposed the grid system of land division that ignored local topography and effectively erased much of the past.[17] Yet many French remained, and their long rectangular lots persisted. One traveler in 1797 thought Detroit then looked much like a much smaller version of Quebec,[18] and when Tocqueville sailed into Detroit in the 1830s, he recognized French features in the architecture.[19]

If some French boundary lines remained visible on Detroit maps, they were engulfed by the American grid.[20] Its geometrical pattern effectively proclaimed that the entire region was open to development, and that every part of it had potential use value, whether wetland or forest, Indian mound or meadow. New roads articulated the grid pattern. Improved transportation opened up Michigan's "gridded wilderness," where "industrious settlers could shape the land." Steamboats first arrived from Buffalo in 1818, and local railways were already being planned in 1836.[21] As John Stilgoe has shown, Americans imposed nearly identical landscapes in all parts of the nation. "By 1845 a great skein of remarkably similar forms overlay the distinctly regional artifacts dating to colonial times," he wrote.[22] In later decades the same skein was overlaid on the lands conquered from Mexico, signaling their absorption into the utilitarian conception of landscape. There was little concern with preservation of either natural or historic monuments. In Detroit, the great mound at the entrance to the River Rouge was "dug away and removed, by wagon load and boat load, and little notice taken of its contents, until now [1887] it is but a miniature of its former self."[23] A local resident noted, "The relic-hunter finds over the whole surface a curious intermingling of the old and the new;—glass, pieces of crockery, iron and other articles of modern housekeeping are in close communion with flint implements, antique pot-sherds, and Indian trinkets, and with bits of brass and iron that once belonged to the accoutrements of the British soldier."[24] The mound was no longer visible in a depiction of the site in 1884 (figure 3.1). Most traces of the first French

Figure 3.1 *Mouth of River Rouge*, Detroit, 1884. The Indian mound had been removed by this time. *Source:* Unknown artist. Courtesy of The Henry Ford.

settlement also disappeared, and the city's layout seemed familiar to any American newcomer.

The countryside was also transformed. Much of the River Rouge area was forested until westward expansion into the treeless Great Plains created demand for Michigan's lumber. Loggers exploited the Rouge watershed, sending logs down to sawmills near the mouth of the river. Part of the demand came from railroads, which needed ties to hold their rails in place. In 1830, the first American railroad line was begun in Baltimore, and by the 1850s railroads linked Detroit to the national market. Tracks were laid alongside the River Rouge as well, and its shores became an industrial zone. In the 1880s, more than $8 million was invested to dredge several miles of its channel, so that factories there could receive larger ships. This new iteration of the site erased hunting, trapping, logging, and farming, as the Rouge Improvement Company built an industrial park. Its factories produced iron stoves and other metal products, and, using the Solvay process, transformed salt into soda ash and caustic soda. By 1890, Detroit employed 38,000 industrial workers,[25] and its population had reached 206,000.[26]

Few traces of these earlier industrial uses of the Rouge remain, however, and one recent publication mistakenly assumed the region remained rural until 1915, when the Ford Motor Company sent anonymous agents into the area to purchase 2,000 acres.[27] The company itself contributed to the myth that the river was undeveloped until it bought land there. A 1935 public relations brochure declared, "Twenty years ago the River Rouge went its placid way, sleepy, unknown and unsung. Drowsy fishermen in flat-bottomed boats formed its major traffic."[28] This was a more accurate description of the Rouge upstream, where Henry Ford and his wife Clara purchased 1,300 acres of farmland. In 1916, they moved into a new fifty-six-room mansion, Fair Lane, which was reflected in the river. Its grounds, including woods, meadows, and gardens, covered an area slightly larger than the Rouge factory built soon afterward.

Like many Americans, the Fords simultaneously embraced both the utilitarian and the pastoral. They became friends with the naturalist author John Burroughs who had written so well about the Grand Canyon. He had known another of Henry Ford's favorite authors, Ralph Waldo Emerson, and was widely perceived as an heir to the Transcendentalists.[29] The two men shared a love of birds and nature, and they visited Walden Pond together in 1913. They also took several vacations in remote rural areas along with Thomas Edison and Harvey Firestone.[30] In 1914 Ford gave Burroughs a new Model T touring car, and in 1916 he dedicated a grotto to him on the grounds behind Fair Lane. It contained a statue of the naturalist, a stone bearing his signature, and a heated bird bath.[31]

The friendship with Burroughs developed during the same years that Ford's company perfected the moving assembly line, which was the culmination of the nineteenth-century drive for efficiency in production through increasing the subdivision of labor, the standardization of parts, and improvements in machine design.[32] A series of incremental improvements coalesced to make possible its quantum leap in productivity. Until 1910 each of the thousands of parts that went into an automobile was carried to the spot where a vehicle was being put together. The procedure was similar to how wagons had been built for centuries. A few years later the parts were being delivered to workers at stations on a long assembly line. Each man stayed in one place and performed one or two tasks as the product moved by. The idea seems simple in retrospect, but it was only possible at a factory that made large quantities of a complex product. Such a factory required electric motors rather than overhead line shafts to transmit power, for this imparted enormous flexibility to the layout of the factory, enabling a conveyor belt, furnace, drill press, lathe, or other tool to be placed anywhere needed along the line. It also required sophisticated machine tools that could make parts to such precise specifications that they were absolutely identical. Once Ford had amalgamated these elements and retrained his workforce, the speed of production at his new Highland Park factory doubled and redoubled. Yet Highland Park had been built before the assembly line was invented, and Ford decided that to scale up production to the maximum he would build a new factory on the River Rouge. Just as New Yorkers tore down and replaced skyscrapers, leading industrialists engaged in what Joseph Schumpeter called "creative destruction," in their quest for greater efficiency, larger market share, and additional innovations.[33] The new River Rouge plant replaced Highland Park and grew into the world's largest industrial complex, yet it too would eventually become the relic of an earlier age.

The River Rouge plant stamped a new geometry on the land, excavating, filling, flattening, and imposing an industrial order. The last two and half miles of the river were transformed into a canal twenty-one-feet deep, and a shortcut was dug to the Detroit River, while the curving older channel was also dredged and maintained.[34] Both entrances could admit larger ships and the banks became docking areas. This reconstruction of nature was not unique to the River Rouge. All across the United States the Army Corps of Engineers and the Bureau of Reclamation were taking control of rivers.[35] The growing electrical utilities also were constructing large dams, and the transformation of the Rouge could be compared to the Conowingo Dam project in Maryland near the mouth of the Susquehanna River. This was an immense undertaking. The dam was 4,700 feet long and as high as a ten-story building. Its powerhouse was as large as the Equitable Building in New York City, and its seven turbines were in 1927 the largest ever constructed, each producing 54,000 horsepower.[36] The transformation of rivers for industrial purposes was characteristic during the 1920s, the era of mass production and high modernism. There is a direct line from such projects to the New Deal's Tennessee Valley Authority, Grand Coulee Dam, and Hoover Dam on the Colorado.[37]

When Ford completed the River Rouge plant, it covered 1,096 acres, not counting access roads and parking lots (figure 3.2). The materials used

Figure 3.2 "Ford River Rouge Plant, the Largest Factory in the World," Detroit Publishing Co., c. 1935. *Source:* Library of Congress.

to build it arrived at the canal slip on freighters and barges that discharged iron ore, limestone, coal, bricks, wood, wire, and tiles.[38] The new factory exemplified the vertical integration of the automobile industry, which meant that Ford could manufacture all of a Model T car's parts, with almost no reliance on outside suppliers. The River Rouge plant eventually employed more than one hundred thousand workers. They smelted fifty-two kinds of steel, made tires and safety glass, produced light and power, and made virtually everything that went into each car from the front bumper to the tail lights. The River Rouge plant also used the byproducts of its production. For example, making coke from coal produced ammonium sulfate (sold as fertilizer), benzol (mixed with gasoline and used in cars), and gas and tar (which the plant burned).[39] The factory's workers and engineers continually innovated. For example, they developed a new method of making plate glass that was faster and required fewer workmen. The River Rouge plant's glass production area was 760 feet long and 240 feet wide, producing four kinds of glass.⁴⁰ The "glass flowed from a continuous melting tank" out "onto an inclined plane that formed the glass into a flat sheet. A roller pressed the ever-moving sheet to proper thickness, then the hot glass sheet exited on to a moving table and into a continuous annealing oven." Ford also "introduced assembly-line principles to the grinding and polishing stages."⁴¹ Plate glass was used not only in automobiles but also in skyscraper windows. A signature material for modernist architecture, between 1890 and 1925 its production increased an astonishing 1500 percent.

At the River Rouge plant, Albert Kahn, a leading industrial architect, used steel-reinforced concrete to create large interior spaces with few columns or other supports, and he worked closely with managers to develop the open floor plan. The complex as a whole had a functionalist design, yet the use of space wasn't rigidly preconceived. William Verner was the builder for the whole project of which Kahn's buildings were a part. He studied the process of making the Model T and laid out each section of the new factory in consultation with Ford's managers. Work flow determined building placement. Since a Model T's main ingredient was steel, Verner began with the railroads and canals that transported the raw materials needed to produce it.⁴² Based on the location of railroads and canals, he built two blast furnaces, a foundry for engine blocks, rolling mills to make sheet steel, and a stamping plant to make car hoods, doors, roofs, and panels. The architectural design anticipated continuous movement of raw materials and parts between buildings. Details were developed in consultation with the managers who would direct production. For example, one noted that "the machine shop setup was more compact. We studied the setup of machinery so there was no wasted space. We tried to move the machines as close together as possible to eliminate the movement of stock." Such changes exemplify what David Harvey has called the "compression of space and time" that is a hallmark of advanced capitalism.⁴³

The flexible factory design encouraged further innovation and greater compression of production. There was no permanent layout for the machine shops, because the "production people . . . had the idea that there were going to be many changes in the makeup of the automobile."⁴⁴ The River Rouge plant accommodated changing production flows, avoiding a rigid arrangement that might constrain innovation. This modern factory was not merely a container for men and machines; it was a master machine that organized and expressed the whole system of production.⁴⁵ Ford concentrated manufacturing there in 1927.⁴⁶

The Ford assembly line became a model for other manufacturers and was so efficient that prices fell for automobiles and other mass-produced goods. The Model T of 1910 cost three times as much as an improved version of the same car in 1925. In a single generation, automobiles ceased to be an expensive luxury for the rich and became the norm for middle-class families. By 1930 automobiles were ubiquitous in the United States, facilitating the growth of suburbia and urban deconcentration. In the Southwest, which urbanized after the motorcar became widespread, Phoenix, Los Angeles, and other cities sprawled across an automotive landscape.

As the center of these transformations, the River Rouge plant became a tourist magnet and a national symbol. It was the apotheosis of the utilitarian conception of nature, and it was often described in the language of the technological sublime. The company tour emphasized elevated views of a vast landscape of harmonious production.⁴⁷ One journalist described the overall effect on a visitor: "He sees these units not only in their impressive individual and astounding collective magnitude, but he also sees each unit as a part of a huge machine—he sees each unit as a carefully designed gear which meshes with other gears and operates in synchronism with them, the whole forming one huge, perfectly-timed, smoothly operating industrial machine of almost unbelievable manufacturing efficiency."⁴⁸ A German engineer, Otto Moug, toured the River Rouge plant in the late 1920s and found it an almost religious experience. "No symphony, no Eroica, compared in depth, content, and power to the music that threatened and hammered away at us as we wandered through Ford's workplaces, wanderers overwhelmed by a daring expression of the human spirit."⁴⁹ The workers on the factory floor had a harsher experience than these words suggest, but this could not be grasped from Olympian viewpoints on the tour.

The artist Charles Sheeler, under commission by the Ford Motor Company, photographed the factory in a series of landscapes in late 1927, just as the Model A was going into production.⁵⁰ These images later became the basis for landscape paintings showing mountains of coal, iron ore, and other raw materials, heaped symmetrically alongside the company's shipping canal and railroad tracks. There was not a single bush or tree or even a blade of grass, and workers were seldom visible. The only signs of activity are the smoke from the powerhouse chimney and the railroad cars along the canal. The immediate impression is one of calm, order, and absolute control over the environment. Sheeler's brushwork seems invisible, as if the canvas were produced without human intervention. He wanted "to eliminate the evidence of painting as such and present the design with the least evidence of the means of accomplishment."[51] He presented the transformed River Rouge as an inevitable part of the narrative of progress.

Simultaneously, Detroit invested in a pastoral landscape. Upstream from Ford's enormous factory, in 1925 the city acquired 1,204 acres and created a contrast to industry's ruthless assimilation of nature. As exemplified by New York's Central Park (1873), American cities landscaped large tracts where it was expected that the individual would be refreshed through contact with an idealized nature.[52] River Rouge Park, like New York's Central Park, erased the grid pattern, notably in "a series of winding automobile drives" and eleven miles of bridal paths for equestrians. The river bordered the east side of the park for half a mile and for two miles was at its center.[53] There were many picnic grounds, and much space was devoted to team sports that had become popular after industrialization, including football, baseball, track and field, tennis, and an Olympic-size swimming pool. During winter, the park offered "a 6-acre skating rink and six 700-foot toboggan slides." More ominously, the park also contained "in a natural hollow" a pistol range for the Detroit police and stables for the U.S. National Guard.[54]

Downstream, in 1927 Henry Ford began construction of another pastoral site, a museum village near his factory that presented an idealized history. At first glance, Greenfield Village seemed a nineteenth-century community, but each building had been moved there from elsewhere.[55] They included a courthouse where Lincoln practiced law and a house where Stephen Foster may once have lived. Several buildings belonged to inventors, including the laboratory where Thomas Edison invented the electric light; the bicycle shop where the Wright brothers invented the airplane; and the garage where Henry Ford built his first automobile. The community also included a church, general store, and other buildings typically found in a village of c. 1880. As its name suggests, this village has large trees and spacious lawns. Its pastoralism seems to contradict Ford's nearby factory. Yet it enshrined the inventors who made the electrical systems, airplanes, and assembly lines that led directly to modernity. Ford may have been nostalgic for the lost world of the village, but he also saw it as the progenitor of progress. Greenfield Village seems to reconcile the pastoral and the utilitarian. The River Rouge plant, the Fair Lane estate, Detroit's public park, and Greenfield Village together erased the previous landscape and exemplify the practice of second creation. They also illustrate how diverse conceptions of nature coexist. Ford's factory epitomized utilitarian values, yet he also read Emerson, Thoreau, and Burroughs, built an estate surrounded by gardens, and collected the buildings that became Greenfield Village. He combined pastoral and industrial values in a narrative of progress that projected second creation into the past as well as into a high-tech future.

This historical narrative became unconvincing, however, after the national economy collapsed in 1929, and almost half the workers in Detroit lost their jobs. By 1932 the unemployed had used up their savings and cashed in their life insurance, and many had lost their homes. More than three thousand people, including many former Ford employees, joined a protest march to the gates of the River Rouge plant. The Dearborn police demanded that they turn back. When they refused, the police fired tear gas and the protestors pelted them with rocks. As the police retreated, the marchers advanced toward the River Rouge plant. There the police and private security forces opened fire, killing four and wounding many more. This "Dearborn Massacre" angered workers in all parts of the United States. In Detroit, more than twenty thousand people marched in a defiant funeral. The River Rouge plant had become a central site in the battle between capital and unionized labor. For the next five years Ford resisted unionization. The confrontation with labor was only resolved when World War II rearmament forced the company to the bargaining table. The union won the right to represent the workers and to hold elections inside the River Rouge plant, which became a symbol of labor's successful struggle for recognition. Decades later, President Bill Clinton summarized the widespread view that "The workers at River Rouge . . . shed their blood for more than their own rights and their own families. Their sacrifice gave all of us collective bargaining and the minimum wage."[56]

After the United States entered World War II, the press rewrote the meaning of the River Rouge plant. It became a military site, where mass-production guaranteed that the United States would never run short of trucks, ships, planes, weapons, or military supplies. In 1940, *Life* magazine devoted eleven pages to a photographic essay on the plant. In addition to a detailed diagram of the factory and photographs of the foundry and various machines, the story included human-interest material, such as a photo of men lined up at a lunch wagon. There was not a critical word.[57] The same issue carried a story on Hitler's rise to power, with more than sixty photographs. Shortly after the United States entered the war, *Time* declared: "Something is happening that Adolf Hitler does not yet understand—a new re-enactment of the old American miracle of wheels and machinery, but on a new scale. This time it is a miracle of war production, and its miracle-worker is the automobile industry." American mass production was expected to overwhelm the Germans and the Japanese. *Time* continued: "Endlessly the lines will send tanks, jeeps, machine guns, cannon, air torpedoes, and armored cars." Ford had "turned its two square miles of self-contained industrial empire to the tools of war."[58] Military production demanded enormous supplies of electricity from coal-fired power plants, including that of Detroit Edison on the River Rouge.[59] The utilitarian conquest of nature morphed into a military narrative, as Ford stopped making cars and produced jeeps, tanks, and bombers. Some of these were tested in the Southwest, where the government established airfields, proving grounds, training facilities, and laboratories.[60]

After World War II, the River Rouge plant again became a popular tourist destination. It was presented as the center of a world automotive empire, with branch factories in Britain, France, Germany, and Japan. Its global reach was highlighted in the Ford Rotunda, where tours of the River Rouge plant began. This structure first had been erected at the 1939 New York World's Fair and afterward was recreated in Dearborn. Ten stories high, it was "cylindrical in plan and modernistic in outline, resembling four different-sized gears, one above the other." Inside, an enormous circular wall was covered by photographic murals that were 190 meters long and 6 meters high, depicting "the Rouge Plant in all its activities." At the center of the enormous room stood a six-meter high revolving globe with Ford's forests, mines, rubber plantations, factories, dealers, and offices clearly marked.[61] It impressed visitors with the enormous and intricate complexity of the company and its global reach. The River Rouge factory complex became an icon of the Cold War. In 1964, 227,561 people went to see it.[62]

However, during the energy crises of the 1970s, Ford's production declined, and it was challenged by lean Japanese production methods that were so efficient American manufacturers had to adopt them to remain competitive. Management gradually abandoned the idea that the Rouge should be a self-sufficient plant producing all the parts for its cars. They outsourced components, which arrived in containers from many parts of the world, and the River Rouge complex became primarily an assembly plant. Many buildings fell into disuse or closed, and parts suppliers went bankrupt. Paul Clemens's moving book, *Punching Out*, describes how the Budd stamping plant in Detroit closed. In 1926, the Budd Company used more sheet metal than any other American corporation, and it became the world's largest producer of automotive parts. It made door panels, more than ten million artillery shells during World War II, and parts for numerous classic Detroit cars, including the Ford Thunderbird. Just one of its many presses weighed one million pounds. Its massive equipment was taken apart, shipped to Mexico, and reassembled there.[63] This "internationalization" eliminated well-paid jobs in Detroit. Asian and Latin American labor markets were less expensive, and their factories had weak (or no) unions, demanded long hours, and spent less on safety. Detroit declined because of the downsizing of the River Rouge plant and other auto factories, along with the outsourcing of parts production to distant suppliers. The city's population slowly collapsed from 1.5 million in 1970 to just over 700,000 in 2010. The narrative of progress through second creation had not anticipated such a decline.

In the twenty-first century, Ford transformed both its factory and its factory tour. The reinvention was based on a narrative about the salvage and recovery of a polluted and despoiled landscape. It began not with empty space waiting to be improved by new settlers, but with a place corrupted and degraded by human misuse.[64] During a century of industrialization, the River Rouge had become seriously polluted. If nothing were done, the area would become an unlivable environment, an anti-landscape. The U.S. General Accounting Office estimated in 1988 that a cleanup would cost at least $1.8 billion.[65] The following year, a binational commission of the United States and Canada "identified the Rouge River as one of the worst pollution 'hot spots' in the Great Lakes area."[66] It contained high levels of heavy metals, organic chemicals, and polychlorinated biphenyls (PCBs). The commission called for a $900 million cleanup that would take twenty years. Companies that had legally discharged into the Rouge watershed under permit included a steel plant, Shell Oil, Mobile Oil, Amoco, Ford, General Motors, and many small factories.[67] Between

1986 and 1992 the Friends of the Rouge organized an annual Rouge Rescue in which 15,000 volunteers removed 19,000 cubic yards of debris and unblocked 500 log jams. Twenty communities participated. But volunteers were hardly enough, and another $1 billion was needed to complete the cleanup. By 1991 state and local authorities had appropriated $500 million for improved sewers and wastewater treatment. More than three hundred illegal points of discharge were eliminated.[68] Finally, in 2005 the river was designated a "Green Corridor."

This transformation was possible in part because in 2000, William Clay Ford, the great-grandson of the founder, decided to spend $2 billion rebuilding the River Rouge complex into a "green" flexible-production factory. A new fifteen-acre grass roof reduced water runoff and provided insulation. Parking lots were redesigned to absorb rain rather than shed it as runoff, and the water now percolates slowly through marshes before entering the river. The soil had been polluted by industrial chemicals, but plantings were carefully selected to neutralize or break down toxic substances. Establishing a wetland area not only addressed the problem at its source, but also cost far less than building new storm sewers. This approach was later expanded to deal with Detroit's storm water, in a $50 million project that also assists development of urban agriculture.[69]

Inside, the rebuilt Ford factory has abundant natural light and many energy-saving features.[70] Other car manufacturers also built green factories, including General Motors in Lansing, Michigan, and Volkswagen in Chattanooga, Tennessee. Elsewhere, Pittsburgh and other industrial cities cleaned up brownfield sites and replaced lost heavy industry with high-tech factories.[71] The architect who retrofitted the River Rouge plant, William McDonough, became a spokesperson for integrating product recycling into the system of production. In 2002, he coauthored *From Cradle to Cradle* that made the case for improving productivity by planning for reuse at every step in manufacturing. "Building a truly sustainable automobile industry," McDonough asserted, "means developing closed-loop systems for the manufacturing and re-utilization of auto parts. In Europe, the End-of-Life Vehicle Directive [passed by the EU in September 2000] makes manufacturers responsible for automotive materials, pushing companies to design for disassembly and effective resource recovery." This legislation exemplified "cradle-to-cradle systems, in which materials either go back to industry or safely back to the soil."[72] McDonough reimagined production as a "technical metabolism" that "can be designed to mirror natural nutrient cycles; it's a closed-loop system in which valuable, high-tech synthetics and mineral resources circulate in an endless cycle of production, recovery and remanufacture." Disassembly lines recover materials without degrading them, for reuse in new products.[73] In its best form, the "technical metabolism" is powered by wind and solar energy.[74] The redesigned River Rouge factory provides a vision of industry appropriate to an ecological age.

Once these changes were underway, Ford recreated its factory tour, which had been closed between 1980 and 2004. As Wendy Lynnette Michael explains, the new tour was a highly mediated event. It began with a bus ride from Greenfield Village to the River Rouge plant, where visitors saw films that presented a somewhat idealized company history and explained assembly line production. At the factory, another film included special effects to heighten audience involvement. They feel heat when viewing a blast furnace and the floor shakes when the film shows stamping machines at work. On the tour, visitors do not see most stages of production but only final assembly. Previously, tourists "used steel catwalks in the foundry, experienced the deafening sound of industrial stamping presses, smelled the stink of oily parts, and walked alongside workers on the assembly line." They saw "an authentic functioning industrial complex, while the contemporary tour shows visitors an assembly line built as part of a museum exhibit," seen from an Olympian position overhead. Ford trucks are being assembled, but it is a "fabricated display."[75] Taken together, the films and the tour aestheticized the assembly line, with no room for counternarratives about deindustrialization, offshore factories, Superfund sites, or tensions with labor over declining real wages since the 1970s.[76]

The history of the River Rouge shows how utilitarianism and pastoralism became the dominant definitions of American nature. The Mound Builders utilized the River Rouge for transportation, hunting, fishing, and agriculture, and they built a ceremonial site at the delta. The French valued the Rouge as part of the fur trade, and only after their defeat did Anglo-Americans settle and farm along its banks. After the arrival of railroads, the area was stripped of trees and converted to industrial uses, including iron making, stove production, and chemical refining, before Ford built the world's largest factory there. It became an icon of mass production in the 1920s, a symbol of labor struggles during the 1930s, a center of military production during World War II, and an exemplar of global capitalism during the Cold War. By 2013, however, some of the area had been returned to wetland, and the roof of the factory was planted with grasses and welcomed wild birds. River Rouge plant managers searched for environmentally sustainable production methods. The imagination of this (or perhaps any) site as a palimpsest mistakenly suggests that nature is merely an original or bottom layer, with additions and erasures above it. In the Rouge watershed, the river and the land have survived many iterations of culture and industry. The new green factory recognizes the persistence of natural forces and seeks harmony with them by developing a technical metabolism, rather than treating Nature as raw materials that exist in order to be exploited. The wetlands of the River Rouge again are valued, and the more modest factory expresses a willingness to live within limits. The River Rouge, once a symbol of the conquest of nature and admired as the epitome of the industrial sublime, suggests the possibility of a new form of pastoralism. The grid system continues to carve the land into identical squares, but much of Detroit has disappeared. By 2010 more than eighty thousand houses and apartments had been abandoned, and forty square miles were vacant. There were vegetable gardens on abandoned lots, and a new forest of maple trees was planted in what was once a middle-class neighborhood.[77]

How should one interpret this sequence of events? Closed automobile factories challenge the utilitarian narrative, which describes a cost-free development from Greenfield Village to the Ford plant. But creationists, including a majority of Republicans, might not narrate the history of the River Rouge as an environmental story. They believe the earth is young and that oil, gas, and other natural resources are of recent origin, with new supplies continually being created. One creationist publication explained that "the rapid formation of oil and gas is not only feasible on the basis of carefully controlled laboratory experiments but has now been shown to occur naturally under geological conditions that have been common in the past."[78] From this perspective, Detroit's collapse was only a local, temporary setback, and the process of second creation should continue with a minimum of restraints. Or as one scholar noted of Reaganomics, it made no sense to economists, but "Economic creationism rests on a fundamental certainty that the economic species of 'free enterprise market economy' is the product of an inspired humanity and represents a mythic truth relevant for all time." From this perspective, "society must be deregulated, government must be reduced, and public responsibilities must be decentralized because that is the way the system was created."[79]

In contrast, environmentalists see the history of the River Rouge in layers of sediment laid down during the last 1,000 years by the societies that once existed along the River Rouge, from the Mound Builders onward. These sediments record the Anthropocene, or the period when the human effects on the environment register in the geological record.[80] They register the disappearance of some species and the importation of others. They register the residue of factories, rising CO_2 levels, and the appearance of steel, plastic, synthetic rubber, and other substances that do not occur in nature. By foregrounding the emergence of human beings as a global force, the Anthropocene implicitly asks humanity to manage its environmental impact.

From this perspective, the history of the River Rouge is one in which American utilitarianism erased both Native American and French colonial landscapes and replaced them with the grid system of land division and industrial development. This second creation also included pastoral zones like River Rouge Park and Greenfield Village that softened the overall transformation. However, this successful amalgam of utilitarianism and pastoralism eventually confronted costly environmental limits. Elsewhere, particularly in the American West, utilitarianism met more resistance, notably from Native Americans and environmentalists. Its triumph was less complete, and more of the pre-industrial landscape survived, including natural bridges, which may be useless but often are considered sublime.

4

NATURAL BRIDGES: CONFLICTS OF MEANING

During the centuries that the French, the British, and then the Americans controlled the River Rouge it was understood in terms of its possible uses. Other natural sites have been understood quite differently, becoming famous for their beauty, sublimity, unique appearance, or illustration of a geological theory. Consider the example of natural stone arches produced by the erosion of wind and water. Bridges are structures made by human hands, designed to get from one side of a stream or chasm to the other. Natural bridges may serve that function, but usually they do not. They were not created for any purpose. Natural forces did not make them for human use or appreciation.[1] Natural bridges arouse interest, especially if they are large, and even more so if they are symmetrical and beautiful. This chapter will examine them from the 1770s to the present, keeping in mind the six different ideas of nature outlined in chapter 1.

Roderick Nash notes that early Christians "judged their work to be successful when they cleared away the wild forests and cut down the sacred groves where the pagans held their rites."[2] Few White Americans accept the Native American understanding that natural bridges can be sacred sites that emanate spiritual power. Because these are often on public lands, White society controls them. As Lydia Grimm notes, federal "agency decisions authorizing the use or development of public lands can harm, or even destroy the attributes that make such lands sacred, and in so doing, diminish the ability of Indians to practice their religions."[3] Government assumptions about nature are often sharply at odds with Native American beliefs. White Americans place animals below human beings in a hierarchy; Native Americans see animals as kin. White Americans understand time as a linear unfolding of events in history; Native Americans often have a cyclical view of time, experienced in natural rhythms. Many White Americans define the world in secular terms as a material reality that can be controlled, but many Native Americans see the world in religious terms infused with supernatural powers and influences. These cultural differences lead to legal conflicts over how to treat particular sites, such as Devil's Tower in Wyoming or certain natural bridges.[4]

Most White Americans perceive natural bridges in terms of science and aesthetics. In *Notes on the State of Virginia*, Thomas Jefferson exemplified how scientific observation of a natural bridge and the experience of the sublime could be combined (figure 4.1). Jefferson began with a series of measurements:

> The Natural Bridge [of Virginia], the most sublime of nature's works ... is on the ascent of a hill, which seems to have been cloven through its length by some great convulsion. The fissure, just at the bridge, is by some admeasurements, two hundred and seventy feet deep, by others only two hundred and five. It is about forty-five feet wide at the bottom and ninety feet at the top; this of course determined the length of the bridge, and its height from the water. Its breadth in the middle is about sixty feet, but more at the ends, and the thickness of the mass, at the summit of the arch, about forty feet. A part of this thickness is constituted by a coat of earth, which gives growth to many large trees. The residue, with the hill on both sides, is one solid rock of lime-stone. The arch approaches the semi-elliptical form; but the larger axis of the ellipsis, which would be the cord of the arch, is many times longer than the transverse.[5]

Modern geology was being invented during Jefferson's lifetime. He was acquainted with the effects of water erosion, the softness of limestone, and the ease with which it could be hollowed out. Yet geology was in its infancy, and there was not even a generally accepted understanding of why rocks found in strata often were tilted. The age of the earth was then reckoned in thousands not millions or billions of years. Jefferson was aware of gradualist ideas about how a natural bridge might evolve, but he thought it more plausible to explain natural bridges through the catastrophe theory. It held that the world had passed through a period of volcanic eruptions, earthquakes, and floods that destroyed many beautiful structures, of which only a few remained. When he suggested that the ridge "seems to have been cloven through its length by some great convulsion," he was reading this landscape as evidence for the catastrophe theory. The French naturalist Georges Cuvier (1769–1832) later systematized such observations into a theory of catastrophe that not only seemed convincing but also could be harmonized with the Bible. From this perspective, the Natural Bridge was a remnant of the perfect world at the beginning of time associated with the

Figure 4.1 "Natural Bridge of Virginia," photographer not identified, Detroit Publishing Company, c. 1900. *Source:* Library of Congress.

Garden of Eden, a world that had been destroyed. Creationists still believe in a version of catastrophe theory to explain the formation and destruction of natural bridges. They believe the world has only existed for about ten thousand years and that floods, earthquakes, and other violent events have shaped it. In short, catastrophe theory has been absorbed into creationism, and it still competes with the uniformitarian theory that James Hutton (1726–1797) formulated in his two-volume *The Theory of the Earth* (1795), which laid the groundwork for modern geology. In 1818, a scientist examined the Natural Bridge and concluded that water erosion produced it, a uniformitarian explanation.[6] But two centuries later, a creationist declared, "The formation of large arches and natural bridges from slow weathering and erosion would take tens of thousands of years. However, the uniformitarian hypotheses for their origin are not observed. A rapid process of erosion in the past consistent with the Retreating Stage of the Flood is more likely."[7] While the National Park Service (NPS) accepts uniformitarian geology, 100 million Americans do not.

Jefferson's description of the Natural Bridge was more than an impersonal record of measurements, placed in the context of a scientific debate. He next described his emotions when viewing it, shifting to the first person and using the language of the sublime:

> Though the sides of this bridge are provided in some parts with a parapet of fixed rocks, yet few men have the resolution to walk to them, and look over into the abyss. You involuntarily fall on your hands and feet, creep to the parapet of fixed rocks, and peep over it. Looking down from this height about a minute, gave me a violent headache. If the view from the top be painful and intolerable, that from below is delightful in an equal extreme. It is impossible for the emotions arising from the sublime to be felt beyond what they are here, so beautiful an arch, so elevated, so light, and springing as it were up to heaven! the rapture of the spectator is really indescribable! The fissure continuing narrow, deep, and straight, for a considerable distance above and below the bridge, opens a short but very pleasing view of the North mountain on one side.

After Jefferson first saw the Natural Bridge in 1767, he had it surveyed and, in 1774, purchased it along with 150 surrounding acres. He considered it an important American site and brought friends to see it.[8] Jefferson urged visitors to seek out the "painful and intolerable" view from the crest of the bridge, even if it caused a headache, as a necessary contrast to the view from below. The natural bridge was sublime because it was both terrifying, painful, and almost intolerable and yet delightful. It was enormous yet graceful, massive yet light. It induced both terror and rapture. These were the feelings evoked by the natural sublime, and in the nineteenth century many Americans visited other sights that provoked such reactions, notably Niagara Falls and later Yosemite.[9]

When Jefferson purchased the Natural Bridge, however, few Americans appreciated the sublime.[10] He persuaded the Marquis de Chastellux to visit in 1782, and he made a survey and published a "Plan Géometral du Pont Naturel."[11] However, Jefferson never convinced an important artist to depict his Natural Bridge. A generation after his death, in 1852 it was painted by one of the finest landscape artists of the time, Frederick Edwin Church (1826–1900). Like his canvas, subsequent paintings and photographs depict the Natural Bridge from below, emphasizing its height above the stream running through the narrow valley. During the nineteenth century, Americans began to read such landscapes as proof of national greatness, which is how Jefferson understood the Natural Bridge.[12] In 1815 he had "no idea of selling the land. I view it in some degree as a public trust, and would on no consideration permit the bridge to be injured, defaced or masked from public view."[13] The bridge was sold ten years after his death, and remained a privately owned tourist site until 2013 when it became a Virginia State Park.[14]

As Americans toured their country, visiting such sublime landscapes became an act of self-definition. John Sears found that "tourism had deeper cultural sources than the need for diversion. Tourism played a powerful role in America's invention of itself as a culture. . . . It was inevitable when they set out to establish a national culture in the 1820s and 1830s, that they would turn to the landscape of America as the basis of that culture."[15] Lacking the rallying points of a royal family, a national church, or a long history memorialized at sites of important events, Americans saw the landscape as the source of national character. Both the painter Thomas Cole and the poet William Cullen Bryant needed "the sublime to celebrate what they felt was peculiar and unique about American scenery, which the concept of the beautiful was incapable of expressing." As Charles Sanford noted, they made the sublime into a patriotic emotion by adapting Edmund Burke's ideas "to the Scotch moralists—chiefly Kames, Blair, and Alison, which united sentiments of the sublime to a great moral idea assumed to exist in and behind nature." In this way, "the passions released into art by the sublime" would "be harnessed to lofty spiritual ends."[16] This philosophy informed travel books that guided early tourists through American landscapes. The Natural Bridge attracted a growing stream of visitors by the time of Jefferson's death in 1826. One, in 1819, wrote of being "so struck with the grandeur and majesty of the scene as to become for several minutes terrified and nailed to the spot, and incapable to move forward. After recovering in some degree from this, I may truly say, agonizing mental state of excitement, the author approached the arch with trembling and trepidation."[17]

Viewing the Natural Bridge was incorporated into Christian religion during the antebellum period, when revivals periodically swept communities into a frenzy. The Baptists constructed a church near the Natural Bridge and used a pool directly beneath its arch for baptisms. One observer noted that these ceremonies were especially impressive, "in that place, always tinged in ordinary times with a semi-religious atmosphere." He noted, "The assemblage of people, whether drawn thither by idle curiosity or by a truly religious motive, were never other than orderly and quiet and attentive. It was as if the concrete evidence right at hand of the Almighty's handiwork in this gigantic structure, touched a chord in the heart of even the most thoughtless."[18] Organized religion appropriated the natural sublime to its purposes. Revivalist religion rejected intellectual approaches to salvation, and insisted on the need to move the sinner's heart. The sublime was easily reconciled with such a doctrine, and the use of the Natural Bridge as a site for baptism is one of many examples of the religious appropriation of the natural sublime. Revivalists sought out dramatic backdrops for their efforts, and visitors to Niagara, Yosemite, or the Natural Bridge wrote poems that professed to see God manifested in these natural works. In 1819, for example, the publisher of the *Lexington Gazette* composed these lines on the Natural Bridge:

> Beneath this noble arch, men wondering stand;
> 'Twas fashioned here, by an Almighty hand,
> An Architect Divine, whose voice can call
> Worlds into being—or, decree their fall.
>
> If I had never known Jehovah's law,
> This scene had taught me reverential awe;
> Inspired my soul its feeble powers to raise,
> Admiring nature–nature's God to praise.

Atheist! contemplate this grand scene, one hour,
And thou shalt own there is a God of Power.[19]

Religious interpretations of the Natural Bridge persisted despite geology's increasing prestige. But for most tourists, it was a natural wonder explained by the uniformitarian theory rather than catastrophe theory. Clifton Johnson visited in 1903 and declared that the bridge's "immensity quite took my breath away. Nothing one has read or imagined can wholly prepare the visitor for this Herculean span of rock across that abysmal chasm. Viewed from below it seems lifted into the very sky. Trees and bushes grow on its tip as on a mountain summit, and the swallows dart under it so far above the spectator as to make the arch appear like another firmament. The grace and regularity of the bridge suggest human handiwork, but doubtless in ages past the stream hollowed out a cavern in the valley, the roof of which all fell in long, long ago, save for this sturdy fragment." Johnson noted that for a century tourists had been writing their names on the underside of the arch. "George Washington" was carved on the rock twenty-five feet above the ground, and his reputed presence at the site had stirred others to surpass him by climbing ever higher up to place their names on the walls. A story circulated in the newspapers about one young man who "after out-rivalling all his predecessors in the height to which he attained, found he was placed in such a situation that it was impossible to descend," and only escaped death by climbing the rest of the way to the top of the arch, doing so by cutting hand grips in the soft limestone with his knife.[20] The boy in the anecdote was a theology student at nearby Washington College named James Hays Piper, who later became president of the University of Tennessee. His feat was witnessed by several fellow students, who recalled that while it was a dangerous climb he managed it without much difficulty.[21]

Neither Johnson's version of this anecdote, nor an earlier one published in 1856 presented the climb as a prank. Rather, the boy, finding that he could carve hand and footholds in the soft stone, kept going higher until realizing that it was more difficult to get down than to continue upward. In some accounts, his exploit is followed anxiously by his family and a crowd of tourists, until finally he is rescued with a rope hundreds of feet above the ground. Then, "such shouting, such leaping and weeping for joy, never greeted the ear of human being so recovered from the yawning gulf of eternity."[22] While this might seem an abuse of the site, climbing up the side of the natural bridge and writing on it was not described as defacement or disrespect. Rather, tourists identified with it, wished to share in its importance, and put their names on it.

By the middle of the nineteenth century, the Natural Bridge had become so well known that Herman Melville referred to it in one of the most dramatic passages of *Moby Dick*. He linked the uncanny symmetry and impressive dimensions of the Natural Bridge of Virginia with the eerie power of the great white whale: "And thus, through the serene tranquilities of the tropical sea, among waves whose hand-clappings were suspended by exceeding rapture, Moby Dick moved on, still withholding from sight the full terrors of his submerged trunk, entirely hiding the wrenched hideousness of his jaw. But soon the fore part of him slowly rose from the water; for an instant, his whole marbleized body formed a high arch, like Virginia's Natural Bridge, and warningly waving his bannered flukes in the air, the grand god revealed himself, sounded, and went out of sight."[23] The whale breeching high in the air and arching his "marbleized body" like the Natural Bridge fuses Kant's mathematical and dynamic sublimes in a magnificent yet terrifying moment before he destroys Captain Ahab's whaleboat. Melville sensed the contradictions inherent in making something natural into a symbol. For when a site or an animal became symbolic, it suggested a supernatural agency at work in the natural world, an agency that might not be benign.

The Natural Bridge of Virginia suggests the wide range of early American perceptions of nature. Ignored by first settlers who focused on utilitarian concerns, in the 1770s it began to be appreciated by Jefferson and his circle of friends, who regarded it as a geological curiosity that exemplified the natural sublime. By the 1820s, it had become a popular tourist site, and, in a fusion of romanticism and religion, it was often seen as a proof of God's existence. This fundamentalist interpretation survived into the twentieth century, alongside the secular appreciation of natural wonders as proofs of scientific theories. It remains a tourist site, but it has been somewhat eclipsed by more spectacular natural arches further west.

The American West served an important role in the creation of a pantheon of national symbols. After the sectional strife of the Civil War, neither the South nor the North could easily serve as the spiritual and ideological home of the nation. It was far easier to overcome the sectional division by focusing on the landscapes of the mountain west, which were then being explored. During the search for irrigable land, mining property, and other resources, unusual sites were discovered, such as Yosemite, Yellowstone, and the Grand Canyon. These began to be set aside as national parks and, after the Antiquities Act of 1906, as national monuments. Some were protected because of their scientific interest, others because they were beautiful and unique. In Utah, there were more than two thousand natural arches and bridges. Eventually three national monuments were established to protect them: Rainbow Bridge, Natural Bridges, and Arches, which later became a national park. These are presented to the tourist in scientific terms, although creationists complain that uniformitarian theory does not explain why such arches are rare in most places but common in a few locations.[24] At Natural Bridges National Monument, the visitor learns that the Owachomo Bridge, Sipapu Bridge, and Kachina Bridge represent the three phases in a natural bridge's history, as erosion perforates rock walls and then creates but ultimately destroys arch formations. Vacationers at Arches National Park learn that new arches are being created even as older ones are being destroyed. Since the weathering process that produces an arch may take seventy thousand years or more, it usually is too slow to be noticed, but substantial changes may suddenly occur. In 1991, a slab of rock 20 meters long and 1 meter thick fell from the underside of Landscape Arch, leaving behind an attenuated span of 291 feet (figure 4.2).

Virginia's Natural Bridge once seemed unique, but Utah's Rainbow Bridge is larger and more spectacular. One early visitor noted that unlike other natural bridges it has "a rainbow-shaped arch, a delicate semi-circle, free-standing on one side, on the other partly imbedded in the rock from which it was born. The dimensions of the Rainbow Bridge, its symmetry, its graceful sweep, its delicate balance, its daintiness, despite its bulk, its picturesque setting and colouring, make it a unique and stupendous monument. It is beautiful from whatever angle it is seen"[25] (figure 4.3). To Native Americans, however, beauty and symmetry were not Rainbow Bridge's most important characteristics.

All Native American tribes hold certain natural sites to be sacred.[26] The Taos Hopi regard Blue Lake, hidden in the 14,000-foot mountain above their pueblo, as the place where their ancestors emerged into the world, and to it their dead return as spirits. They make a pilgrimage to Blue Lake every August.[27] Likewise, the Sioux believe that the Black Hills are holy,

Figure 4.2   David Hiser (1937–), *Landscape Arch, in the Devil's Garden section of Arches National Park, is believed to be the longest natural stone arch in the world. It has a span of 291 feet and a height of 105 feet*, May 1972, Environmental Protection Agency. *Source:* National Archives.

Figure 4.3   Eugene La Rue (1879–1947), *Rainbow Natural Bridge, Utah, is 300 feet high, 40 feet thick at the crown and has a span of 275 feet*, October 30, 1922, U.S. Geographical Survey. *Source:* Library of Congress.

and many other tribes consider a particular lake, rock formation, or mountain to be sacred. To most White Americans, natural arches do not manifest divine intervention in the world; they are only curiosities. Yet Native Americans often have a religious view. The Navajo believe that their gods created Rainbow Bridge. They associate it with the sacred Navajo Mountain, which stands behind it, and with the nearby confluence of the San Juan River, understood to be male, and the Colorado River, understood to be female. Their union produces clouds and rain. For centuries, the Navajo have prayed and made offerings at all three sites in order to maintain spiritual harmony and to ensure rainfall from "the storm spawning peak of Navajo Mountain." Unlike Christians, who pray directly to God, they pray "where they are connected to Mother Earth, Father Sky, holy mountain, or holy water." These "prayers and offerings of corn pollen" prompt "holy beings to bless the land with water," and Protectionway rituals held there provide protection from non-Navajo enemies. The Navajo always avoided walking under the stone arch, but visitors often do not respect this tradition. Worse still, the stone altar beneath the bridge, seen by Theodore Roosevelt in 1913 and by other early visitors, had disappeared by 1930, apparently destroyed by careless tourists.[28]

The arrival of mass tourism created tensions.[29] Rainbow Bridge attracted ever larger crowds because it is one of the largest natural stone bridges in the world. It is a little higher than and three times longer than the Natural Bridge of Virginia: 290 feet high and 275 feet wide, forming an almost perfect half circle. Peter Nabokov concluded that its spiritual significance for the tribe cannot be doubted. It has long been a holy place of pilgrimage.[30] The legal case *Badoni v. Higginson* arose because the Navajo "believe if humans alter the Earth in the area of the bridge, [tribal] prayers will not be heard by the gods, and their ceremonies will be ineffective to prevent evil and disease."[31] After the Glen Canyon dam was built, they could not perform rituals at the river junction, which had disappeared beneath Lake Powell. Worse still, tourists so disturbed Rainbow Bridge that the Navajo found it "no longer desirable for ceremonial use. The holy beings have fled."[32]

The arch's transformation from a Navajo holy place to tourist site was rapid. Until the early twentieth century it was unknown to White society. When the famous Grand Canyon photographers, the Kolb brothers, boated down the Colorado River in 1908, they could not find the site, and they later made a separate trip to photograph it.[33] Before then, in 1909 a party of whites, guided for four and a half days by two Native Americans through a canyon wilderness, claimed to have "discovered" Rainbow Bridge. A year later, on May 30, 1910, President Howard Taft declared it a national monument.

The Antiquities Act of 1906 gave Taft the right to make this declaration. It granted presidents the power to establish national monuments, whose size was "limited to the proper care and management of the objects to be protected."[34] While vague about how much land could be set aside, the Antiquities Act was intended to preserve archaeological remains like those of the Southwest. It was less sweeping than the Forest Reserve Act of 1891, which gave presidents the right to set aside millions of acres. President Theodore Roosevelt immediately used the Antiquities Act to preserve Devil's Tower in Wyoming as the first national monument. The tracts set aside soon grew. Devil's Tower National Monument covered only 1,152 acres, but the Petrified Forest in Arizona, established the same year, contained 84,597 acres. Two years later, Roosevelt made the Grand Canyon an 806,400-acre monument. Woodrow Wilson tripled that figure in 1918, when he created Katmai National Monument (now Katmai National Park and Reserve) in Alaska.[35] Taft allocated Rainbow Bridge a modest 160 acres.

In 1910, to reach Rainbow Bridge one needed permission to hike thirteen miles through the Navajo Nation, or one could take a wooden boat down the Colorado, difficult in itself, and then hike seven miles up a side canyon. Most early visitors, including Teddy Roosevelt and the novelist Zane Grey, rode through the Navajo reservation with a guide, carrying provisions for themselves and their mules. After arrival, the occasional band of visitors could enjoy the majestic view in silence. In 1916, the government created the National Park Service, and Rainbow Bridge came under its jurisdiction. There were no nearby accommodations until 1924, when Rainbow Lodge was constructed some miles away. In the 1940s, Barry Goldwater became part owner, which also entailed upkeep of a trail to the natural bridge, because the guests came to see it exclusively. Like Jefferson at the Natural Bridge of Virginia, Goldwater promoted tourism with little success. In his best year, only four hundred guests stayed and he lost over $1,000. When the lodge burned down in 1951, it was not rebuilt.[36]

To visit remote Rainbow Bridge demanded time and stamina, but it was a rewarding experience. In 1930, a party of four, alone at the site, could gaze in silence as the moon rose over Navajo Mountain to cast its silvery light over the bridge. This vision often stirred religious emotions, for as one visitor declared: "Nothing could be more marvelous, nothing more beautiful; nor could anything more perfectly attest the definite existence of a Supreme Being, a mighty architect of the universe."[37] The anthropologist Clyde Kluckhohn often heard that no one remained an atheist after visiting Rainbow Bridge. In a visitor's book, many shared passages from the Bible and their religious feelings. A visitor in 1920 wrote, "A wonderful work of your God, remain and worship Him in all His glory."[38]

Until the 1950s, visits to Rainbow Bridge increased slowly, but more tourists arrived after 1963, when Glen Canyon Dam closed its gates and began to collect the water that become Lake Powell. Suddenly tourists could cruise the 100-mile round trip to Rainbow Bridge in a day or include it on a longer voyage to the many interesting side canyons. These visitors upset the Navajo, and in 1974, members of the tribe brought suit in the U.S. District Court against the secretary of the Department of the Interior, the commissioner of the Bureau of Reclamation (who had built the dam), and the director of the NPS (who administered national monuments). The court ruled that the value of water storage outweighed Native American religious concerns. As the waters continued to rise, more Navajo religious sites were threatened, and several medicine men sought an injunction, to close Rainbow Bridge so that they could conduct religious rituals there undisturbed.[39] But the Tenth District Court of Appeals rejected this request on the grounds that the U.S. Constitution protects the religious freedom of all citizens. In practice, this meant that soon three hundred thousand people were visiting the bridge every year. The Superintendent responsible for protecting Rainbow Bridge tried to appease the Navajo by placing signs at the entrance that told visitors the Navajo regard the site as sacred and asking them to voluntarily refrain from walking under the bridge, climbing on the rocks, or otherwise causing disturbances. He recognized "an inherent conflict between the large number of people coming to Rainbow Bridge and how Native Americans view it. . . . What we're trying to present is the whole story, not just the Anglo side of it, but also the Native American perspective of what this place is and what it means to them."[40]

Figure 4.4   Eugene La Rue (1879–1947), *A View of Glen Canyon at the Lee's Ferry Damsite, Colorado River*, October 30, 1922, U.S. Geographical Survey. *Source:* Library of Congress.

The water route to Rainbow Bridge was an unintended result of a struggle between environmental activists led by the Sierra Club and the Department of the Interior and politicians from western states. In the 1950s, the Sierra Club protested when the federal government proposed to place a dam on the upper Colorado River, inside Dinosaur National Monument. The compromise worked out in Congress was to build a dam in Glen Canyon instead (figure 4.4). Since national monuments were supposed to be inviolable, a promise to protect Rainbow Bridge was written into the Colorado River Storage Project Act of 1956. The Bureau of Reclamation testified in Congress that it could build a barrier dam without an additional appropriation. But as Glen Canyon Dam neared completion, it realized that a dam below the bridge would block the small stream that ran under it, making necessary a diversion dam and pumping station above the bridge. Construction of dams both above and below the natural bridge would mar the landscape, block access to the site, and require continual maintenance. The alternative was to allow the streambed to gradually fill up with sediment, which seemed a less intrusive solution.[41] Congress concurred, and the waters spilled into the national monument. Conservationists sued, won in federal court, but lost in the Court of Appeals, and the Supreme Court refused to review the case.[42] Since then sand and debris have been left beneath Rainbow Bridge as the lake's level rises and falls.[43]

The refusal to protect Rainbow Bridge was also based on economics. Glen Canyon Dam was to generate income and eventually to pay for itself by selling irrigation water and electricity. Indeed, some Navajo supported construction of the Glen Canyon Dam in order to acquire precisely that water and electricity. As Erika Bsumek noted, there were Navajo in a lobby group working against the Sierra Club. Called the Aqualantes, they embraced utilitarian arguments and asserted that the dam would "uplift" the Navajo and make them more self-sufficient.[44] A public relations effort, including paintings and photography commissioned by the Bureau of Reclamation, presented the Navajo as a people awaiting modernity. In contrast, the Sierra Club disseminated images of an idealized ecological Native American who preferred a simple life close to nature, and it reprinted on its calendars a speech attributed to Chief Seattle but that had been written by a White screenwriter from Texas.[45]

Ever since its first discovery by White Americans, access to Rainbow Bridge had been difficult. As Jared Farmer nicely summarizes: "Rainbow Bridge became famous not simply as a wonder but as the center point of the most remote country. . . . Surrounded by a sea of slickrock, the natural bridge was removed from the profane: the world of modern cities, politics and wars."[46] After riding to the bridge, the western novelist Zane Grey declared that "this trip is one of the most beautiful in the West. It is a hard one and not for everybody. There is no guide except [John] Wetherill who knows how to get there." Grey recalled it was "the only place I have ever visited which I am not sure I could find again alone."[47] Only rugged travelers went, and the next party included Theodore Roosevelt.[48] Grey caught the ethic of this early era: "The tourist, the leisurely traveler, the comfort-loving motorist would never behold it. Only by toil, seat endurance and pain could any man ever look at Nonnezoshe," which was his rendering of the bridge's Navajo name into English. After riding for days through the desert and Monument Valley, he encountered the Rainbow Bridge at sunset. It "was the one great natural phenomenon, the one grand spectacle which I had ever seen that did not at first give vague disappointment. . . . But this thing was glorious. It absolutely silenced one. My body and brain, weary and dull from the toil of travel, received a singular and revivifying freshness. I had a strange, mystic perception that this rosy-hued, tremendous arch of stone was a goal I had failed to reach in some former life, but had now found. Here was a rainbow magnified even beyond dreams, a thing not transparent and ethereal, but solidified, a work of ages, sweeping up majestically from the red walls, its iris-hued arch against the blue sky."[49] In Gray's *Riders of the Purple Sage*, it became the portal to a beautiful hidden valley: "The curve of the great stone bridge had caught the sunrise, and through the magnificent arch burst a glorious stream of gold that shone with a long slant down into the center of Surprise Valley. Only through the arch did any sunlight pass, so that all the rest of the valley lay still asleep, dark green, mysterious, shadowy . . . [with] walls as misty and soft as morning clouds."[50]

The thousands of casual visitors who walked from a nearby dock to Rainbow Bridge had not "earned" the right to see it,[51] which infuriated environmentalists and upset many Navajo. The Sierra Club's president, David Brower, bitterly regretted that he and most of the other directors had not seen Glen Canyon when it was proposed as an alternative dam site. Later, they were outraged that the Bureau of Reclamation refused to build the barrier dam that Congress had specified. They worried that saturating the ground might destabilize Rainbow Bridge and cause its collapse.[52] Later, during years of hearings on the wilderness bill, its advocates distrusted the Bureau of Reclamation, and argued that new dams were a desecration, forever destroying unspoiled scenery and wildlife habitats. In part because Glen Canyon had been flooded and Rainbow Arch left unprotected, the Wilderness Act of 1964 laid down strict guidelines prohibiting development.

The battle over Glen Canyon Dam is not over. Its reservoir filled until the early 1980s, but levels have fluctuated since then. In 1998, Congress held hearings on a Sierra Club proposal to drain Lake Powell, which was considered unrealistic, as the dam generated an average of 5.2 billion kilowatt hours each year and had an estimated life of five hundred years.[53] The lake was nearly full when the hearings were held, but it dropped 100 feet during the next five years. As waters receded, they revealed again the red cliffs and winding river channel.[54] By 2016 the reservoir was not even half full, and less water was available to generate electricity or to irrigate (figure 4.5).[55] Moreover, each month 160 billion gallons of water evaporated. Downstream, Lake Mead behind Hoover Dam was also evaporating

Natural Bridges

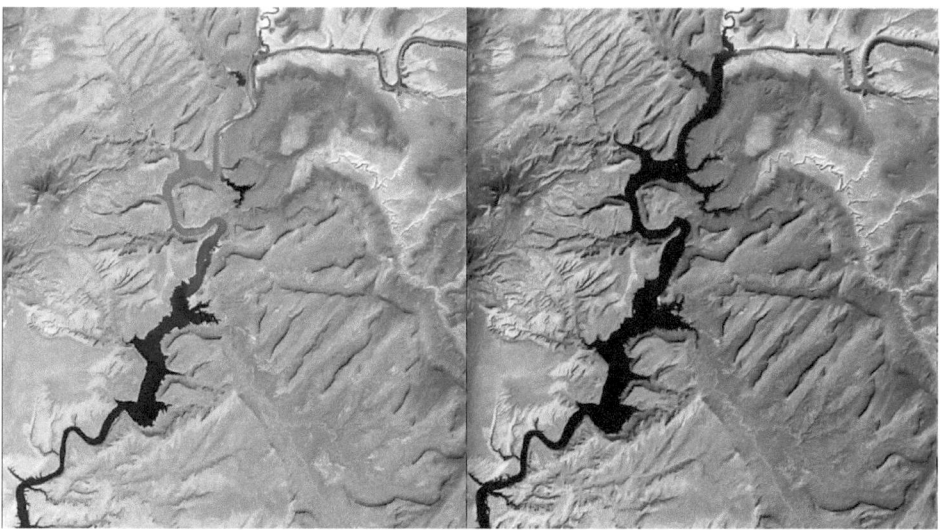

Figure 4.5 "Shrinkage of Lake Powell, from 1999 to 2017." *Source:* Satellite photography, Library of Congress.

and leaking away, and it was little more than one third full. There was enough water for only one dam, and Glen Canyon Dam had proven a poor investment. From a business point of view, it would save water to use only Lake Mead. It is deeper, and concentrating the water there would save the evaporation loss of billions of gallons. Concentrating water in one place would exacerbate other problems, however. As early as 1961, in Lake Mead "spontaneous bacterial accumulation in lake sediments . . . forced closure of many areas to the public. The U.S. Geological Survey has compared these contaminated sediments unfavorably with raw sewage."[56]

Worse still, on the bottom of Lake Powell lie tons of radioactive waste. From the 1940s until 1953, the White Canyon Mill alone had daily crushed and treated twenty tons of ore, to extract five or six pounds of uranium. Debris from more than a dozen other uranium mills and mines also polluted the watershed, and washed down the river. Muddy uranium waste laced with 26,000 tons of heavy metals is buried in the lake's sediment.[57] Draining Lake Powell would create a Superfund site more costly to clean up than the River Rouge in the 1990s. Exposing this waste to rain and periodic flooding would be an economic and environmental disaster. Moreover, tourism around the lake stimulates the local economy. In 2014,

Glen Canyon Dam, Lake Powell, and Rainbow Bridge together attracted 2.4 million tourists, who spent $155 million in nearby communities.[58] At Glen Canyon, the utilitarian ideology of nature once justified a dam with an irrigation reservoir that doubled as a recreation area. But by 2016 the dam was no longer much help for irrigation. Instead, it was justified by tourism and waste containment.

Lake Powell's recent condition has been thoughtfully photographed by Peter Goin.[59] His images suggest the hubris of the great dam projects, and they acknowledge the sometimes destructive intrusion into and transformation of Glen Canyon. But they move beyond ironic commentary to explore the places that emerged when the lake's water level fell due to lower rainfall and higher temperatures. Goin shows us neither an old river nor a new lake, but rather the landscape below the bathtub ring left by the high-water mark. While there are sunken boats and some debris, the side canyons have emerged back into the light. Rainbow Bridge seems safe from inundation, and tourists must walk a mile from the shrinking lake to reach it. The landscape no longer looks pristine, but much beauty remains.

As was the case with the Glen Canyon Dam, the second creation story has often been used to support logging, mining, oil and gas extraction, ranching, or irrigation, overriding environmental concerns. In 1948 and 1949, the NPS fought off several proposals to treat the lands under their jurisdiction as raw material waiting for development. These included an electrical transmission line through Rocky Mountain National Park and a request from the Army Corps of Engineers to construct a dam inside Glacier National Park that would have destroyed 20,000 acres of wilderness. Conservation groups opposed both proposals. The director of the NPS declared at a public hearing: "Civilization is encroaching on the wilderness all over our land. What remains of it becomes increasingly precious to present-day Americans, and will be in even greater degree to Americans of the future. Here, threatened with permanent destruction, is an extraordinarily fine example of 'Original America.'"[60] Much the same thing could once be said of Glen Canyon.

For a century, wilderness areas, national monuments, and national parks have been assailed by the Bureau of Reclamation, the Army Corps of Engineers, mining corporations, oil companies, the military, and real estate developers. Yet this dominant utilitarianism was far from the whole story, as it competed with five other conceptions of nature. The popular response to natural arches traces the history of non-utilitarian attitudes toward nature. They have been seen as Native American sacred space, as proof for competing geological theories, as illustrations of the aesthetic of the natural sublime, as proof of the existence of God, as manifestations of America's national greatness, and as remnants of wilderness that need protection. At the Grand Canyon, a similar sequence of attitudes unfolded, to counter an intensive utilitarian effort to treat it as real estate, discussed in the following chapter.

5

DISCOVERING THE COLORADO RIVER: BEYOND USE VALUE

Today's visitor to the Southwest arrives with expectations far different from those of explorers and early settlers.[1] The Grand Canyon has become sacrosanct to most Americans, and it is among the most popular national parks.[2] But early U.S. expeditions along the Colorado River did not have the goal of discovering such a shrine. They saw the West as almost empty land, awaiting improvement. In the utilitarian vision, exploration was the first stage in its settlement. New Mexico, Arizona, California, Utah, Nevada, and parts of Colorado had belonged to Mexico until a decade before the Civil War, and to Americans in 1850 the area remained terra incognita. They perceived the region in terms of Manifest Destiny, and the intentions of early explorers were much the same as those who had been first on the Hudson, Ohio, Mississippi, Missouri, Rouge, or Columbia Rivers. These rivers were gateways to new regions. Americans expected that along their banks farmers would settle and towns would rise.

Yet the Colorado was not developed like other American rivers. It never had a major port near its mouth, and although it could be navigated several hundred miles upstream it never carried much trade. Neither Spanish nor American settlers built an important town along its banks. After the Mexican War man-made boundaries ignored the river's geography, leaving the delta in Mexico while most of the river became part of the United States. Transportation routes ignored the river's north-south flow and established east-west trajectories. The wagon roads, the overland mail, the railroads, and finally the highways all treated the Colorado as an obstruction. When dams were built, navigation was not considered important. There were canals to siphon off water to Arizona and California, but no locks for ships. Dams blocked the Colorado as a transportation artery, and it was used for pleasure boating. Americans valued the river for water and to generate electricity, and every state bordering the river demanded as much water as it could get. Were this allocation based on each state's runoff, then California and Nevada would get almost nothing. Arizona and California fought a bitter legal battle over allocations, on one occasion leading Arizona to call out the National Guard.[3] Today, water is parceled out according to legal agreements.[4]

In 1852, Americans knew little about the Colorado River. A few small steamboats were operating on the lower river, but from the government's perspective the region was a blank. Because navigable rivers were considered the key to development, the federal government ordered an expedition, and the War Department selected Lieutenant Joseph Christmas Ives to lead it. He used a steamboat manufactured in Philadelphia, tested on the Delaware, disassembled, shipped to the mouth of the Colorado, and put together again. Ives explored upstream to see how far he could travel without serious impediment and to assess the resources. The national government, laissez-faire in many areas, actively mapped and cleared waterways as a boon to development. The fifty-foot stern-wheeler started in December and for two months carefully beat its way upstream (see figure 5.1). Often stuck on sand bars, Ives reached Black Canyon, near the present site of Hoover Dam, before striking a sunken rock.[5] Leaving the damaged boat behind,[6] the expedition proceeded on foot into the Grand Canyon, bringing back the first American descriptions and drawings of the site. Ives went a considerable way into the canyon, passed Diamond Creek, and with Hualapai guides climbed 5,000 feet up to the rim. The party scrambled with difficulty into side canyons but found the way blocked by vast natural obstacles. On the rim to the east of his camp, Ives wrote:

> The extent and magnitude of the system of cañons in that direction is astounding. The plateau is cut into shreds by these gigantic chasms and resembles a vast ruin. Belts of country miles in width have been swept away, leaving only isolated mountains standing in the gap. Fissures so profound that the eye cannot penetrate their depths are separated by walls whose thickness one can almost span, and slender spires that seem tottering upon their bases shoot up thousands of feet from the vaults below. . . . Our reconnoitering parties have now been out in all directions, and everywhere have been headed off by impassable obstacles. The positions of the main water-courses have been determined with considerable accuracy. The region last explored is, of course, altogether valueless. It can be approached only from the south, and after entering it there is nothing to do but to leave. Ours has been the first, and will doubtless be the last, party of whites to visit this profitless locality. It seems intended by nature

Discovering the Colorado River 69

Figure 5.1   Heinrich Balduin Möllhausen (1825–1905), *Mohave Canyon, Colorado River*, in Joseph C. Ives, *Report upon the Colorado River of the West: Explored in 1857 and 1858* (Washington, DC: U.S. Government Printing Office, 1859), 62–63. *Source:* Wilson Library, University of Minnesota.

that the Colorado River, along the greater portion of its lonely and majestic way, shall be forever unvisited and undisturbed. . . . The country could not support a large population.[7]

If the Colorado River was "profitless" and "valueless," Ives judged the Moqui tribe's irrigated lands to be "the most promising looking for agricultural purposes of any yet seen."[8]

The Colorado River would be little help to White settlers because it had an irregular flow and was difficult to navigate. Ives's "Hydrographic Report" stated that in the delta region, "Memory assists but little in selecting the channel, for it has been known to change from one bank to the other in a single night. The water being turbid and perfectly opaque, it is impossible to determine the depth as in the case of a clear stream." Only an experienced pilot could manage the job. "From the formation and relative positions of the islands and banks, from the eddies, the direction of the currents, from the pieces of driftwood, and other floating substances, the experienced navigator can generally determine the proper course." Upstream, the river contained rocks, rapids, and rough gravel shoals. The further north one went, the shallower it became, and at Black Canyon, near the present site of Hoover Dam, navigation was only possible during moderately high water. Given these conditions, Ives suggested that a 100-foot stern-wheel iron-hulled steamboat, with a draught when light of not more than twelve inches, be built for service from the delta to Black Canyon. Ives estimated that such a boat could make eight or nine trips a year, transporting freight for $30 a ton.[9] As such calculations suggest, he saw the Colorado River valley as an empty space to be settled and exploited.

After explorers came surveyors, and some expeditions performed both functions. As was the case when Americans displaced the French and the British in Detroit, surveyors divided the formerly Mexican land into a grid, establishing the framework for land claims, new roads, and railroads. A decade after Ives's trip, Clarence King surveyed a 100-mile-wide band along the 40th parallel, including part of the route for the first transcontinental railway, completed in 1869. King's report, *Mining Industry* (1870), suggested rich possibilities.[10] More than half of it focused on the Comstock Lode in Virginia City, Nevada, which had produced immense quantities of silver since 1859. Mark Twain provided a popular account of these mining camps in *Roughing It*.[11]

Before King's report was published, in 1869 the Army Corps of Engineers sent Lt. George Montague Wheeler from San Francisco to Nevada and the Colorado River area, with a party of thirty-six people, seventy-nine mules and horses, and eight wagons. His five-month expedition focused on "mining districts, their access to transportation routes, and the disposition of the Nevada Indians."[12] At the same time, the Treasury Department had "a special commissioner of mining statistics, Rossiter Raymond" who was "covering the same mining districts and providing in annual reports the same kinds of information."[13] Henry Adams noted in 1871 that the pursuit of gold and silver in the Great Basin between western Colorado and California created "a feverish, or even furious, spasm of speculative excitement, during which roads and stage lines traversed the region in every direction, while mining camps, towns, and even cities shot up like mushrooms."[14] In the canyons of the Colorado and its tributaries miners found small quantities of gold, copper, and asbestos.[15] All these explorers saw a Colorado River basin awaiting second creation.

Yet these surveyors, travelers, and prospectors were not immune to the pleasures of landscape. Wheeler appreciated the rugged scenery, calling the

Colorado River canyon "the most wild, picturesque and pleasing of any that it has ever been my fortune to meet."[16] King also had lofty sentiments, cultivated by a wide reading, knowledge of art, and personal acquaintance with John Ruskin, who once gave him two paintings by the great British landscape artist J. M. W. Turner.[17] Powell's descriptions of the Colorado River still inspire preservationists,[18] but he spent years promoting dams and irrigation. Even so, he knew that much of the fertile region could never be irrigated from the scant sources available.[19] As Donald Worster noted, "Powell was deeply moved by the sublime geology and brilliant colors of the canyonlands, by sweeping desert vistas, by mountain forests and rills." Yet Powell also "favored turning as much of the wilderness into 'productive' agricultural landscapes as possible—and so did virtually every other white man of his age, except John Muir."[20]

This utilitarian vision of nature as raw material has by no means disappeared. Floyd Dominy, the commissioner of the Bureau of Reclamation from 1959 to 1969, relished building dams during the 1950s and 1960s. His career began in rural Wyoming during the drought years of the Great Depression, when he built small earth dams to help local farmers survive. He was the driving force behind construction of the Glen Canyon Dam, creating Lake Powell (discussed in chapter 4). Dominy made no apologies. Like Edward Everett, who justified building a railroad from Boston to Montreal in 1851,[21] Dominy told John McPhee that Colorado dams made nature democratically available. "Preservation groups claim we destroyed this area because we made it accessible to man. Six hundred thousand people a year use that lake now."[22]

Native Americans have not always opposed mining, and some have worked in mines. However, this does not mean they subscribe to the same utilitarian land ethic as the Bureau of Reclamation. In the nineteenth century, observers noted that Native Americans did not see the land in abstract terms, whether the numerical abstractions of the surveyor or the visual abstractions of the landscape artist. Powell described his Native American guides as follows: "There is not a trail but what they know; every gulch and every rock seems familiar. I have prided myself on being able to grasp and retain in my mind the topography of a country; but these Indians put me to shame. My knowledge is only general, embracing the more important features of a region that remains as a map engraved on my mind; but theirs is particular. They know every rock and every ledge, every gulch and cañon, and just where to wind among these to find a pass; and their knowledge is unerring. They cannot describe a country to you, but they can tell you all the particulars of a route."[23] Native Americans recalled details more than patterns, and they could visualize precisely. Archaeologists have unearthed a drawing on the walls of a kiva from 800 AD. When excavated, the archeologists "noticed discoloration on the lower half of the walls" that they at first thought could be water damage. Once the whole surface was revealed, however, "the outline looked familiar" and they saw that "the forms on the kiva walls were practically a photographic reproduction of the skyline of the Peaks" of the area, which were inscribed with dots that appeared to be "calendrical markers for various positions of the sun throughout the year."[24] This native imagery emphasized the summer and winter solstices, when to plant and when to harvest. Their imagery linked spatial relationships to the rhythm of time.

Powell understood the landscape in terms of geology, and devoted pages of his government report to classifying the forms of desert valleys, first in general terms (diaclinal valleys, which pass through a fold in sedimentary beds; synclinal valleys, which follow synclinal axes, etc.). He then used this terminology to delineate the Green and Colorado Rivers and their tributaries.[25] Combining this knowledge with his appreciation of landscape, Powell had a "map engraved on my mind." He linked the sublime with the new science of geology, and this sensibility could even be made congruent with a pious interpretation of nature.[26] As had been the case with the Natural Bridge of Virginia, Americans saw the Grand Canyon as a proof against atheism, as they subsumed it within the aesthetic of the sublime.[27] The geologist Clarence Dutton wrote a detailed study of the Canyon's rock formations, yet retained a reverential awe toward the site. As Stephen J. Pyne put it, "For Dutton, the scenic cliff and the geological cliff were the same cliff. Both could be understood by similar acts of critical imagination, and one could be trusted to reinforce the meaning of the other."[28] Dutton wrote a passionate scientific analysis that put into words an enthusiasm many felt but could not express. Even before his descriptions were published, the sublime vision of the Grand Canyon was embodied in Thomas Moran's large-format painting *The Chasm of the Colorado*, 1873–1874, which Congress immediately bought for $10,000 and displayed in the Capitol Building.[29] This vision was further expressed in other Moran paintings that the Santa Fe Railroad purchased, reproduced, and distributed nationally.[30]

In contrast, Native Americans did not think in terms of maps or paintings. They knew every nook and cranny of the land, which they imbued with spiritual significance. They often used descriptive place names, as the linguist Keith Basso discovered in research among the Apache. One tribal chairman, Ronnie Lupe, told Basso that White men need maps, but "his people's maps were in the place-names they kept in their visual memories."[31] Every place name is embedded in stories that further fix its significance, so that to tell a story evokes precise visual images through place names such as "Juniper Tree Stands Alone" or "Gray Willows Curve Around a Bend." Given this structuring of knowledge, Basso realized that the Apache were not only a face-to-face community but also a face-to-place community, where the meaning of sites was handed down through the generations by their naming. Similarly, other researchers have found that the Ute tribes "had a descriptive classification system that helped locate a spring, canyon, or resource."[32] These are not names invented by real estate developers, such as "Sharon Street," or "Cedar Avenue," nor are they mere enumerations such as 162nd Street or 11th Avenue. They are descriptive visualizations that are embedded in narratives and rituals.

For most White Americans landscape remained more abstract, and a feeling for the sublime could coexist with the impulse to exploit a region. Wheeler admired the scenery but also made special note of good agricultural land, the possibilities for irrigation, and, most of all, existing and potential mines. In 1871, he led a second expedition into the Grand Canyon area, taking along photographer Timothy O'Sullivan, who produced not only some of the most famous early photographs of the Canyon, but also images of mines, including smokestacks, shafts, and mounds of tailings. Wheeler's expeditions also included San Francisco investors, whose names soon appeared on land claims in Arizona and Nevada.

The early explorers often rejected Native American rights to the land. Wheeler, a recent graduate of West Point who had finished first in his class in philosophy and mathematics and second in engineering, hardly held enlightened views.[33] In 1879, he attacked what he called the "peace-at-any-cost-policy" that he felt the federal government pursued with Native Americans. He declared, "The ever-restless surging tide of population, almost a law unto itself, already in many cases crowd over the borders of these [Native American] reservations, and the time is not far distant when the question of the surrender of these lands to actual settlers will naturally be answered in the affirmative, on the plea of the greatest good for the greatest number."[34] The view that only Whites were "actual settlers" was widespread, and the appeal to "the greatest good for the greatest number" was a repeated utilitarian justification for taking Native American land. In Wheeler's view, their disinheritance provided a suitable topic "for the ethnologist and philosopher, but scarcely for the practical man of affairs, intent on wresting from productive nature the largest bounty."[35] For Wheeler, bounty often meant mining. His 1872 survey examined forty-eight mining districts in Utah, Arizona, and Nevada.[36] For others, the bounty of the West meant lumbering, irrigated farming, or ranching, but it seldom meant creating a national park.

Robert P. Porter, who helped compile the U.S. Census of 1880, wrote a book summarizing its findings that celebrated with no misgivings "the march of civilization" from east to west.[37] In writing about Arizona, he devoted only one sentence to the Grand Canyon.[38] Of the Colorado River, he remarked that although it is the largest in the arid west, it "cannot be used to serve any large quantity of land, owing to its bluff, high banks, and cañon walls, and its slight fall where it flows through open country." Exploiting other streams to the maximum, however, Porter estimated that 3.5 million acres could be irrigated in Arizona, roughly an area 100 miles long and fifty miles wide.[39] He also mused on the human history of the region, where, he reported, "are found abundant signs of a former dense civilization, a civilization far in advance of that of the Indians proper now inhabiting those regions, and resembling in many essential features that of the Moquis and Pueblos." The similarity was "so striking as to lead to the irresistible conclusion that the latter peoples are but the remnant of a large and powerful race that once covered with a dense population this great region." Porter then described the ruins of large towns, which he thought were the last resort of a people under attack. The conclusion was clear: "The Navajos, Apaches, and Utes obtained this country by conquest from this people, and can show no other title."[40] Thus Porter offered a second rationale for conquest in addition to Wheeler's utilitarianism: Native Americans had despoiled a lost civilization. They therefore had no ancient right to the land. If the rationales differed, the conclusion was the same: White settlement was inevitable, desirable, and justifiable.

After the public sensation of his first exploration of the Colorado River, Powell immediately went to Washington and raised money for a second expedition, which took place in 1871–1872. Valuable scientific work came out of this later trip, including maps of the region and considerable exploration of side canyons. As William H. Goetzmann has noted, Powell later "telescoped his labors of 1869–73 into one exciting report, which made it seem as if his two expeditions down the Colorado had actually been one great and all-encompassing voyage of discovery."[41] He waited more than two decades before composing this book, which by the time of its publication in 1895 seemed to have been a journey that set out to discover the Grand Canyon. The book's fifteen chapters culminate in a description of the canyon that is still a useful introduction, though it can mislead the reader about what the region meant to first explorers.[42]

The diary of Powell's photographer Jack Hillers, first published only in 1972, clarifies the early river trip.[43] His laconic entries remind the reader that while Powell was the first to explore the Colorado River systematically, in the same years many others were searching its banks for gold and minerals. Hillers wrote, for example, that on October 6, 1871, they ran into "two prospectors" who "were anxious to reach some cañon where the water ran swift. They said that they had come all along up the river from the Virgin [River]. Found gold everywhere, averaging from 3–5 dollars a day."[44] The following week Powell hired another miner to take rations down river "to the mouth of the Pa Weep."[45] Ten days later, Hillers was exploring away from the river and camped with another surveying party and "had a pleasant time."[46] As such encounters suggest, prospectors and surveyors crisscrossed the area. In addition, it was being settled by Mormons. As early as 1866, the Hualapai Mountains of northern Arizona had been extensively explored, and more than 2,500 mining locations discovered and claimed.[47] Hillers did not have a modern tourist's sensibility. At no point does he sound disappointed to find that someone else had arrived before him. On the contrary, in the difficult situation of taking wooden boats down an uncharted river full of rocky rapids, encounters were welcome. Four decades later the Kolb brothers had the same attitude on their expedition to photograph the canyons of the Colorado, as they gladly hailed any trapper, prospector, or explorer whom they happened to encounter. In short, they conceived the Colorado River more as a resource than as a tourist site.

This attitude suffused an 1882 publication with the descriptive title *From River to Sea: A Tourists' and Miners' Guide from the Missouri River to the Pacific*

Ocean, with alternating chapters on promising mining claims and on natural wonders of the West. A detailed chapter on the mining law came after one on sport fishing.[48] A similar attitude toward the region was evident in another full-fledged expedition down the Colorado River, led by Robert Stanton in 1889–1890. It surveyed several hundred miles of the Colorado as a potential route for the Denver, Colorado Canyon and Pacific Railroad. The idea of a railroad along the Colorado River seemed plausible enough in the abstract. A line connecting Grand Junction, Colorado, to the Pacific coast would take advantage of a water grade by going down through the canyons to southwestern California and leave the river near Las Vegas to cut across to the Pacific. An engineer, Stanton kept meticulous notes of his explorations, filling more than one thousand pages he never published. As Smith and Crampton noted, "Stanton's objective was to find a way to open the canyons to commercial traffic."[49] To this end, he ran a continuous transit line over 350 miles along the Colorado, sketched contour topography, and made detailed maps, until his funds ran low in Glen Canyon. From there on, he did only preliminary work. He argued that such a railroad would not require many tunnels but a great deal of blasting to create stone benches for the tracks. It would have run at a gentle grade through spectacular scenery. Free from ice and snow because of its low elevation, it might have competed effectively with lines through high mountain passes. Its trains could have carried Colorado coal to California, whose coal came from Australia or British Columbia. The line would have appealed to tourists and made extensive mining operations feasible all along the Colorado and its tributaries. Gold placer deposits had been found, including several claimed by the expedition itself. It seemed likely that in the vast system of canyons there would also be copper, silver, lead, and other minerals. Indeed, at the Chicago Columbian Exposition some particularly rich copper ore was displayed from the Grand Canyon.[50]

Stanton's diary reveals that he saw no contradiction between scenic grandeur and railway development. One day he writes that "the views become more grand. The marble mountains come near the river and rise towering over it. . . . The bright colors are entirely wanting, but the nearness of the peaks to the river give one a more correct idea of the greatness of the *whole canyon*" [emphasis in original]. The next day Stanton evaluated the scene with an engineer's aesthetic: "Beautiful railroad bench on granite under the sandstone all around this left turn, 1–40-foot opening, 1–10-foot opening,

Figure 5.2 "Robert Brewster Stanton in Glen Canyon, Colorado River about 1893." *Source:* The Miriam and Ira D. Wallach Division of Art, Prints and Photographs, New York Public Library.

or if the grade will suit, a beautiful line on flat on top of the sandstone."[51] The same rock formation could be both sublime and a "beautiful railroad bench." Stanton's 1,100-plus photographs document not only the railroad, but also his interest in sublime landscape and Native American petroglyphs that would later be submerged under Glen Canyon Dam (figure 5.2). Stanton's railroad never attracted enough investors, but he did raise money to dredge Glen Canyon for gold. He staked 145 claims and brought in ten tons of equipment. He estimated that there were half a billion cubic yards of gravel with gold content at $0.25 a yard, and in 1901 his dredge began to operate. But it produced only a few ounces of gold after a month, when he abandoned the venture.[52]

If mining preoccupied early settlers, prospectors, and surveyors, using the Colorado River for irrigation became a regional obsession. Homesteading the desert through irrigation seemed a logical extension of Manifest Destiny. In the early 1870s, both Wheeler and Powell advocated extensive use of the river for this purpose. In 1875, Lt. Eric Bergland, another West Point graduate, prepared a detailed investigation into "the feasibility of the diversion of the Colorado River of the West from its present channel, for the purposes of irrigation."[53] Small-scale irrigation had been practiced on the Colorado's tributaries, first by Native-Americans and later by Spanish and American pioneers. Near present-day Phoenix, Arizona, the Hohokam tribe built up an extensive canal system focused on the Gila and Salt Rivers that was in use for one thousand years.[54] Five hundred years later the Pima tribe was redeveloping that irrigation system when the United States conquered the Southwest. Native Americans lost many conflicts over water rights, as irrigation became the foundation of regional growth. Along the Nevada-California border, however, there were few tributaries to exploit. Yet the land was suited to agriculture, especially southeastern California, which was once part of the Colorado River delta. Here Bergland wanted to irrigate, but in 1875 no private developer possessed the resources, and the federal government was not willing to be involved.

Elsewhere in California, irrigation developed rapidly. The first combination irrigation-electrification project came in the 1880s, when a self-educated engineer, George Chaffey, created the California communities of Etiwanda and Ontario. From the experience gained in such projects came more grandiose designs. In the 1890s, Chaffey showed investors how to divert the Colorado into an old channel near Yuma, and then run the water through a loop into Mexico and back, to irrigate a portion of the Sonoran Desert that they renamed "The Imperial Valley of California." Settlers arrived even before the water began to flow in 1901, many coming from Arizona's Salt River irrigation area.[55] In the next decade, however, the Colorado River overwhelmed the floodgates, deserted its channel, flooded the settlers' claims, rampaged over the region, and flowed into a desert sink called the Salton Sea. Local investors had insufficient resources to deal with the catastrophe and called on the railroads and the federal government for help.[56]

Congress had stimulated settlement of the lower Colorado through railroad construction and homesteading. This approach had sparked settlement in the Great Plains, but farming the desert also required water. Therefore, in 1902 Congress established a Reclamation Fund to construct and maintain dams and irrigation works in arid and semi-arid lands under the direction of the Secretary of the Interior.[57] Worster, in *Rivers of Empire*, presents the creation of the Bureau of Reclamation as part of the centralization of economic and political power.[58] Because of their high cost and complexity, irrigation systems require central management and tend to concentrate economic resources in a few hands. Enthusiasts saw western irrigation as a way to recreate Jefferson's nation of small farmers in a new geographic setting, but western water projects usually did not sustain a new kind of yeoman farmer. Instead, they favored either large landholders or tightly knit groups, such as the Mormon towns. The startup cost of irrigation was high; accessible water was limited. Congress originally established a maximum of 160 acres that any individual could irrigate from publicly supplied water, but the Bureau of Reclamation's relaxed interpretation of this limit allowed large landholders to get irrigation water at subsidized prices. In fact, a single family could subsist on less land if it always had water and sunshine. In the 1890s, Powell advocated a maximum of eighty irrigated acres per family, creating a denser population than in rural Illinois or Iowa.[59] Something resembling this vision was realized at a few sites, such as the Snake River in Idaho, where in 1920 the Bureau of Reclamation completed a hydroelectric dam and a 630-mile canal system. There, 121,000 acres of formerly arid land produced alfalfa, potatoes, sugar beets, and garden crops, and made possible a dairy industry. These farmers also had electric light and power, at a time when 90 percent of American farmers did not.[60] But communities of small farmers seldom resulted from the Bureau of Reclamation's activities, which tended to concentrate water and wealth in a few hands.

The fundamental premise behind dam building was stated baldly on the cover of the Department of the Interior's *The Colorado River: A Comprehensive Report on the Development of the Water Resources of the Colorado River Basin for Irrigation, Power Production, and Other Beneficial Uses in Arizona, California, Colorado, Nevada, New Mexico, Utah, and Wyoming:* "A Natural Menace Becomes a National Resource." This concluding phrase was taken up in the foreword: "Yesterday the Colorado River was a natural menace. Unharnessed, it tore through deserts, flooded fields, and ravaged villages. It drained water from the mountains and plains, rushed it through sunbaked thirsty lands, and dumped it into the Pacific Ocean—a treasure lost forever. Man was on the defensive. He sat helplessly by to watch the Colorado River waste itself, or attempted in vain to halt its destruction."[61] The Colorado was a thief on the rampage, but it was a wastrel that could be reformed. The report continues: "Today this mighty river is recognized as a national resource. It is a life giver, a powerful producer, a great constructive force." Like a wild horse that had been tamed, its energies were under control: "Its water is providing opportunities for many new homes and for the growing of crops that help to feed this nation and the world. Its power is lighting homes and cities and turning the wheels of industry. Its destructive floods are being reduced. Its muddy waters are being cleared for irrigation and other uses."[62] The *Comprehensive Report* celebrated the domination of nature: "Tomorrow the Colorado River will be utilized to the very last drop. Its water will convert thousands of additional acres of sagebrush desert to flourishing farms and beautiful homes for servicemen, industrial workers, and native farmers who seek to build permanently in the West. Its terrifying energy will be harnessed completely . . . only a nation of free people have the vision to know that it can be done and that it must be done."[63]

The river's meaning had been reduced to use value; its water existed primarily for man, and its energy was to be subjugated. The development of the Colorado River became a part of America's historical fate, an actualization of its Manifest Destiny. A free people could see that they must dominate nature. To realize their freedom, they had to recognize, paradoxically, that they had no choice. Similar plans had been expressed by every previous Secretary of the Interior, including John W. Noble who in 1893 declared, "All through that region, much of which is now arid and not populated, will be a population as dense as the Aztecs ever had in their palmiest days in Mexico and Central America. Irrigation is the magic wand which is to bring about these great changes."[64] The Southwest was to be transformed in a second creation story, which the Bureau of Reclamation still celebrates in photographs of dams and irrigated fields on its website.[65]

The Bureau of Reclamation came under attack during the 1960s, when the Wilderness Act was passed and activists established Earth Day as a countercultural holiday. In response, between 1968 and 1973 the Bureau commissioned forty artists to produce 355 paintings of water projects and the new landscapes they made possible. The artists went on tours to select landscape subjects, and their works were displayed at the National Gallery in *The American Artist and Reclamation* show that then became a traveling exhibition.[66] Some works are images of lush irrigated fields juxtaposed with arid lands, such as Michael Frary's *Irrigation* (figure 5.3). This was the sort of public relations the Bureau of Reclamation wanted. Norman

Figure 5.3   Michael Frary (1918–2005), *Irrigation*, commissioned by the Bureau of Reclamation, c. 1970. *Source:* Bureau of Reclamation.

Rockwell's painting of Glen Canyon Dam has proved to be more problematic. In it, a Navajo man and his wife and son gaze at the dam in the distance (figure 5.4). Mrs. Rockwell photographed the family against the side of a barn, and her husband then painted them into his foreground.[67] Rockwell's career as an illustrator for the middle-brow *Saturday Evening Post* suggests he might have seen the dam in unambiguously positive terms, as the source of irrigation water and electricity for the Navajo reservation. When commissioning him the Bureau of Reclamation presumably hoped to obtain an uncontroversial depiction of progress. However, some critics think Rockwell's canvas is reminiscent of the "last of his race" theme of the Victorian era, which was "a popular nineteenth-century commemorative allegory" in which a Navajo family fatalistically surveys the advance of White society, embodied in a powerful technology that will eliminate the Native American way of life.[68] But Rockwell specialist Jane Allen Petrick

Figure 5.4 Norman Rockwell (1894–1978), *Glen Canyon Dam*, oil, commissioned by the Bureau of Reclamation, c. 1970. *Source:* Bureau of Reclamation.

rejected such a reading and concluded that "in the rigid back of John Lane, the drooping shoulders of his son, the fixed glare of his wife, even the bewildered expression of the dog, Rockwell painted not only the dam, but more significantly, the Indians' condemning reaction to it."[69] Rather than celebrating a second creation narrative, his painting depicts the dam but also suggests the cultural conflicts that surround it.

While the original justification for such dams was irrigation, the lower Colorado basin developed quite differently. The largest city near the river was Las Vegas, and the largest consumers of its water would be Tucson, Phoenix, and Los Angeles, all distant from the Colorado River watershed. The Bureau of Reclamation's most grandiose scheme was the Central Arizona Project (CAP), authorized by Congress in 1968, to pump Colorado water through tunnels, over mountains, and along a 173-mile aqueduct. That authorization took twenty years, followed by surveying and construction for sixteen years. The cost ballooned from an estimated $832 million to $4.4 billion. As conceived in the 1940s and revised in the early 1960s, CAP depended on two new dams to be erected inside the Grand Canyon, which would then supply cheap electricity needed to pump all that water over the mountains. These proposed dams met overwhelming opposition. When it became clear in 1967 that they would not be built, CAP was reconceived. The energy needed to pump water over the mountains would come not from hydroelectric dams but from a new power plant built between 1970 and 1976 that burned coal mined on the Navajo reservation.[70] When the water finally became available in the Phoenix area in 1985, however, irrigated farming was in decline. Many farmers found CAP water too expensive, and they sold their lands to developers. By 1993, when CAP reached Tucson, the agricultural need for the project was disappearing, replaced by urban demand. Since the project had been conceived, the population of the Tucson and Phoenix areas had quadrupled to almost six million people. However, CAP's water quality proved a problem. Tucson residents "complained that the water was foul colored, had a poor taste and smell, and was corrosive to household appliances."[71] The city stopped buying CAP water for a short time and then began to pump much of that water into its aquifer where it blended into the existing supply. By 2000, more than one fifth of CAP water was not used for farming or for domestic consumption. Rather, it was pumped into Arizona aquifers to replenish the diminishing groundwater.[72]

Neither poor water quality, nor cost over-runs, nor the decline of irrigated farming were mentioned in the brochure handed to tourists at Hoover Dam in 1996 (see figure 5.5). It was a precis of the Department of Interior's 1946 report, *The Colorado River*. The dam was "an engineering wonder" with "multi-purpose benefits." The brochure ended with an almost-verbatim quotation from that old report: "Hoover Dam changed the Colorado River from a natural menace to a national resource, strengthening the economy of the Southwest and the Nation."[73] It had paid off the original construction cost, plus 3 percent interest, and its seventeen generators were being "uprated" to increase their peak load by almost 50 percent. Utilitarianism was the gospel of the publications in the Hoover Dam gift shop. But as with Glen Canyon Dam, the costs of second creation had been far higher than expected. Some CAP irrigation districts risked bankruptcy, and it seemed unlikely that even half the $4.4 billion spent on the project would ever be recovered.[74]

Tourists, however, are seldom aware of the huge federal subsidies that made CAP possible. Instead, like the explorers of the 1870s, they shift aesthetics effortlessly when moving through the region. At the Grand Canyon

Figure 5.5 Carol Highsmith (1946–), *Aerial View of Hoover Dam, Arizona*, c. 2005. *Source:* Library of Congress.

most appear imbued with the ideology of "America as nature." But at Hoover Dam, they adopt the utilitarian ideal. Americans still embrace the contradictions found in Powell, King, Wheeler, Stanton, and other nineteenth-century explorers. Resource development has seldom been seen as merely utilitarian; it also has a redemptive quality. The same sensibility that appreciates the sublime view, with its linear perspective into an uplifting infinity, embraces a topographical approach to space itself, in which the gaze encompasses vastness and power, whether in terms of the natural or the technological sublime.[75] An individual could expand the self through an encounter with the absolutely great in nature or through the sense of power gained from the exploitation of resources. The Cartesian sense of space, whether expressed in terms of development or in terms of the sublime, made Native Americans picturesque figures in the landscape.[76] "Natives" were remnants of the frontier, a counterpoint to modernity.

Like the Colorado River, other natural wonders have appealed to developers. Yellowstone's thermal springs might have been harnessed to produce electricity, but such ideas were successfully quashed. But for more than a century, much of the water that cascaded over the brink of Niagara at night has been siphoned off to make electricity, but the tourist does not notice.[77]

At such sites, contradictory forms of sublimity battle for supremacy.[78] The vast and powerful objects of nature seem to offer themselves up for both contemplation and use. Like Ives, Powell, and Stanton, often the same person embraces both ideas. Jefferson sponsored the gridiron land division of the nation but he also celebrated the sublimity of the Natural Bridge of Virginia. Henry Ford built both factories and pastoral retreats. Frank Waters, in a book on the Colorado River, both admired the Grand Canyon's sublimity and enthused over the newly constructed Hoover Dam, which he called "a fabulous unearthly dream. A visual symphony written in steel and concrete."[79] Americans want both wilderness and rapid development, often in the same place. They have internalized the conflicted landscape.

6

GRAND CANYON, 1870–1940: SUBLIME GEOLOGY

Lt. Joseph Christmas Ives thought his antebellum expedition into the Grand Canyon would be the last party of White Americans who would ever visit "this profitless locality." He could not have been more mistaken. A 1974 poll found that the Grand Canyon was the country's most popular national park. The 1991 film *Grand Canyon*[1] suggests its status. All of the dramatic action occurs in Los Angeles, and it concerns the tensions of race, family, and careers, in the intersecting lives of a mechanic, a lawyer, and a film producer. The film's title refers not to the action but to the cultural frame around it. The Grand Canyon is named or discussed three times, but it is not seen until the very end, when the protagonists pile into a van, drive to Arizona, and are united in their encounter with its immensity.[2] The movie viewer is not told where they are driving, and on arrival the camera focuses on their faces, to show their reaction to the view. The immediate response is silence. Lines relax in the adult faces, and the skeptical look of the teenagers grudgingly gives way to wonder. Only at the last moment does the camera swing around, and the vista opens up. As the credits start to roll, the camera moves out over the canyon to display its apparently infinite vistas.

The film assumes the Grand Canyon's iconic value as an uplifting alternative to ordinary life. This view is articulated by a mechanic (played by Danny Glover) as he sits outside his service station. He has just towed a car, rescuing its driver from a gang. The two men sit talking about the incident, putting it in perspective. The mechanic eventually asks, "Have you ever been to the Grand Canyon?" The White lawyer has not, but says he had "always meant to go." He supposes it must be beautiful. The mechanic had hiked to the bottom and spent a night there, realizing it "took so long for that thing to get to look like that. And it ain't done either. It happens right while you're sitting there watching it. It's happening right now while we're sitting here in this ugly town." He pauses to toss an emptied beer can into the trash, and concludes "you just realize what a joke we people are. . . . I figure our time here means diddly to those rocks. It's a split second we've been here. The whole lot of us. And one of us? That's a piece of time too small to give a name." The lawyer asks if this recollection is meant to cheer him up, but the mechanic continues to muse: "Yeah. Those rocks are laughin' at me. I can tell. Me and my worries. It's real humorous to that Grand Canyon." He ends one of the longest speeches in the film with the observation that the canyon made him feel "like a gnat that lands on the ass of a cow that's chewing its cud next to the road that you ride by on at 70 miles an hour."[3]

This speech reprises the sublime response to an immense natural object. Kant described the mathematical sublime as something incomparably and absolutely great. Since every phenomenon in nature is measurable, and therefore only relatively great in relation to other things, the infinity of the sublime ultimately is an idea, not a quality of the object itself. In the presence of the immensity of the Grand Canyon, the mechanic experiences insignificance, feeling like a "gnat on the ass of a cow." But after experiencing awe and insignificance, he reaches a heightened awareness of his place in the universe. Paradoxically, through this negative experience he recuperates a sense of self-worth, because he is able to conceive something more powerful and immense than the momentary reality that his senses can grasp.[4] His visit to the canyon has a therapeutic function, making both his problems and his achievements insignificant. The film *Grand Canyon* suggests that the natural sublime remains a vital part of American culture. Most tourists are awed and many are humbled when confronting its apparent infinity.[5]

Spanish explorers who saw the Grand Canyon in 1540 had difficulty perceiving its size, and, looking down from the rim, thought the river at the bottom was only a few meters wide.[6] For the next three centuries the area was ignored as an impassable barrier to transportation. Havasupai who lived there were less disturbed than tribes elsewhere. The Navajo and the Hopi consider the canyon sacred. The Hopi believe that a supernatural being, Maasaw, greeted them when they first emerged "out of the netherworld." He "bestowed the Grand Canyon to them."[7]

In contrast, White Americans could not plausibly claim to originate in this land. Instead, shortly after they annexed it from Mexico, they relocated it in a geographic imaginary of iconic sites such as the Hudson River Valley, Mammoth Cave, Niagara Falls, and Yosemite. After the Civil War,

Americans expanded this list to include new national symbols in the West.[8] The Grand Canyon was explored at the same time as Yellowstone, but it became a national icon more slowly. Few saw it until near the end of the nineteenth century. Just as importantly, those who did see the canyon often found it so immense and complex that they had no aesthetic to make sense of it. It required a half-century for the Grand Canyon to be defined as a quintessentially American space.[9] Photographs and paintings played an important part in this redefinition, as they both articulated and constituted its significance. The Grand Canyon only became a national park in 1919, seventy years after the Ives expedition stumbled upon it.[10] Why did it take so long?

When Ives entered the Grand Canyon, he saw two kinds of space, neither of which he called "grand." From his utilitarian perspective, it was a "profitless locality" and "altogether valueless." Yet he was fascinated with the "fissures so profound," the "slender spires," and "gigantic chasms." Later explorers experienced a similar ambivalence. They were searching for mines, navigable rivers, and arable land, but they also recognized the site was strange and even "majestic."[11] Yet eyes trained to admire alpine scenery or verdant river valleys had difficulty seeing either the sublime or the beautiful in this enormous cavity with its fantastic landforms.[12]

In 1872, William Cullen Bryant edited a two-volume work, *Picturesque America; or the Land We Live In*, which he called "a delineation by pen and pencil of the mountains, rivers, lakes, forests, waterfalls, shores, cañons, valleys, cities and other picturesque features of our country."[13] The book turned American attention to native landscapes. Bryant insisted that the United States contained "a variety of scenery which no other country can boast of," which offered the artist a gallery of new subjects.[14] He stressed that the transcontinental railroad completed in 1869 gave Americans "easy access to scenery of a most remarkable character." These western landscapes were untainted by the fraternal bloodshed of the Civil War. All citizens, North and South, could identify with Yosemite and Yellowstone, which were prominent in the volume. Bryant also noted that the West had "enriched our vocabulary with a new word . . . cañon, as the Spaniards write it, or *canyon,* as it is often spelled by our people," which he defined for his readers as "one of those chasms between perpendicular walls or rock—chasms of fearful depth and of length like that of a river."[15] He did not mention the Grand Canyon by name, for no stretch of the river had been designated as *the* canyon. Instead, he briefly described the entire Colorado River north of Black Canyon. Grand Canyon was not yet a name or distinct physical location, and the taste for desert landscape and canyons was undeveloped. Bryant allotted the Colorado less than half the space he gave to the Susquehanna River or the Housatonic.

The largely eastern audience had a taste for the sublime, and it had seized upon Niagara Falls, the Hudson River Valley, and the Natural Bridge of Virginia.[16] Initial depictions of the Grand Canyon worked out of this sublime tradition. In 1871, Timothy O'Sullivan made large plates and stereographs of the Grand Canyon as part of the Wheeler Expedition.[17] His images emphasized the enormous scale of the canyon and showed the comparative insignificance of tiny individuals in the foreground. O'Sullivan and other photographers[18] were so early on the scene that government expeditions could name mountains after them, including the newly trained photographer, Jack Hillers, who accompanied Powell on his second trip down the Colorado in 1872.[19] Photographers literally went over the ground together with the first painters. When Thomas Moran visited in 1873, for example, he met Hillers, who guided him to several views. Moran studied Hillers's work as the basis for his own, at times depicting scenes he had not seen first-hand, notably a drawing of Kanab Cañon that appeared in Bryant's compilation.[20] Photographers helped define how Americans would see the Grand Canyon—whether in paintings, engravings, or photographs—from the moment they first became aware of its existence.

Bryant devoted only nine pages to the entire length of the Colorado River, as well as the Green River, for the Grand Canyon was not yet iconic. The initial inability to perceive the canyon as a sublime object was also demonstrated by J. H. Beadle's more than eight hundred pages on *The Undeveloped West*, written between 1868 and 1873. He described a descent into the canyon of the Colorado, but the name "Grand Canyon" did not appear, and the landscape was not his focus but rather the hardships of the journey. The lack of interest in the Grand Canyon is surprising, because Beadle met the photographer of the Powell Expedition, E. O. Beaman, and he used one of Powell's boats to get across the river. In contrast, his book described Yosemite and Yellowstone in detail with accompanying engravings.[21] A decade later, Charles Gleed's massive, all-purpose guide *From River to Sea: A Tourists' and Miners' Guide from the Missouri River to the Pacific Ocean* touted the scenery along the newly completed Santa Fe Railroad, but did not mention the Grand Canyon by name, though it briefly praised the canyon country of the Colorado.[22] Gleed included woodcuts of Yellowstone, Yosemite, The Garden of the Gods, and many other western scenes, but no image of the canyon. The works of Bryant, Beadle, and Gleed together show that during the 1870s, Americans still did not comprehend the Grand Canyon.

Instead, other natural wonders represented the nation and visualized the transcendental conception of nature and a sense of Manifest Destiny. As John Sears has noted: "The strong religious tradition of many Americans predisposed them to construct the symbolic landscape of their own country. . . . America was the Promised Land; God had guided people to its shores for some transcendent purpose; America was the place where the millennial expectations of Christians would be fulfilled." Natural tourist attractions "provided points of mythic and national unity" in a nation without a state religion or ethnic homogeneity.[23] Barbara Novak has also noted how in America nature served as a powerful contrast to European culture. "The opposition between Europe's antiquity and their own wilderness had given Americans an alternative past. They could not look back on a long tradition as could other cultures. . . . But they could relate to an antiquity still unspoiled by man—purer and by implication closer to God."[24] The tourist experienced the natural sublime and learned to interpret it in nationalistic terms.

Powell's 1869 expedition down the Colorado River drew national attention to the Grand Canyon. Until then the name "Grand Canyon" had only appeared on one map, a railway survey the year before,[25] and no one had descended the Colorado River, the last large blank area on U.S. maps. Powell's ten-man expedition disappeared for three months, and newspapers reported it a disaster. He emerged with five other survivors to read his obituary. His survival was a sensation, and when his report of the expedition appeared, supplemented by articles in the popular press, the public learned of a fabulous canyon that dwarfed all other national landscapes.

During the last decades of the nineteenth century a who's who of nature writers and celebrities came to see it. John Muir reported that visitors were struck dumb: "I have observed scenery-hunters of all sorts getting first views of Yosemite, glaciers, White Mountain ranges, etc. Mixed with the enthusiasm which such scenery naturally excites, there is often weak gushing, and many splutter aloud like little waterfalls. Here, for a few moments at least, there is silence, and all are in dead earnest, as if awed and hushed by an earthquake."²⁶ Mark Twain's neighbor and fellow novelist Charles Dudley Warner concurred: "No one could be prepared for it. The scene is one to strike one dumb with awe, or to unstring the nerves; one might stand in silent astonishment, another would burst into tears."²⁷ Buffalo Bill wrote in a visitor's book that the Grand Canyon was "too sublime for expression, too wonderful to behold without awe, and beyond all power of mortal description."²⁸ These were characteristic sublime responses to a site whose size and scale no painting or photograph could capture. Its sublimity was seen as American, and nationalism was a recurrent theme of those who recorded their impressions at the rim. One man declared, "Doubtless, God might have made something more wonderful or more magnificent, but doubtless he never did. America for Americans."²⁹ A woman proudly proclaimed her credentials as a traveler and her judgment of the canyon: "I have visited the whole world. I travel nine months in the year. I have never seen anything so grand as a sunset view of the Grand Canyon."³⁰

Many more visited after September 17, 1901, when the Santa Fe Railroad opened a branch line from Williams, Arizona, that reduced travel time from two days on rutted roads to three comfortable hours. However, early tourists found the Grand Canyon littered with mining claims. A prominent local entrepreneur, James Cameron, fought government plans to make the canyon into a park, eventually taking the fight to Washington after he was elected to the Senate in 1920. Two decades before then he had constructed a small hotel on the rim. Based on mining claims that stretched over seven thousand acres,³¹ Cameron briefly "ran Bright Angel Trail as a toll road," and also claimed the springs at Indian Gardens, which he ran as a tourist camp. Many other locals set up lodgings or tents and made a modest living from tourists. As late as 1917, a witness testified in Washington, "From the rim of the Grand Canyon to the Colorado River there is a string of lode claims covering every foot of the ground. Every foot of the plateau under the El Tovar Hotel is covered by mining claims. In fact, if I remember correctly, there are something like 225 [mining] locations in this neighborhood."³² The land disputes even prevented laying out "a footpath along the rim of the Grand Canyon for the convenience of visitors. The rocks are so sharp along this rim that I have seen women return from this trip of 1¼ miles with their shoes literally torn from their feet."³³ In 1916, Aldo Leopold coauthored a report on the condition of the Grand Canyon for the U.S. Forest Service that then was responsible for it. It described haphazard commercial development that included electric signs, unsanitary conditions, views from the rim blocked by businesses, and a dangerous public enthusiasm for rolling stones over the edge.[34] To deal with such problems, in 1919 Congress transferred jurisdiction from the Forest Service to the newly established NPS. Meanwhile, the courts declared many of Cameron's mining claims invalid.[35] In short, between 1890 and 1920, at the Grand Canyon visions of the sublime quite literally battled utilitarian exploitation.

Yet photographs and paintings from these years seldom depicted these mines or the ore-processing mills constructed at Indian Gardens. Rather, artists disseminated visions of the glory of the Grand Canyon, as they had since Powell invited Moran to come in 1873. Some of his drawings appeared in Powell's 1875 government report. Born in England, Moran came to America at the age of seven. Studying with the Philadelphia painter James Hamilton, he early admired Turner's landscapes, which later he closely examined in England. Moran did not wish to paint European scenery, however. He found it "an anomalous fact, that American artists are prone to seek the subjects for their art in foreign lands, to the almost entire exclusion of their own." He maintained that "no foreigner can imbue himself with a spirit of a country not his own. Therefore, he should paint his own land."[36] Moran's *The Chasm of the Colorado* is a composite of many views sketched in 1873 and completed as a painting the following year (figure 6.1). The scene, partially shrouded in clouds and mists, depicts primal chaos within the great chasm. A storm and an incomplete rainbow near the center of the composition suggest an Edenic world emerging from the energies of creation.[37] A serpent and an American eagle underscore this mixture of the Book of Genesis and nationalism. The impressive rock formations are indistinct, and no scientist could deduce anything more than the existence of sedimentary layers near the top. The avoidance of literalness was precisely what Moran sought: "I place no value upon literal transcriptions of Nature. My general scope is not realistic; all my tendencies are toward idealization." The first great interpreter of the Grand Canyon concluded, "Topography in art is valueless."[38] He disparaged geological drawings that show every sedimentary bed and topological feature with the precision of an architect. Such colorless exactitude was common in early drawings of the Grand Canyon.[39] Moran made details of a scene subservient to a

Figure 6.1 Thomas Moran (1837–1926), *Grand Canyon of the Colorado*, photomechanical print, 1912, based on oil painting of 1874. *Source:* Library of Congress.

visionary transformation. Joni Kinsey's exhaustive study of his *The Chasm of the Colorado* shows that he constructed a "single view from a variety of vantage points and individual vignettes, often rearranging proportions and relationships to create what he called his 'impression.'"[40] It did not mirror a particular scene. Rather, Moran fused observation and memory with his conviction "that the cañons of this region would be a Book of Revelations in the rock-leaved Bible of geology."[41]

Yet if photographers and painters were continuously present after Americans discovered the canyon, it proved hard to depict and difficult to grasp. What were its landmarks? At Yellowstone, an erupting geyser or a hot spring was comparatively easy to frame, and the waterfalls of its river could be depicted using the older conceptions of the sublime and the beautiful. But the Grand Canyon was too large and too complex to be contained in a single image, or even a sequence of images, and it lacked quintessential landmarks like the Old Faithful geyser at Yellowstone or El Capitan at Yosemite. Roughly 2,000 square miles in extent, the Grand

Canyon contained no central feature. Its rim was invisible from the river, and vice-versa. One had to represent the whole on the basis of a selection, but what to select? What, if anything, made the canyon meaningful? Why should a tourist seek it out? If one saw it, what had one seen?

The first photographers who wrestled with these questions arrived with the explorers, and most of their images were made near the river. While they showed its size, power, and effects, the height and the extent of the Grand Canyon as a whole were difficult to represent from the bottom of the inner gorge. Some photographers, notably Bell, Hillers, and Kolb, tried to solve this problem by photographing from elevated locations in the inner gorge, showing the river below.[42] This approximated what river explorers saw if they climbed into side canyons (see figure 6.2). Often, such views emphasized the buttes and rock formations that towered above as much as the river below. Such landscapes transformed Grand Canyon scenery into mountains, but such views were inaccessible to tourists on the rim. They looked down and, to their surprise, were unable to see the river from many outlooks. A river voyage was then dangerous, time consuming, and expensive. As late as 1950 fewer than one hundred people had ever passed through the Grand Canyon in a boat.[43] The few who walked down into the gorge only briefly saw the canyon from one riverside location. The early expedition images, taken near the river, did not depict what early tourists saw from miles away and 5,000 feet higher up.

This disjunction existed in part because of technical constraints. The photographers of the 1870s had to employ a large, viewfinder camera, mounted on a tripod, using heavy glass plates with slow exposure times. Because they worked before the introduction of the dry plate, they needed a portable darkroom nearby in order to prepare a wet plate immediately prior to exposure. Then, immediately afterward, photographers had to wash the plate and "fix" the image.[44] Carrying a darkroom, processing chemicals, and a supply of clean water placed extra demands on an expedition. Frederick S. Dellenbaugh recalled: "The camera in its strong box was a heavy load to carry up the rocks, but it was nothing to the chemical and plate-holder box, which in turn was a featherweight compared to the imitation hard-organ which served for a dark room. This dark box was the special sorrow of the expedition, as it had to be dragged up the heights from 500 to 3000 feet."[45] Preparing a wet plate, a demanding process in a studio, was arduous in the dusty desert. The weight of the equipment and

Figure 6.2 William Bell (1831–1910), *Grand Canyon, Inner Gorge, Near Paria Creek, Looking West*, 1872. *Source:* Metropolitan Museum of Art.

the time required to deploy it before making an image restricted the photographer's range of movement and the number of images one could make in a day. The temperature extremes of the Southwest further increased the difficulties. In cold weather the collodion solution froze, and in hot weather it "ran" on the plate.

The steep trails out of the Grand Canyon compounded these technical difficulties. The Bright Angel Trail, with its many switchbacks, still the easiest route down from the South Rim, suggests the challenges photographers faced: precipices, uneven footing, searing heat, and no water. Therefore, most images were made near the boats. Carrying nothing more than a light pack with the obligatory food, water, and clothing needed for sudden changes in the climate is strenuous; transport and use of a full photographic outfit required several men. Today's hiker has a trail and a map, but the first photographers in the Grand Canyon had no maps, no trails, and no mules. They also faced the time pressures of an expedition hastening down the river before food supplies ran out. All photographic equipment had to be packed into boats with great care after each stop, so that it could not shift about or fall out, even if the boat capsized, which was by no means unusual. Glass plates could break, muddy water could foul the chemicals, and constant exposure to mist and spray could damage a camera. Roll film and handheld cameras became available by the 1890s, but the images produced were not of high quality, and for another generation all serious photographers at the Grand Canyon still used large viewfinder cameras resting on tripods.[46]

Yet these difficulties created one advantage. It was unthinkable that any expedition would casually select its photographer. Expedition leaders understood that good photographs were essential documentation when seeking public support and further funding.[47] They required experienced professionals who could improvise in the field and who knew how to protect glass negatives as they moved through rough terrain. For their part, the photographers expected to make a living not from the scanty wages but from selling prints, particularly stereographs. Prior acquaintance with the taste of the eastern audience was therefore essential.[48] Yet if expedition photographers made landscapes that would satisfy that audience, the official justification for having them along was scientific record-keeping. Explorers knew the power of the image to publicize their journeys, and they understood the profits to be made from selling reproductions.[49] Stereographs were particularly effective in conveying a three-dimensional sense of vast landscapes, and they helped to make the Grand Canyon famous. Powell played a central role in this process. Directed by the Smithsonian to hire a photographer for his 1871 expedition, he employed E. O. Beaman, who made 350 images. Beaman's contract with Powell and the expedition's topographer divided the reproduction rights to stereographs equally. Powell later purchased Beaman's share and long profited from sales made by the Jarvis Company of Washington, DC.[50]

Photographs authenticated verbal descriptions of new places. They played a role in the creation of the first national park at Yellowstone. The images made there in 1871 by William H. Jackson were displayed to Congress, which unanimously passed a bill establishing the park in the following year. (Earlier, Carlton Watkins's images had played a similar role in promoting Yosemite.) In subsequent decades these images of the hot springs, geysers, and waterfalls were generally thought to have accomplished "a work which no other agency could do and doubtless convinced everyone who saw them that the region where such wonders existed should be carefully preserved to the public forever."[51] The written report and lectures of F. V. Hayden, the Yellowstone expedition leader, also played a decisive role.[52] The often-repeated tale about the impact of these photographs was enhanced by a naiveté characteristic of the nineteenth century. People thought that while words could exaggerate, the "camera told the truth; and in this case the truth was far more remarkable than exaggeration."[53] The camera seemed a scientific instrument, and photographs even understated reality, since they were in black and white. Precisely because photographs were taken to be objective they were an effective means of promotion.

The early availability of Grand Canyon photographs did not prompt immediate creation of a national park. Images from the inner gorge failed to represent what most tourists saw. They authenticated the heroism of explorers, depicting the spectacular hardships they endured. The hardships were a good story, but they did not define a tourist site, much less a national icon. Photographs from the water's edge and looking up at monumental scenery relied on the conventions of mountainous landscape, which was not what tourists saw. Photographs from the rim, however, provided a view that did not fit conventional ideas of alpine landscape. From above, the canyon was a chaotic jumble beneath a disconcertingly flat horizon.

Before the Grand Canyon could be considered the equal of Niagara or Yellowstone, three things were necessary: easier access, vigorous promotion, and, most important, a convincing way for the public to understand the site. The creation of such an interpretative schema was already underway from the moment that Ives first pushed into the area. In his expedition was John Newberry, one of the central figures in the development of geology in the United States. Newberry grasped the scientific value of the canyon as a series of sedimentary beds that exposed to view millions of years of history. His student Karl Gilbert returned to the area with the Wheeler expedition. Newberry and Gilbert realized that in walking down to the bottom they walked toward the origins of the earth. As Stephen J. Pyne explains, armed with this insight, "the Colorado River became one of the scientifically great rivers of the world, and its canyon not merely an indescribable and impassable tangle of gorges."[54] As Newberry put it, the canyon was the "most splendid exposure of stratified rocks that there is in the world."[55]

Geology was still a new field during the 1870s, however, and much of the public did not understand wind and water erosion to be the major forces shaping the earth's contours. Even the leading geologist Charles Lyell had believed that the movement of the ocean was more important than streams and rivers, and Cuvier's catastrophe theory was still taken seriously. Armed with such ideas, early Canyon visitors could not imagine that the Colorado River could have created the vast and chaotic landscape. Many then believed the earth was but a few thousand years old, and they correctly saw that gradual erosion would require much more time than that. Symptomatically, Moran's *The Chasm of the Colorado*, 1873–1874, could not be read as a representation of the erosive power of water, nor as a representation of the passage of time. Rather, Moran presented the Grand Canyon as a massive wonder. With self-proclaimed artistic license, he represented no actual place or point of view, but arranged a composite of impressions on a canvas that converted the actual downward gaze into a look upward. Moran's canyon was a strange and remarkable sight, but it did not represent the natural laws at work in the Grand Canyon.

To most who first saw it, the Grand Canyon was a magnificent oddity—not a scientific exhibit. Only after the centrality of water erosion to its formation became accepted among scientists and the public would there be a new way to grasp its meaning. The canyon became the central proof of this fluvial theory,⁵⁶ particularly in the work of the geologist Clarence Dutton. His detailed study of its rock formations retained a reverential awe toward the site, in a government publication that contained alternating chapters on science and landscape. Dutton established the view from the rim as the standard, both for aesthetic appreciation and for scientific observation.⁵⁷ Yet his 1882 publication was not read by a wide audience. Scientists alone do not create national icons, which also require promotion and good access to the site.

Photographers and painters together developed conventions to depict the canyon. Successful images combined sublimity and geology, while emphasizing the enormous scale, often through inclusion of a miniscule human figure in the near distance.⁵⁸ The Kolb brothers, who built a studio on the rim of the Grand Canyon at the head of the main trail, did far more than make a living taking photographs of tourists.⁵⁹ The Kolbs knew Moran and they shared images with him, and of course viewed his paintings. When the Kolbs made a river journey from Wyoming to the Grand Canyon, taking photographs all the way, Moran was one of the first people to see their prints, and the painter already knew many places they had photographed, and could name them. The two mediums were not in conflict but complementary. These artists strove to convey the immensity of the scene, preferring broad views and high perspectives. Their work adorned publications distributed by the major railroads. Moran provided engravings to *Scribner's* for Powell's articles on the discovery expedition, and these were frequently reprinted. Moran was also sought out by other magazines for illustrations, and he contributed to the widely read *Picturesque America*.

The Atchison, Topeka, and Santa Fe Railway recognized the importance of artistic representations in luring passengers to the Southwest in general and the Grand Canyon in particular. The railroad company began to use Moran's illustrations in advertising and brochures as early as 1877, and increased their dissemination once it had built a branch line to the Grand Canyon and spent $500,000 on the luxurious one-hundred-room El Tovar Hotel and the more modest Bright Angel Lodge.⁶⁰ The railroad financed annual trips by Moran and other artists to the South Rim where they were given hotel rooms.⁶¹ Moran came every year from 1901 until his death in 1926, and an outlook is named after him. In 1901, the Santa Fe Railway produced 174,000 copies of *Grand Cañon of Arizona*, 15,000 copies of a pamphlet, *Titan of Chasms: The Grand Canyon of Arizona,* and a smaller run of a 123-page anthology "of words from many pens" as well as artistic illustrations.[62] These publications encouraged Americans to seek out their country's scenic wonders, and they included an essay and illustrations by Moran.[63] Other railroads reproduced his work or found illustrations of a similar nature. From its discovery, the Grand Canyon was represented as sublime.

In 1906, Henry Ford, his wife Clara, and son Edsel visited the Grand Canyon by train on their way to California (figure 6.3). They returned again in 1911 and spent New Year's Eve at the canyon's bottom. The next day they walked up to the rim. Edsel photographed the canyon and watched the Hopi dances staged outside Hopi House. Edsel visited again with some friends in 1915, and the following year took his bride there for their honeymoon, booking rooms at the El Tovar.[64] The railway did not monopolize transportation to the Grand Canyon for long. The highways of 1902 were so poor that an automobile trip to the Grand Canyon was a

Figure 6.3   Henry and Clara Ford at the Grand Canyon, 1906. Photographer not identified. *Source:* Courtesy of The Henry Ford.

feat. A steam-powered six-wheeler needed two days to rattle from Flagstaff to the South Rim.[65] But cars and roads improved, and in 1920 ten thousand people drove to the canyon. The price of an automobile made on Ford's assembly line fell rapidly, and by the end of the 1920s there was one car for every six Americans.[66] They cruised the countryside on weekends and toured national parks during summer vacations. In 1927, for the first time more people arrived at the Grand Canyon by automobile than by train, even though Arizona had only 219 miles of paved roads.[67]

By 1912, the Grand Canyon was being proclaimed one of the *Three Wonderlands of the American West*[68] on a par with Yosemite, and Yellowstone, despite the fact that when it became a national park in 1919, only a tiny minority of Americans had seen it. Instead, they knew it from the paintings of Moran, Henry F. Farny, and F. H. Lungren, from the photographs of Jack Hillers, Timothy O'Sullivan, and the Kolb brothers, and from stereographs. These images, like the tourism they promoted, often depicted the view from a hotel, as in "Man Hath No Part in this Glorious Work" (figure 6.4). As this title suggests, by the 1920s the view from the rim could be both sublime and geological. This view was also presented in the Grand Canyon diorama at the 1901 Pan-American Exposition in Buffalo, and in

Figure 6.4 *Man Hath No Part in All This Glorious Work—From Grandview Hotel. Grand Canyon, Ariz.*, c. 1925, Keystone View Company. Photographer not identified. *Source:* Library of Congress.

a larger three-dimensional model at the 1915 Panama-Pacific Exposition in San Francisco.[69] These dioramas further established the downward gaze into the canyon as the correct one rather than its construction as a mountain landscape seen from the river.

The Santa Fe Railroad, which sponsored these dioramas, made its hotels and other conveniences into subsidiary icons. The text on the back of one postcard read, "From the wide, comfortable porch of Hermit's Rest, the most recent building erected by the Santa Fe for the convenience and comfort of the traveler at Grand Canyon, a far reaching and most interesting view can be had." The card depicted the porch, and the accompanying text insisted that, "The finest effects at the Grand Canyon are altogether uncommunicable by brush or pen. They give themselves up only to personal presence.... You cannot paint a silence, nor an emotion, nor a sob."[70] It told the reader the emotions proper to the site: awestruck silence or an inarticulate cry. The photographic image itself was defined as being always inadequate to the immensity and complexity of the scene. The image represented the experience and yet was disparaged as being inherently deficient. The photograph, no matter how spectacular, was a mere suggestion of the powerful experience a tourist could enjoy in person. Therefore, it was appropriate to represent the bench, the porch, or the hotel from which the canyon might be studied. The tourist was assured of both comfort and awe.

The need to observe the canyon for long periods of time also became a theme of its photographic representation. Once the chasm's general appearance had been established, it became popular to depict the Grand Canyon when engulfed with fog, which obscured its depths and made it more mysterious. In 1905, the Detroit Photographic Company sold an image of "Fog effects near Hotel El Tovar," which provided only glimpses of the famous view. The Grand Canyon had many moods. One needed to stay at the hotel for days to see it in sunshine, storm, lightning, shadow, wind, snow, and fog. Its multiplicity became part of its allure, suggesting once again the impossibility of full photographic representation. Only a stay at the El Tovar could make good this deficit.

Since static representations were insufficient, cameramen turned to film. In 1911, the Kolb brothers took the first moving images from a boat trip down the river. By 1915 they had expanded their studio on the South Rim, putting in a small theater for the tourists.[71] The Ford Motor Company, which provided short subjects to movie theaters across the country, also made a film about the Grand Canyon that was distributed in 1920. It began with a map of the Colorado River plateau and a diagram illustrating the sedimentary layers that the river had cut through. It then showed tourists on horseback descending into the canyon on what had become the typical trip down Bright Angel Trail to Phantom Ranch.[72] In 1920, 67,315 people visited the park; a much larger audience saw the Ford film.

Even as the mule trail became familiar, new views of the Grand Canyon were also becoming available. In 1917, Orville Wright told a conference on the national parks in Washington, DC, that airplanes could take small groups to national parks once airstrips were established. He thought, however, that parks "must be viewed from the ground to be fully appreciated. The giant sequoia, when viewed from on high will be no more impressive than a modest shrub, and the Grand Canyon of the Colorado will flatten out almost to a plain. Though the shining river will be seen winding its tortuous way in a mass of variegated colors, the grandeur of the gorge in size and sculpture will be gone."[73] In 1919, the Army Air Service began a series of flights across the United States to map air routes for commercial use. On February 24, a DeHavilland DH-4 bomber flew over the Grand Canyon, and its pilot found that "the river was like a pencil. Every wiggle, every shade every shadow of the giant gorge was visible at once and there is nothing comparable to it." The next day a second army plane carrying a Fox News motion picture photographer cruised over the rim and dropped down 2,000 feet for a closer look.[74] Even as the wire services hummed with the story, Congress made the Grand Canyon a national park. The following year a daredevil pilot flew within 100 feet of the river, negotiating the tight confines of the inner gorge.[75] In 1923, aerial photographs were made over the entire length of the canyon and published in *National Geographic*.[76] This suggested a new tourist experience, but few paid to see it in the 1920s. Attempts to establish commercial air service failed until 1931, when the demand for aerial views had increased enough for Grand Canyon Airlines to begin regular flights.[77] It signed a contract with the two park concessionaires, Fred Harvey Company on the South Rim and the Utah Parks Company on the North Rim, granting them a percentage of sales in exchange for exclusive rights to provide air transport. Park superintendent M. R. Tillotson approved this arrangement.[78]

However, Tillotson successfully opposed demands from motorists for a road across the Grand Canyon, so they could quickly see it from multiple perspectives. Automobile traffic had been officially permitted in national parks in 1913, and it grew rapidly during the 1920s. When construction began on Hoover Dam, Grand Canyon tourism increased. By the end of the 1930s, it had become the central tourist site in the American Southwest, with four hundred thousand annual visitors.[79] However, to get from the North Rim to the South Rim was time consuming. It was only a dozen miles away, but to get there one had to drive 200 miles, crossing the river at Hoover Dam. Yet the NPS considered a direct route through the canyon a desecration of the site. Tillotson declared: "To break the age-long silence of the Canyon with the honking of horns, to carve roadways into its formidable rainbow walls, to impair the normal impregnability of Nature, to make it easy for anyone to conquer the Grand Canyon, that would be sacrilegious indeed."[80] His defense of the canyon against road building established a precedent that was respected as tourism multiplied from about four hundred thousand visitors a year in 1940 to almost six million in 2016.[81]

After World War II, the NPS contested the Bureau of Reclamation's proposal to divert the Colorado River through a fifty-four-mile "tunnel under the Kaibab Plateau to a powerhouse on Kanab Creek." If built, it would have transformed much of the Grand Canyon into a dry ditch, except for sporadic freshets from the Little Colorado River.[82] At the south end of the canyon, visitors would have seen the diverted Colorado River cascading from a minor tributary, Kanab Creek. These waters would then have been impounded behind the proposed Bridge Canyon Dam that the Bureau of Reclamation wanted to construct, creating an eighteen-mile lake inside the canyon. The overall result would have been a dry Colorado riverbed in the northern half of Grand Canyon leading to an artificial lake. Fortunately, this project was defeated.

It had taken Americans generations to understand the Grand Canyon as a sublime landscape. By the middle of the twentieth century, it seemed that art and nature appreciation had triumphed over utilitarian values. But the conflict was by no means over. Some corporations wanted to mine Navajo coal and the federal government permitted uranium mines near the rim. Mass tourism also would become a problem. But before examining these matters, the following chapter examines the conquest of nature in the skyscraper city.

7

SKYSCRAPER AND SKYLINE: UTILITARIAN SUBLIME

The stress and the pace of city life spurred interest in preserving nature, and the national parks were set aside at the same time that the United States was becoming an urban nation. A Chicago clergyman, Charles W. Gilkey, spoke to the National Parks Conference of 1917 on "The Spiritual Uplift of Scenery as Exemplified by the Grand Canyon." He told the audience, "better than any place I know, the canyon creates that awe and reverence which are at the very foundation of all spiritual life. . . . What the canyon does for you is to pick you out of circumstances and scenes and away from people and ways of living that do little to stimulate your awe and reverence, and to set you down in the place where, try as you will to resist, try as you will to hold yourself in another mood, you cannot help yielding to your awe and reverence."[1] Once back in Chicago, Gilkey "tried, in a series of three addresses to my own people there, to review some of the spiritual uplift of such scenery as that in our western parks, and particularly in the Grand Canyon." He wanted his Hyde Park congregation "by proxy, as it were, . . . [to] enjoy the spiritual uplift of our western scenery." Many other Americans agreed that the psychological pressures of urban life seemed to require the counterbalance of sublime nature. As the Secretary of the Interior put it in 1915: "Just as the cities are seeing the wisdom and the necessity of open spaces for the children, so with a very large view, the Nation has been saving from its domain the rarest places of grandeur and beauty for the enjoyment of the world."[2] Or, as the Secretary of the Smithsonian averred, "Men and women with minds weary from the constant turmoil of business will inhale the elixir of life in the parks."[3] If American conceptions of nature were contradictory, these differences were useful. The Director of the United States Geological Survey reflected, "Where better than in these wide spaces telling of the infinite past can tired and troubled humanity find relief from the petty things of the city street, and win that true recreation of spirit to fit us for the duties of life?"[4]

The national parks offered psychological release from the city, but the two realms were nevertheless linked in many ways. During the same decades that Americans explored the Southwest and began to see the Grand Canyon not as a "profitless locality" but rather as a sublime creation, they were also inventing the skyscraper and completing the world's largest railroad system. These activities were intimately connected in their timing, technology, and psychology. The first skyscrapers were built after the Chicago Fire of 1871, at the very moment when Yellowstone was designated the first national park and Powell was exploring the Colorado River. The national enthusiasm for the "wonders" of the West coincided with a renewed enthusiasm for the technological sublime that the railroads had embodied since the 1830s, but which by the 1870s began to include the towers of Brooklyn Bridge under construction in New York, and the first skyscrapers in Chicago. Railroads stimulated the explosive growth of American cities, and they enabled tourism to the new national parks. The urbanite wanted Pullman sleeping car service to and from the wilderness, and wealthy families owned private rail cars. Every line advertised the attractions of its particular park. The Central Pacific touted the Rocky Mountains. The Santa Fe made the Grand Canyon its iconic site with a branch line that ended a stone's throw from the South Rim. The Great Northern promoted Glacier Park and ran tracks by its entrance.[5] In fact, the railroads not only provided service to the parks but also promoted their establishment. The financiers of the Northern Pacific vigorously lobbied Congress for the first park at Yellowstone, and then advertised their line as "The Yellowstone Route" to the West.[6]

Railways also drove expansion of the steel industry. They transported coal and iron ore to the mills and demanded improved steel for their rails and bridges. Steel was also the indispensable material in skyscrapers. By abandoning masonry construction it was possible to build tall structures without bulky walls at street level. Just as important, as Thomas Misa has shown, building with steel was fast. In Chicago, "with steel-skeleton construction it took only twelve months from turning out the old tenants and destroying the old building to installing new tenants in a new building."[7] By 1891, in just three months a steel framework was erected and walls, plumbing, elevators, and windows were added to create a Chicago department store. Streetcars and subways, which like the railroad ran on steel rails, concentrated offices and shopping in the downtown area. As Misa concluded, "New York and Chicago would have been inconceivable without steel-lined transport systems and steel-framed buildings. They were the first cities of steel."[8] The horizontal city with its slowly constructed beaux-arts architecture remained characteristic of Europe, where building heights were restricted to four or five floors. Americans built enormous towers more quickly.

The skyscrapers and the great steel bridges were erected to a surprising extent by Native Americans, particularly Mohawk from the Canadian border region. They first showed an aptitude for work in high steel when employed as day laborers during bridge construction over the St. Lawrence River. They proved fearless, agile, and sure-footed, and they excelled at the difficult job of riveting. They worked on bridges all over Canada, and gradually spread out to work in Cleveland, Chicago, Buffalo, Detroit, and New York, and San Francisco. They put up the steel framework of the Chrysler Building, Rockefeller Center, and the Golden Gate Bridge. In New York they worked on the "R.C.A. Building, the Cities Service Building, the Empire State Building, the Daily News Building, the Chanin Building, the Bank of the Manhattan Company Building, the City Bank Farmers Trust Building, the George Washington Bridge, the Bayonne Bridge, the Passaic River Bridge, the Triborough Bridge, the Henry Hudson Bridge, the Little Hell Gate Bridge, the Bronx-Whitestone Bridge, the Marine Parkway Bridge, the Pulaski Skyway, the West Side Highway, the Waldorf-Astoria, London Terrace, and Knickerbocker Village."[9] Native Americans were central figures in the high steel construction of the skyscrapers and bridges in all parts of the country. They typically divided their time between work in the city and leisure on the reservation, often driving hundreds of miles to be at home for a few days.[10]

Like them, urban Americans found national parks a restful escape from the tensions of the city. In 1908, President Roosevelt convened a conference of state governors, where the president of the American Civic Association praised "the renewing of strength and spirit that comes from even a temporary sojourn amidst natural scenic delights. The President has but just returned from a 'week-end' visit to his castle of rest in the Virginia Hills. Could he have had equal pleasure in Hoboken? [Laughter] Mr. Carnegie's enterprise built Homestead—but he finds the scenery about Skibo Castle much more restful! Who of us, tired with the pressure of Twentieth Century life, fails to take refuge amid the scenes of natural beauty . . . ?"[11]

Yet if American leaders at times grew weary of commerce, they found exaltation in its spectacular expression, the skyscraper, which projected the grid of the land survey skyward.[12] The skyscraper embodies the logic of the utilitarian vision of nature, as raw material being worked up to its highest expression. The skyscraper cannot be understood simply as the logical outcome of property values. If it were, then no skyscraper would rise higher than justified by the rental return on investment. The builder of the Woolworth Building warned its owner that the building was going to be too tall, with no economic justification for its higher floors. But the dime store magnate explained that his building's value lay not only in offices but also in public relations. It would be the tallest building in the world in 1913, and such a landmark was worth millions in publicity. Moreover, tourists would pay admission for a skyscraper view of the city.

American cultural preferences encouraged skyscrapers. Many European cities were more densely populated than New York or Chicago in 1900, but they built few tall buildings before World War II. London's first skyscraper went up in the 1950s, and it was an American Hilton Hotel. In 2020, Copenhagen still resisted tall buildings. When a European city did build them, for example in Frankfurt after World War II, they seldom included observation decks. More than Europeans, Americans liked and encouraged skyscrapers.

Gertrude Stein's stream-of-consciousness meditation on New York's skyscrapers suggests how these buildings were understood when new. "When I used to try to explain America to Frenchmen of course before I had gone over this time, I used to tell them you see there is no sky over there there is only air, when you look up at the tall buildings at the time I left America the Flatiron was the tallest one and now it is not one at all it is just a house like any house but at that time it was the tallest one and I said you see you look up and you see the cornice way on top clear in the air but now in the new ones there is no cornice up there and that is right because why end anything. . . ."[13] Stein saw skyscrapers as American cultural experiences. France had no such buildings, and many Europeans found them vulgar and pretentious. Mark Girouard notes that in turn-of-the-century London, Paris, and Berlin "a sense of hierarchy led to high buildings being prohibited by law: it was for long unthinkable that cathedrals, palaces or public buildings should be overshadowed by commercial structures."[14] Henry James disliked skyscrapers, and much preferred the horizontality of the "great Palladian pile just erected by Messrs. Tiffany. . . . One is so thankful to it, I recognize, for not having twenty-five stories."[15] Architects trained in Italian and French traditions felt skyscrapers violated classical proportions. The Columbian Exhibition in Chicago intentionally rejected the tall building in favor of the beaux arts style and the horizontal city. Its planners had absorbed classical culture and sought to reproduce and sustain it.[16] They meant to show that they valued a European sense of the sky, framed like paintings by the cornices of long horizontal buildings and reflected in great lagoons. The skyscraper violated the sense of the sky by thrusting up so high, and by eliminating the cornices, crowning domes, and other traditional ways of framing a building. Why, as Stein asked, end anything? Like her verbal stream of consciousness, the skyscraper was a continuously unfolding sequence that ran into the future, and it would later find expression in sheer glass towers and skyscrapers with mirrored surfaces.

Unlike Stein, most architecture books presented skyscrapers as isolated things in themselves, not as part of an ensemble of buildings, and not as a rewriting of our relationship to air and sky. In such criticism, each structure represents a particular style or movement, placed in a sequence like paintings hung on a gallery wall. Too often these buildings are decontextualized, idealized, and shorn of human presence. In older architecture books, skyscrapers are not presented as part of the flow of everyday life. Even very good critics such as Paul Goldberger tend to see them as things apart, like art objects in the white space of a museum.[17] Photographs in such volumes tend to present each building alone, excluding as much as possible of the surrounding architecture. The buildings are then discussed in terms of their formal qualities, as seen by architects, not in terms of how the public receives them in their urban context. The building's appearance is discussed either from the perspective of someone standing on the ground, or from an idealized position in midair. The classic view is from the outside, looking at the building.

In contrast, for the public the skyscraper achieved much of its meaning as a vantage point that created new experiences of space. In popular culture the skyscraper is a platform that changes one's relationship to the city. When people look at skyscrapers from the ground, it is seldom from immediately in front of the building. Even a colossus like the Empire State Building may be ignored by people walking right by it, not only because of the many distractions of the street, but because the building is literally quite hard to see from nearby. Skyscrapers are recognized at a distance as part of a general pattern. Except for the most famous buildings, few people can name them, much less their architects. Instead, the public learned to appreciate a landscape of skyscrapers, and a new word entered the American language to describe the cluster of tall buildings in a city center: the "skyline." In short, there were two popular ways of understanding the skyscraper: as part of an ensemble that composed a skyline and as an Olympian vantage point. Public appreciation of skyscrapers was part of shift from the horizontal walking city to the vertical city of mass transportation.[18] A new aesthetics of the technological sublime presented urban space in the terminology that had been used to describe spectacular natural sites since the eighteenth century. The sense of awe before an overwhelming natural power and infinitude, which Kant and Edmund Burke had identified as the characteristic emotion of the sublime, Americans transferred to great bridges and skyscrapers.[19]

During the 1920s, exhibitions, magazine articles, displays in department stores, and works of art manifested the public enthusiasm that Merrill Schleier has called "skyscraper mania." In 1924, the *New York Times* ran an article on "The Excelsior of Architecture," with illustrations by Hugh Ferriss, that compared skyscrapers with gothic cathedrals, both of which seemed "to hang from heaven."[20] The following year, a magazine article admired "America's Titanic Strength Expressed in Architecture," and said of the new skyscrapers: "Man enjoys overwhelming effects of extraordinary power. The simpler these titanic expressions are, the more they satisfy him. They appeal to his imagination, to his reverence, they transcend all petty things."[21] As Schleier summarized, the image of the skyscraper as a sublime object "was adopted by optimists and pessimists alike. The numerous paintings and photographs of boundless towers rendered from disorienting perspectives" manifested amazement at the skyscraper's ungraspable monumentality.[22]

In Sinclair Lewis's novel *Arrowsmith*, his medical researcher-hero who has recently moved to the city with his wife is awed by the New York skyline. Riding the elevated on his way to the research center where he was to start his new job, he "beheld the Woolworth Tower" then the world's tallest building, and "he was exalted. To him architecture had never existed; buildings were larger or smaller bulks containing more or less interesting objects. His most impassioned architectural comment had been, 'There's a cute bungalow; be a nice place to live.' Now, he pondered, 'Like to see that tower every day—clouds and storms behind it and everything—so sort of satisfying.'"[23] For Arrowsmith, the sublimity of the skyscraper objectified his desire to excel.[24]

In 1926, the year after Lewis's novel appeared, Claude McKay published "Song of New York" in the *New Masses*.[25] McKay celebrated "the world's most splendid town, / Grey stone and iron rushing to the sky." Comparing New York favorably to Paris ("a lovely whore, / In jeweled dress attracting everyone") and Berlin ("a raw and bleeding sore") he has a double vision. On the one hand, he "realized New York" was a "demon holding in his hand a whip / Driving me through the cold straight streets to work." Arrowsmith likewise feels the pulse of the city and works harder in New York than anywhere he has lived before. It doesn't take long, as he hurries to and from work each day, until he scarcely looks up at the skyscrapers. "The city of Magic was to become to Martin [Arrowsmith] neither a city nor any sort of magic but merely a route: their flat, the subway, the Institute, a favorite inexpensive restaurant."[26]

On the other hand, the fast pace of the city gave way to a different experience, when, from a distance, Martin experienced the skyline. Or, as McKay put it:

> Yet once you stand upon New Jersey's soil
> With a child's attitude and turn your face
> Toward the first citadel of modern toil,
> A great rock jutting grandly out in space,
> You'll never forget that marvel of these years,
> Around which wash the world's increasing tides,
> And, spurred by loves and hopes and stinging fears,
> Six millions scrambling up her steel-ribbed sides.[27]

Lewis and McKay could assume their readers knew the skyline. McKay did not need to describe it, but focused on what it represented: a "citadel," a "great rock" that six million people were trying to scale. He fused several responses; this marvel evoked awe, love, fear, and hope.

McKay and Lewis had internalized the meanings of the skyscraper, as had their readers. To explore what the panorama of New York first meant one has to go back a generation to when it was new and its meanings were openly discussed. By the 1890s, people realized the unintended outcome of skyscraper building would be a new view of Manhattan, seen from the harbor or its two rivers. The term "skyline" emerged to describe this new vertical city.[28] The architectural critic Montgomery Schuyler remarked that the silhouette of Manhattan visible from the surrounding shores had a symbolic quality that was not a conscious intent of architects, but a concatenation of the whole: "It is in the aggregation that the immense impressiveness lies."[29] Schuyler's generation witnessed the creation of an artificial New York horizon, a man-made substitute for the geology of mountains, cliffs, and canyons. This horizon would become iconic by the 1930s (see figure 7.1).

In 1909 the mayor of New York told a delegation of foreign guests that few of the city's buildings "even by a stretch of the imagination can of

Figure 7.1 Berenice Abbott (1898–1991), *New York Skyline, c. 1933. Source:* The Miriam and Ira D. Wallach Division of Art, Prints and Photographs, New York Public Library.

themselves be called beautiful." Yet despite their inadequacies, he continued, "Take the city altogether, the general effect of the city as a whole, the contrast of its blotches of vivid color, with the bright blue of the sky in the background, and of the waters of the harbor in the foreground, the huge masses of its office buildings, towering peak on peak and pinnacle above pinnacle to the sky, making of lower Manhattan, to the eye at least, a city that is set on a hill, and New York does have a beauty of her own, a beauty that is indescribable, that seizes one's sense of imagination, and holds one in its grip."[30] When the mayor spoke, the Singer Building was the tallest, and the Woolworth Building would not be completed for three more years. The heights reached by the Chrysler and Empire State Buildings were scarcely imagined. Yet already he articulated what would become standard praise for the skyline. He referred to the biblical "city on a hill" that was to be a model for all humankind, and claimed for New York what the early Puritans had wished for their colonies. The "huge masses of office buildings" were metamorphosed from undistinguished commercial structures into representations of destiny. Montgomery Schuyler expressed a similar sentiment in 1903 when he wrote, "We can imagine quarters and avenues in New York in which a uniform row of skyscrapers might be not merely inoffensive but sublime."[31] The British novelist Arnold Bennett concluded that "a great deal of the poetry of New York is due to the sky-scraper. At dusk the effect of the massed sky-scrapers from within, as seen from any high building up-town, is prodigiously beautiful, and it is unique in the cities of this world. The early night effect of the whole town, topped by the aforesaid Metropolitan tower, seen from the New Jersey shore, is stupendous, and resembles some enchanted city of the next world rather than of this."[32]

This landscape told citizens that civil engineers and architects could perform wondrous feats, and that the owners of these buildings—insurance companies, newspapers, and captains of industry—were colossal. While banks and museums still clung to the low, horizontal building as being more refined, new businesses and new money adopted the tall building, both to concentrate energies in a single location and to trumpet their importance. The publicity value of a great tower made additional stories well worth the investment.[33] The striving millions whom McKay saw swirling around the base of these towers were reminded daily of the Singer sewing machine, the Woolworth stores where they shopped, the newspapers they read, and the insurance they bought. Skyscrapers also became landmarks that provided spatial orientation. It paid to give people a reason to look at a corporate headquarters, and they installed giant illuminated clocks that could be seen from across town, day or night. The towers were more than giant billboards. They justified the social order. If they manifested the economic might of corporations, they did so not in terms of tradition and taste, as in the horizontal city, but in terms of startling change. They asked Stein's question—"why end anything"?"

Arrowsmith gazed at New York from his new laboratory inside in a Manhattan skyscraper. Alone in his lab for the first time, "He looked out of the broad window above his [work] bench and saw that he did have the coveted Woolworth Tower, to keep and gloat on. Shut in to a joy of precisions, he would nevertheless not be walled out from the flowing life." He could also see the Singer Building and "the arrogant magnificence of the City Investing Building. To the west, tall ships were riding, tugs were bustling, all the world went by. Below his cliff, the streets were feverish. Suddenly he loved humanity as he loved the decent, clean rows of test-tubes."[34] Arrowsmith gloats over the skyscrapers because they provide him with a fantasy of dominance over a new domain. Lewis could quickly sketch Arrowsmith's response because he knew that in 1920s readers had become familiar with precisely such a view from the high office window. The city viewed from a skyscraper had become a central part of popular iconography. Millions of postcards were sold of views from atop famous tall buildings. Likewise, artistic photographers such as Edward Steichen and Alfred Stieglitz explored the new upper world of glass and steel.[35] The skyscraper view also became a recurring motif in magazine advertising. These images typically silhouetted an executive against a window, as he looked out over the city, and the reader was expected to identify with the captain of commerce. Roland Marchand, the historian of advertising and public relations, has noted, "The panorama view through the window was always expansive and usually from a considerable height. It was never obstructed by another skyscraper across the street."[36] From this vantage point, the businessman's magisterial gaze dominated the new man-made landscape (figure 7.2).

From his upper floor, Arrowsmith saw an abstract humanity, shorn of particularity. One cannot in practice "love humanity as he loved the decent, clean rows of test tubes." The magisterial vision applies abstract

Figure 7.2 "View from the top of the Woolworth Building," Bain News Service, c. 1918. Photographer not identified. *Source:* Library of Congress.

reasoning to accounting, engineering, finance, geology, or medicine, and becomes the normal way to think about the world. When Arrowsmith leaves his laboratory for the first time, he is in a buoyant mood and races back to the hotel, "seeing nothing yet in a blur seeing everything."[37] This blurred vision of the people around him is paralleled by his failure to think of his own needs. When he gets to the somewhat shabby hotel where he and his wife are staying, she congratulates him on the new job, but is dismayed to discover that he has no idea what salary he will be paid. The exaltation of the view has literally distracted him from asking.

Executives still covet offices with a view. The psychic economy of the skyscraper is far different from that of the horizontal city of c. 1860, whose characteristic office buildings had four or five stories. Before the elevator made building high attractive, the value of offices declined with each staircase one had to climb. Shops generally occupied the street level, and the most successful accountants, doctors, and lawyers were no more than one flight up. Close to the street, they could observe the life around them from a slightly elevated position, but they were not cut off from scrutiny of the passers-by. They remained tied to the vitality of the street, its bustle, noise, and occasional traffic jams and confusion. During the warm months of the year the windows were usually open, partially breaking down the distinction between inside and outside. The skyscraper changed this relationship completely. Built into its very architecture were exclusivity, remoteness, and climate control. The street ceased to be a vibrant theater filled with identifiable people, and instead became a distant realm inhabited by figures so small as to become abstractions. The higher floors offered a fantasy of domain where individual personalities disappeared. By the time Lewis wrote *Arrowsmith* it seemed natural to speak of the flow of life as represented not by people, but by the spectacle of other skyscrapers in the distance.

The world seen from such towers assumed a new aspect. As early as 1905 a journalist who visited the top of the Flatiron Building, observed "things that you would take for beetles, others that seem to you ants. The beetles are cabs, the ants are [human] beings—primitive but human, hurrying grotesquely over the most expensive spot on earth."[38] The brightness of the unobstructed sunlight at the top further heightened the sense of contrast between the observer and the people below. The perpetual twilight of that nether realm contrasted with the dazzling light at the top of the city, literally removed from the dirt, din, and darkness of the surface. Pedestrians were reduced to tiny figures without personal characteristics, mere insects whose humanity had disappeared. If the sublime view made one appreciate human skill and ingenuity, at the same time it disconnected the observer from the masses below. In "People Who Must," Carl Sandburg described the view from the top of skyscraper:

> They were the same as bugs, many bugs on their way—
> Those people on the go or at a standstill;
> And the traffic cop a spot of blue, a splinter of brass,
> Where the black tides ran around him.[39]

O. Henry's 1905 short story "Psyche and the Pskyscraper" contrasts the response of a philosopher and a shop girl to the view from the top. The philosopher gazing down thinks, "What are the ambitions, the achievements, the paltry conquests and loves of those restless black insects below compared with the serene and awful immensity of the universe that lies above and around their insignificant city." The shop girl complains, "I think it's awful to be up so high that folks look like fleas."[40] A quarter century later, the tallest buildings were more than double the height of those in O. Henry's story. When the Empire State Building opened in 1931, a characteristic newspaper item proclaimed: "From this highest vantage point steamers and tugs which appeared to be little more than rowboats could be seen far up the Hudson and the East River. Down the bay, beyond the Narrows and out to sea, a ship occasionally hove into view or faded in the distance. For miles in every direction the city was spread out before the gaze of the sightseers."

The natural sublime emphasized human weakness and insignificance in the presence of a mountain or canyon, and skyscrapers could induce a similar sense of personal unimportance when dwarfed by an immense building. But the experience pointed to a different conclusion, for this was not a feeling of inconsequence compared to enormous natural forces but compared to the powerful individuals who had imagined, erected, and owned the skyscrapers. The natural sublime reduced all humanity to the same level before the absolutely great in nature; the technological sublime exalted some at the expense of others. The sense of greatness rubbed off on those with offices on the upper floors. Their skyscraper view of an enormous man-made landscape stretching to the horizon provided a sense of empowerment, a fantasy of domain that was shared by tourists who paid to see such views.

The observation platforms at the top of the tallest skyscrapers offered the public this reconception of urban space, miniaturizing the city into a pattern. The congestion of the streets below became a detail, and from "a height of more than 1,000 feet pedestrians were little more than ants and their movements hardly could be detected"[41] (see figure 7.3). Lifted up to the sky, one was invited to see the city as a vast three-dimensional map and to accept a new relationship between the self and this concrete abstraction. As one reporter from Boston wrote, "You may be awed by it, you can even be a little afraid of it; you cannot deny that it is Today in Steel and Stone."[42] Roland Barthes noted that visiting the Eiffel Tower "is to enter into contact not with a historical Sacred, as is the case for the majority of monuments, but rather with a new nature, that of human space."[43] The skyscraper provided a spectacular perch from which to contemplate a

Figure 7.3 Berenice Abbott (1898–1991), *Seventh Avenue looking South from 35th Street, Manhattan, 1935*. *Source:* The Miriam and Ira D. Wallach Division of Art, Prints and Photographs, New York Public Library.

manufactured world. Michel de Certeau made a similar point in discussing the skyscraper view: "To be lifted to the summit . . . is to be lifted out of the city's grasp. One's body is no longer clasped by the streets. . . . It transforms the bewitching world by which one was 'possessed' into a text that lies before one's eyes. It allows one to read it, to be a solar Eye, looking down like a god."[44] The paradox that the tall building is at once within and outside the scene makes it an attraction, but it is not an ideologically neutral space. The panoramic vision permits any tourist to view the city not as disconnected parts but rather as a unified structure. The skyscraper seems to make the many parts of the city, in Barthes's words, comprehensible as "intelligible objects, yet without—and this is what is new—losing anything of their materiality; a new category appears, that of concrete abstraction."[45] This category visualizes the capitalist "romance" of rationalization, abstraction, and growth. One momentarily adopts the perspective of the captain of industry. One does not merely escape from the clasp of the street; one enters the panopticon of corporate power. The gaze from the top invites one to celebrate the utilitarian view of nature.

This new version of the sublime was an emotion of awe and fear. There was an element of terror in looking at the city from a high place, in gazing down a sheer wall. This experience was further dramatized by the contrast between the confinement of a crowded elevator that whisks up from ground level, to emerge suddenly on a windswept platform facing an urbanized horizon. Many experience this sudden opening as psychological expansion, and then strain to link the details of the scene with the city they know on the ground. The mental activity of triangulation requires an apparently infinite series of mental transpositions of scale and orientation. The vast region visible from the top of a skyscraper appears intelligible, offering itself for decipherment like a huge hieroglyphic. Yet like all sublime landscapes, its meaning remains unutterable, and for this very reason, the sense of power does not abate, but can be constantly renewed, as one looks out over the metropolis.

The view provided a sense of mastery, and rents ascended with the elevator. The businessman hero of James Oppenheim's 1912 novel, *The Olympian*, reaches his apotheosis the first time he stands at the top of his new skyscraper: "He was utterly alone in the skies," with "slanting glimpses of deep streets busy with tiny black people and darting traffic, and from their tips curled white smoke in the boundless swim of sunlight. He saw the waters that circled the city like a hugging arm of the sea, and on the level stretches harbor-craft and ocean-liners. He saw the bridges suspended between Long Island and Manhattan, Brooklyn beyond; he saw the Jersey heights. . . . All the mighty metropolis stretched like a map below him, crowded to the circling horizon with millions of human beings." Oppenheim interprets the view to mean, "Science tearing off the crust of the earth and releasing the powers and riches of Nature." It is the product of "mines, manufactures, laboratories, exchanges." In modern civilization, the "railroad came, the post, the mill and farm machinery, the typewriter, the telegraph, the telephone, the automobile. And all these were like nerves and blood vessels laid out through the chaos till it began to coalesce, the parts aware of each other, the Earth gradually shaping into one body."[46] The magisterial gaze materialized a new historical relationship between human beings and their environment. The skyscraper was not merely a center of commerce. It mediated the relationship between the ordinary citizen and great corporations. From the outside, it was an emblem of corporate power that awed the man in the street. From the top it was the site of the magisterial gaze. To experience either the immense vistas aloft or the insect life of the street below validated corporate power.

To describe the sublimity evoked in seeing the city from the top of a skyscraper, the term "geometrical sublime" is useful. Kant distinguished between the mathematical and the dynamic sublime, both of which refer to nature. In contrast, the geometrical sublime refers to the experience of man-made infinitude, which evokes in the viewer not awe of the divine or the natural world but rather of human invention.[47] The skyscraper's fantasy of domain altered the phenomenology of the city, adding a new psychological dimension to everyday life. The skyscraper manifested both domination of those below and visions of transcendence for those at the top. The American public was eager to pay for the experience of the magisterial gaze. The "concrete abstraction" glimpsed from the skyscraper filled them with half-articulated visions that suggested the conquest of nature, the triumph of science, the rationalization of the modern city, the certainty of progress, and the apotheosis of corporate will. These emotions were only superficially similar to the experience of the natural sublime at the Grand Canyon, for they exalted not nature but human domination.

The skyscraper could also be etherealized with lighting. A photograph of the Singer Building once hung in the dining room of the British author H. G. Wells. Taken at twilight in 1912, it looked up at the tower from the street. The photographer, Alvin Langdon Coburn, also had made a portrait of Wells himself and provided illustrations for the uniform edition of Henry James's novels.[48] Wells admired American technological achievements in general and skyscrapers in particular. His generation had observed the shift of American cities from horizontal to vertical, and saw the skyscraper as the hallmark of a new kind of urban space. The fact that skyscrapers were illuminated was intensely felt by those who first saw them. As Wells noted in 1906, "New York is lavish of light."[49] In the image he chose for his dining room, the Singer Building is a dark silhouette, punctuated by lights from office windows. Taken in a pictorialist style, the hard edges of the roof lines have become slightly fuzzy, while the brightest lines in the image are white horizontal streaks connecting the streetlights. Coburn explained: "The lines connecting the lights were made by passing trams, and I believe they improve the pattern."[50] The skyscraper and the street were only visible because of electric lighting in the office windows, the streetlights and the streetcars. What Coburn and Wells saw in the image was not only one of the tallest buildings in the world, but also a revisualization of the city in terms of electricity.[51]

Once the skyscraper became a central icon in American cities, its appearance at night became its most salient feature.[52] As in Coburn's photograph of the Singer Building, this was at first an unintended effect of lighted office windows seen from a distance. Gradually, between c. 1890 and 1920, people witnessed the emergence of the night skyline, a new landscape, entirely man-made and festooned with lights. The photographic critic Sadakichi Hartmann enthused over the new landscape shortly before World War I: "Every night, as the darkness comes on and all the electric light and places of amusement are lighted, a new world of solemnity, beauty, and mystery lies before our gaze."[53] At night, New York "becomes another city entirely. Out of the darkness, like some magical effulgence, emerges a dazzling shower of light, a myriad of beaming sparks. Buildings and objects that were of no pictorial consequence in the daylight may assume quite the first place in our favor, and ugly things, not to be dodged anyhow by day, most kindly retire out of sight, or else are turned into things of beauty."[54] The electrified skyline visualized American modernity.

The skyscraper city could be viewed from the ground, from observation decks at the top of the tallest towers, from the ferries plying the waters of the harbor, from the walkway across Brooklyn Bridge, from the head of the Statue of Liberty, and from airplanes and blimps flying overhead. Many painters and photographers active between 1900 and 1930 explored this multiplication of perspectives, including Robert Henri, Joseph Stella, John Marin, John Sloan, Alfred Stieglitz, and Georgia O'Keefe. Like the Grand Canyon, New York's vistas challenged them to capture the totality of a vast scene. The canyon evolved slowly, suggesting the eternity of nonhuman time. In contrast, New York expressed the frantic pace of a capitalist economy. The city constantly changed, adding and subtracting vantage points, as older structures were razed and taller towers rose in their place. The building where John Sloan had his studio, whose roof provided the vantage point for his wonderful 1922 painting, *The City from Greenwich Village at Night*, was torn down in 1927. The Singer Tower, depicted in the upper left-hand corner of that canvas, was the tallest building in the world in 1908, but it was demolished in 1967 to make way for a taller building. This was the utilitarian vision taken to its logical extreme. As Sloan remarked in 1936, "Landmarks are torn down so rapidly that your canvases become historical records almost before the paint on them is dry."[55] What had once been sublime could be ripped down and replaced. New skyscrapers represented the future, especially if they were depicted with "primitive" or rural people in the foreground, as in a 1929 image showing three Native Americans looking at the Chicago skyline (figure 7.4).

Most objects of the technological sublime decayed rapidly in value. The great railways that took tourists to the national parks had once been considered sublime, but after 1945 few Americans wanted passenger service. The sight of a small airplane drew a crowd into the street in 1910 but two generations later people scarcely looked up at a passing jet. A building of twenty-five stories was once considered immense, but later generations were only impressed by much higher structures. In contrast, the natural sublime does not wane but persists and even becomes more powerful with longer acquaintance. The tourist who hikes in the Grand Canyon for a week is more awed by its immensity than a visitor who only spends a few hours on the rim, and those who return to Niagara Falls or Yosemite do

Figure 7.4 *Princess O-Me-Me, a Chippewa; Sun Road, a Pueblo; and Chief Whirling Thunder, a Winnebago, looking over Chicago's skyline from the roof of the Hotel Sherman,* 1929. Photographer not identified. Underwood and Underwood. *Source:* Library of Congress.

not find its power diminishes on further acquaintance. But the objects of the technological sublime rapidly decomposed into familiarity, becoming antiquated, with attributes less impressive with each passing year, because they were no longer the tallest, fastest, brightest, or the most spectacular. The urban skyline required constant renewal to remain impressive. Otherwise, it risked appearing quaint, as was the case with Boston in 1960, Minneapolis in 1970, or Buffalo in 1980. By the 1990s, Las Vegas had erected a skyline that was a pastiche of older icons, including an Egyptian pyramid, the Eiffel Tower, and New York's skyscrapers (see figure 7.5). The satisfactions of the technological sublime prove transient because they are rooted

Figure 7.5 Carol M. Highsmith (1946–), *Compressed Manhattan Skyline, New York, New York Resort, Las Vegas*, c. 1999. *Source:* Library of Congress.

in time, in contrast to the natural sublime that points toward eternity. Today's cutting-edge architecture becomes tomorrow's obsolete tradition, ripe for the tongue-in-cheek homage of the Las Vegas Strip.

Anti-landscapes of death and destruction, however, retain a lugubrious fascination.

8

NUCLEAR ANTI-LANDSCAPES

The utilitarian conception of land that justified skyscrapers, bridges, dams, mines, and factories, if taken to extremes, could lead to damaged landscapes and Superfund sites like the River Rouge of the 1990s. The American Southwest also suffered such exploitation. Beginning with nineteenth-century government expeditions, Anglo-Americans saw much of the region as empty wasteland. This perception was based on centuries of living in the colder, wetter climates of northern Europe and the eastern United States. The Spanish were more familiar with arid regions like the Southwest, and for Native Americans it was not a wasteland but a homeland. After 1900, their architecture, rituals, and culture attracted anthropologists to the region. By the 1920s, some of the latter, notably Edward Sapir, admired the "well-rounded" culture of Native Americans in contrast to the "spurious" industrial culture of White Americans.[1]

A positive desert aesthetic emerged in the writings of John Muir, Mary Austin, John C. Van Dyke, Willa Cather, and some late works by D. H. Lawrence.[2] The small city of Santa Fe in New Mexico became an important center for the arts,[3] and the region inspired paintings by Georgia O'Keeffe and photographs by Alfred Stieglitz and Ansel Adams. Its landscapes became iconic, including the Grand Canyon, Rainbow Bridge, Sunset Crater, Sedona, Saguaro National Monument, Chaco Canyon, Monument Valley, Bryce Canyon National Park, Zion National Park, and many more. Southwest landscapes formed the backdrop to many films, notably those of John Ford, and the region became a familiar part of road trips from Chicago to Los Angeles on Route 66.[4] In short, the Southwest became an important site of American identity.

Yet if the cultural value of the Southwest was recognized in anthropology, literature, art, film, and tourism, on the eve of World War II Washington policy makers still regarded the region as a largely empty zone where the military could locate airfields, training sites, and the secret laboratories that developed the atom bomb at Los Alamos, New Mexico. Near Flagstaff, Arizona, the army established Camp Navajo, a forty-four-square-mile training facility. Large air bases were built near Phoenix and Tucson in Arizona and Ogden, Utah. In 1950, Nellis Air Force Base in Nevada opened to train pilots. When the U.S. Department of Defense decided to test nuclear weapons domestically rather than on Pacific islands, it required absolute control over an area in Nevada the size of Rhode Island, adjacent to a weapons testing area the size of Connecticut. (An 1853 treaty specifies that much of this land belongs to the Shoshone, who still refuse to sell it to the government.[5]) Later, in New Mexico, the Defense Department established the White Sands Missile Range, almost twice as extensive as the Grand Canyon. These vast military sites contain weapons depots, toxic storage facilities, fields of debris, and areas that have been repeatedly bombed.

A century earlier, George Perkins Marsh described sites devastated by human actions in *Man and Nature* (1864). He studied the gradual destruction of European and Mediterranean landscapes, beginning in ancient times. Marsh rejected the idea that the land was raw material waiting for development. Rather, he saw the natural world evolving slowly until mankind disturbed it. Marsh saw that nature was not indestructible, nor could it always heal itself. He was hardly a spokesman for the idea of second creation. As David Lowenthal put it, Marsh believed "that each living creature creates and destroys the ambience of its own and its successors' lives," and "saw all life destined ultimately to fade from the earth."[6] Marsh understood that any landscape might become unsustainable, and he knew that human beings could hasten the process.

The concept of anti-landscape inverts J. B. Jackson's definition of landscape as "a composition of man-made or man-modified spaces to serve as infrastructure or background for our collective existence."[7] In contrast, anti-landscapes cannot support human life. They have become more numerous as human beings command more powerful technologies. Environmental studies of mining, the oil industry, and warfare[8] developed terminology to deal with damaged places, including "toxic landscape" and "sacrifice zones." In the 1970s, the Trilateral Commission proposed that the U.S. government might officially "designate certain parts of the Dakotas, Montana, and Wyoming as 'National Sacrifice Areas'" and declare them "uninhabitable as a consequence of uranium mining and processing."

Fortunately, this designation was not made, for it would have set a precedent for ruining land without restitution. In 1987, the United Church of Christ Commission for Racial Justice used government data to establish that 75 percent of U.S. toxic waste dumps were located in poor communities of color.[9] Black Americans and Native Americans were far more likely to live near radioactive waste than White Americans.

The anti-landscape implies the post-human. Desertification, erosion, deforestation, pollution, or poisoning often occurred so slowly in the past that it was difficult to anticipate long-term consequences. But highly technological societies create anti-landscapes quickly, for example in Hanford, Washington. There, beginning in World War II uranium was concentrated into plutonium. General Electric (GE) built several nuclear reactors at Hanford between 1948 and 1955 that "cut corners on design" and "had no containment shells in case of an explosion" (figure 8.1). They "had a single pass system where water poured through the reactors once and exited into the basins from which the effluent, contaminated with radioactive isotopes, flowed into the Columbia River." The government first tried to ignore the pollution, but eventually forced residents to move away and sealed off the area.[10] Another example is the town of Picher, Oklahoma, which mined much of the lead used by the U.S. military in the World Wars. Left behind were 170 million tons of mine tailings that covered 7,000 acres and leached toxic substances into the ground and water[11] (figure 8.2). Its residents were evacuated, and it too became a ghost town. By definition, anti-landscapes are uninhabitable.[12]

The anti-landscape is the result of extreme environmental degradation. Marsh was thinking along similar lines. He realized that settled societies often were more destructive than nomads and that deforestation could destroy rich soils: "When the forest is gone, the great reservoir of moisture stored up in its vegetable mold is evaporated and returns only in deluges of rain to wash away the parched dust into which the mould has been converted. The well-wooded and humid hills are turned to ridges of dry rock." Slowly the land became "an assemblage of bald mountains, of barren, turfless hills, and of swampy and malarious plains. There are parts of Asia Minor, of Northern Africa, of Greece and even of Alpine Europe, where the operation of causes set in motion by man has brought the face of the earth to a desolation almost as complete as that of the moon."[13] Archeologists and cultural geographers later documented societies that abandoned

Figure 8.1 *Hanford 100-B reactor area in Benton County, Washington, January 1945.* Photographer not identified. *Source:* Library of Congress.

regions after they were stripped of trees, overgrazed, or irrigated too intensively.[14]

For millennia, human beings have created wastelands, but as the means became more powerful the speed and scale of destruction increased. Timothy LeCain's *Mass Destruction* (2009) explains how copper mines became devastating after they adopted high-speed blasting and enormous steam shovels. They extracted millions of tons of low-grade ore, pulverized it into dust that contained no more than 3–4 percent copper, and then mixed it with water and a small amount of oil that adhered to the particles of metal. Blowing air into the mushy mixture made it frothy and brought copper to the surface where it could be skimmed off. These processing techniques were perfected between 1910 and 1930, making it profitable to refine ores that contained less than 1 percent copper, and the other 99

Nuclear Anti-landscapes 131

Figure 8.2 Fritz Henle (1909–1993), Office of War Information, *Zinc and lead production leaves a growing mountain of waste, Eagle-Picher plant, Cardin, Oklahoma, 1943.* Source: Library of Congress.

percent of the pulverized rock was thrown away. The devastation to land, air, and water was so vast that restoration became prohibitively expensive. Mining engineers who ravaged whole regions nevertheless felt justified in what they did. Daniel Jackling who owned many large copper mines saw engineers as the vanguard of progress. He declared that the engineer was "responsible, primarily, basically, and almost wholly, for mankind's welfare and the progress of civilized advancement in practically all phases of human endeavor."[15] This was a widely held view among industrialists and corporate leaders during the first half of the twentieth century.[16]

Most people respond to degraded landscapes with dread, foreboding, and aversion. In *Landscapes of Fear* Yi-fu Tuan notes, "Fear is in the mind," but "has its origins in external circumstances that are truly threatening."[17] This emotional response often arises directly from sensory impressions, but fear can also be based on knowledge of pollution or radiation that the senses cannot detect. A dangerous chemical may be tasteless, a lethal gas may have no odor, and radioactivity is invisible. People must rely on scientific measurements and experts to assess the danger. In the aftermath of Hiroshima, a dark vision emerged of atomic destruction so severe that the damage could not be reversed. Another apocalyptic story reached a large audience with the publication of Rachel Carson's *Silent Spring* in 1962.[18] She made Americans aware of the dangerous overuse of pesticides, fertilizers, and chemicals. The first pages of *Silent Spring* described an idyllic town where indiscriminate use of pesticides killed fish and birds, entered the food chain, was ingested by the local population, and posed a menace to society. Her book increased the prominence of what Lawrence Buell later called "toxic discourse."[19]

During the 1970s, the suburban town of Love Canal near Niagara Falls, New York, became a nationally famous anti-landscape. Its residents smelled noxious odors, planted seeds that never sprouted, saw their shrubbery blighted, and found that vegetables grew poorly. Women suffered aborted pregnancies, gave birth to deformed babies, and watched healthy children succumb to unusual diseases. The community learned that it was built on polluted land. Between 1942 and 1952, the Hooker Chemical Company supplied the U.S. Army with explosives, disinfectants, defoliants, and other chemical products.[20] Using a legal permit, it placed 21,800 tons of toxic waste in a disused canal. Hooker Chemical covered the barrels with clay, planted grass, and sold the site to the Niagara Falls school board for $1. In 1957, when the land was sold to private developers, Hooker Chemical Company reminded the school board that the land was not suitable for housing, but homes were built there nevertheless. A generation later, the barrels began to disintegrate and rain flushed out more than thirty carcinogens. Home values collapsed, although the city government resisted lowering property taxes accordingly.[21] Press coverage of residents desperate to move but unable to sell polluted houses forced the federal government to purchase the homes, relocate the families, and clean up the site. The

Department of Justice sued the polluters, and the courts forced them to pay $250 million.

As sites like Love Canal were identified in all parts of the United States, the Environmental Justice movement emerged. Congressional hearings established that between 1950 and 1980 1,605 chemical plants had disposed of 762 million tons of toxic waste, most of it casually dumped into pits, landfills, ponds or streams.[22] By 1980, more than fifty thousand toxic waste dumps had been identified, and others were later discovered.[23] In response, Congress passed the 1980 Comprehensive Environmental Response, Compensation, and Liability Act (CERCLA), which ordered the Environmental Protection Agency (EPA) to designate sites eligible for federally funded cleanups.[24] The money came from Congressional appropriations, from lawsuits against polluters, and from a tax levied on the petrochemical industry.

By 1995, that tax had provided $18 billion—two-thirds of all Superfund funding—and it had been used to clean up hundreds of sites that were later declared free of hazardous waste. The Love Canal Area Revitalization Agency removed, destroyed, or contained waste inside impermeable clay barriers. It then rebuilt 234 houses, sold them for 15 percent below the market price, and renamed the town "Black Creek Village."[25] However, tons of toxic chemicals are buried behind a chain-link fence around an area larger than two football fields. Below the sod is a plastic liner and a thick layer of clay to make the ground impermeable. This off-limits area is a reminder of the pollution that once oozed through the neighborhood.[26] In 2004 Love Canal was declared clean and safe.[27] An anti-landscape had become an exemplar of recovery. Another cleanup took place in Nevada, where mercury used in silver mining during the nineteenth century had contaminated fifty miles of the Carson River. The polluted sediment was removed and replaced with clean soil.[28] The restoration of the Detroit's River Rouge, discussed in chapter 2, is an example of a recovery narrative. Another was the cleanup of a water supply polluted by Pacific Gas and Electric, which had to pay $333 million in damages. That story is told in the film *Erin Brockovich* (2000), for which Julia Roberts won an Oscar.[29] But despite such success stories, many polluted sites have not been cleaned up. Some are difficult to detoxify, and many of the worst cases are on (or near) Native American reservations in Oklahoma, Wyoming, New Mexico, Arizona, Washington, and Utah.

Removing waste and cleansing or replacing damaged soil is costly, and the petrochemical industry did not want to foot the bill indefinitely. In 1995, it sought relief from the Republican-dominated Congress, which obligingly eliminated corporate contributions to the Superfund. Congressional appropriations dwindled during the Bush administration, but between 1980 and 2007, the EPA received an average of $1 billion each year in penalties and cost recoveries from culpable parties.[30] In the utilitarian view of nature, pollution is not the responsibility of the chemical industry or the government but of individual polluters. The EPA was told to rely on litigation to pay for the costs, with the presumption that a company was innocent of dumping harmful waste until proven guilty. Yet often it was difficult to discover who dumped chemicals or buried waste, and some of those responsible had gone bankrupt. Even when a case was brought to trial, some defendants minimized their legal obligation to pay by restructuring their assets. The EPA could point to more than 450 sites that had been restored and put to new uses. Yet there were thousands more, and some difficult cases were so expensive that whole towns had to be abandoned, such as Hanford or Picher.

Many anti-landscapes were a direct result of government demands for uranium. Building a nuclear arsenal created radioactive pollution at multiple locations. Most early U.S. uranium mining took place in Arizona, New Mexico, and Utah. The Navajo had long resisted mining, but after the attack on Pearl Harbor, they permitted mining of vanadium, used to harden the steel in weapons. Next, between 1943 and 1945 tailings from these vanadium mines were processed to extract 76,000 pounds of uranium oxide.[31] Government geologists and prospectors then searched for uranium ore, while pretending to look for other minerals. Navajo, shown samples of uranium ore, could pinpoint promising sites. But they were not informed about the radiation risks, and they saw uranium mines in terms of jobs and tribal revenue.[32]

After World War II the federal government promoted uranium mining. It predicted a boom to rival the gold and silver rushes of the nineteenth century, and disseminated a book that was a classic second creation story. In it, an Atomic Energy Commission (AEC) engineer explained how heroic men "explored and developed a vast mining province once considered worthless."[33] The AEC sold 70,000 copies of *Prospecting for Uranium*, and ran a public relations campaign promoting the mineral wealth of the

Colorado plateau. It publicized "rags to riches" stories of prospectors who found large deposits, and downplayed or ignored questions of native sovereignty in the region.

In 2018, the Grand Canyon Trust counted more than 430 active mines in national forests close to the Grand Canyon,[34] which did not include those on Navajo land. In the words of the Environmental Protection Agency: "From 1944 to 1986, nearly 30 million tons of uranium ore were extracted from Navajo lands under leases with the Navajo Nation. Many Navajo people worked the mines, often living and raising families in close proximity to the mines and mills." This left "a legacy of uranium contamination" at more than five hundred abandoned mines, "as well as homes and drinking water sources with elevated levels of radiation. Potential health effects include lung cancer from inhalation of radioactive particles, as well as bone cancer and impaired kidney function from exposure to radionuclides in drinking water."[35] Dire as this description sounds, the situation was worse. Roughly 90 percent of the first U.S. uranium mines were located on the Colorado Plateau, many on Navajo land. More than five thousand Navajo worked these mines and labored in the ore mills. Private companies operated both, and their production was sold exclusively to the U.S. government. Mine safety was left to individual states, but they had little expertise in dealing with radioactivity. Nor, legally speaking, did they have jurisdiction over Native American reservations. The Bureau of Indian Affairs (BIA) approved mining leases. In theory, BIA represented the tribes, but in practice its agents seldom negotiated a good price, they signed contracts that Navajo opposed, and they paid too little heed to health and safety issues.[36]

Some uranium mines were in the Grand Canyon, notably the Lost Orphan Mine (figure 8.3). After it closed in 1969, it annually emitted 26,280 millirems of radiation.[37] The normal, or background radiation in that area is 150 millirems a year. A cluster of uranium mines lay between Flagstaff and Page, Arizona, near the South Rim of the Grand Canyon; others were concentrated south of Monument Valley. These mines contaminated the air, soil, and water. Their thousands of tons of tailings contained lead, arsenic, selenium, cadmium, and radium, which decays to produce radon, a carcinogenic gas that causes lung cancer. The Navajo could not smell, taste, or see radon. The latency period before radioactive materials cause disease in the human body is roughly twenty years. By the 1960s,

Figure 8.3 David Killam, Headframe, *Lost Orphan Uranium Mine, South Rim of the Grand Canyon, 2005. Source:* Library of Congress.

uranium miners suffered lung and bone cancer ten times more than the general population.[38] Government inspectors and scientists were alarmed by the dangers of the mines in the late 1950s,[39] but only in the 1960s, prodded by protests and press reports, did Congress respond.[40] These fatalities did not surprise historians of medicine. In fifteenth-century Bohemia, Agricola, a famous early author on mining, observed that miners extracting pitchblende (now known to be radioactive) suffered from respiratory disease and early death.[41]

Miners were seldom informed of uranium's dangers, and state and federal agencies were slow to protect them.[42] After exposure to radioactive dust and radon, they contracted lung cancer.[43] By 1980, of 150 Navajo miners who worked at one Ship Rock mine between 1952 and 1970, 38 had died of lung cancer and 95 more had contracted it. In 1990, Congress recognized that uranium miners had suffered "an epidemic of lung cancer and respiratory diseases." The Radiation Exposure Compensation Act

(RECA) apologized, declared that their health had been "sacrificed to the national security interests of the United States," and offered them compensation of up to $150,000.[44] By 2009, more than 21,800 miners, ore mill workers, and local residents had been compensated, at a cost of $1.455 billion. Yet many received nothing. Mining after 1971 was not compensated, nor was work done above ground. Miners were covered for lung cancer, but workers in uranium mills were not. Other cancers known to be caused by uranium were excluded from compensation. The applicants who were rejected included more than 70 percent of onsite workers (i.e., not miners), 44 percent of "downwinders" the name used to describe residents subjected to air pollution after above-ground nuclear blasts; and 46 percent of children with leukemia.[45] Families who lived at mining sites were not eligible, even though a study of two Navajo communities in 1969–1970 found that they suffered birth defects at five times the national average. Another study of children in uranium mining towns found they contracted ovarian and testicular cancer fifteen times more than the national average. RECA did not cover these children.[46] Those compensated often found it did no more than pay their medical bills.

The Navajo live near "more than half of the many small, abandoned uranium mines from the middle of the 20th century," and illnesses still plague them. Radioactive dust from abandoned mines has contaminated the air and aquifers. Waste rock and tailings used as building materials in houses later proved to be radioactive. Drivers "traveling on roads made with waste rock were in danger of breathing radioactive dust." In Grand Junction, Colorado, 4,000 radioactive properties and yards were decontaminated at a cost of $250 million.[47] Decades too late, the 1978 Uranium Mill Tailings Radiation Control Act prohibited use of mine waste in construction.[48] Some areas were declared Superfund sites, which released more than $1 billion to move families out of radioactive houses, supply them with safe drinking water, and begin the cleanup.[49] Yet decades after the uranium mines closed, the EPA still had not contained all the radioactive waste. In 1978, Congress passed a law to ensure mine tailings would be "safely managed," but not until the 1990s did the Nuclear Regulatory Commission transport millions of tons of radioactive material from Monument Valley to a former ore-processing site in Mexican Hat, Utah. Other former processing plants became disposal sites at Shiprock, New Mexico, and Tuba City, Arizona.[50]

After mining, ore was trucked to mills and processed into "yellowcake." Raw ore was seldom even 3 percent uranium, usually less. The mills broke it into pieces that were milled into fine sand and then processed. One thousand pounds of ore might produce as little as one pound of uranium. The rest was discarded. In 2017, the United States imported 90 percent of its uranium, most of it from Canada, Australia, and Kazakhstan. But during World War II and the early Cold War, the supply was mined and refined domestically, supplemented by imports from the Belgian Congo. In 1955, the United States was the world's largest producer of uranium, with mines and processing plants concentrated in Arizona, Utah, Colorado, and New Mexico.[51] Ore from just one of the Navajo mines produced more than five million pounds of yellowcake.[52]

There are two processes for separating uranium from ore. A recently developed method leaches uranium from the ore underground, without digging a mine, but only drilling holes. In some cases, fracking is used to break up the rock before sulfuric acid is pumped in, dissolving the uranium. The liquid collects in wells, is pumped to the surface, and is transported to processing plants, where the solution is treated with chemicals to precipitate out the uranium. This method is less expensive than conventional mining, but it requires large amounts of water and leaves behind toxic residue that pollutes the groundwater.

The other method resembles making coffee on a large scale. The ore is mined and brought to the surface. Then it is ground into sand and placed in large tanks where sulfuric acid is poured over it. This leaches out uranium and other heavy metals, which dissolve into the acidic solution. It drains out of the tank and then is precipitated out of solution. The White Mesa Mill near Blanding, Utah, has used this process to produce up to eight million pounds of yellowcake a year.[53] It also stores a toxic cocktail of radioactive waste that includes uranium, thorium, radium, polonium, radon, and arsenic in ponds, impounded behind dams. Tailings remain dangerous long after extraction and can spoil the water supply.[54] A study of northern New Mexican mines found, "The discharge of such highly contaminated mine effluents to streams and seepage from tailings ponds, creates a long-lived source of ground-water contamination."[55]

The largest radioactive spill in U.S. history occurred in 1979 not at Three Mile Island but at Church Rock, New Mexico, sending a flash flood of 93 million gallons of wastewater roaring down the Puerco River toward

Arizona. It contained 1,100 tons of mill waste including heavy metals, and traces of uranium, thorium, radium, and polonium. Aquifers were contaminated, as the waste flowed through the Painted Desert into the Little Colorado River and the Grand Canyon. In May 1979, Elsie Peshlakai, a Navajo activist, addressed 85,000 antinuclear demonstrators in Washington, DC, along with Jane Fonda, Barry Commoner, and then-governor of California Gerry Brown. Peshlakai said, "You people from Harrisburg, my heart is with you. In twenty years, you will see what we already went through at Red Rock [Arizona]. I saw the widows of former uranium miners. I saw former uranium miners who were dying of cancer break down in tears. I talked with the old people who have been misled by trusting the companies." She denounced the injustice that came with these mines. "The companies have cleared our grazing land, they have cut down our trees, they have bulldozed over our religious sacred sites and grave sites. They have dried up our wells. The uranium drillers that have moved into Crown Point have running water and electricity in their mobile homes while my people, not even two miles away, do not have these conveniences. These people working for the uranium companies have come onto our land with no respect for our way of life."[56]

The media focused far less on the Church Rock disaster than on White communities affected by Three Mile Island and Love Canal. For two years, Navajo drinking water was trucked in, but then this assistance ended, even though the radioactive waste remained. The Navajo asked the EPA to declare the region a Superfund site, but it delayed, in hopes of winning a lawsuit to force those responsible to pay for the cleanup. Then the EPA declared a cleanup impossible because there was no baseline study to establish the level of radioactivity before the spill. Nor was there long-term monitoring of community health. After the Church Rock disaster, the Kerr-McKee mine still discharged radioactive waste into the local watershed.[57] Decades later, this pollution was not adequately cleaned up, and the federal government, the states, and the corporations all escaped legal accountability. Stewart Udall, former Secretary of the Interior in the Kennedy administration, spent years championing the Navajo cause. His lead medical witness, the founder of the biomedical unit at the Lawrence Livermore National Laboratory, declared the Navajo miners had cumulative radiation exposures forty-four times higher than the Japanese survivors from Hiroshima and Nagasaki.[58] The court concluded that mining had caused cancer but it did not hold the federal or state governments liable. Nor were the mining corporations held liable. It was worse than Love Canal, but the guilty parties escaped on technicalities.[59] The Navajo had not filed the proper paperwork. In 2014, the EPA began to clean up 50 of the 500 closed mines on or near the Navajo nation, at an estimated cost of almost $1 billion.[60]

The trail of radiation exposure, disease, injustice, and death is long. After refining, the concentrated uranium, or yellowcake, was packed into metal barrels,[61] and transported to Hanford, Washington, or to Oak Ridge, Tennessee, where it was transformed into reactor plutonium for atomic plants and weapons-grade plutonium for atomic bombs. Hanford was the larger facility, established on 560 square miles of "lands traditionally used for hunting, fishing, and gathering by the Yakima and Umatilla" tribes. It was also "adjacent to the homeland of the Nez Perce." By the end of World War II, Hanford "would rival in size and cost the entire U.S. automobile industry."[62] Like Ford's River Rouge plant, it too polluted its surroundings and became a Superfund site. "Hanford released radioactivity intentionally and routinely during its operations, from the start of production in 1944 until the reactors and processing plants closed down in 1986–88."[63] Its eight nuclear reactors and processing plants discharged 440 billion gallons of contaminants into the soil and the Columbia River, whose waters were used to cool the reactors. Radioactivity spread throughout the area.[64] By 1954, the Atomic Energy Commission knew that it was unsafe to eat local fish, mussels, and birds, but it kept the problem secret.[65] Unaware of the dangers, Native Americans continued to harvest berries, hunt, and fish for salmon. Soon, they suffered high rates of cancer. The reactors have closed, but the contamination remains. Hanford stores forty-three million cubic meters of radioactive waste, and in 1987 held "about two-thirds of the nation's total volume of waste involved in the production of nuclear weapons."[66] The town was so toxic that in 1989 all residents were evacuated. In 1994 the federal government was spending $4 million a day to contain and clean up Hanford's nuclear waste.[67]

Much of the weapons-grade plutonium Hanford produced was shipped to the Pantex weapons plant, eighteen miles northeast of Amarillo, Texas, where most U.S. nuclear weapons were assembled. The Pantex grounds cover 16,000 acres, an area larger than the Ford River Rouge plant, and there are more than six hundred buildings in the complex. The last new bomb was assembled there in 1991. Since then, workers have maintained or dismantled old weapons. In 2005, a W-56 nuclear warhead almost exploded during disassembly. In October 2011, the workers took apart one of the largest bombs ever built in the United States, the B53. It weighed 4,500 kilograms and was a thousand times more powerful than the Hiroshima bomb.[68] It was so old that no one who had built it remained on the work force. Disassembly required careful research and preparation. Despite the delicacy and danger of such tasks, workers have complained of being pressured to work seventy-two hours or more a week. They also criticized factory conditions in a letter: "Look around the plant. You will find leaking roofs, crumbling buildings, waist-high weed-infested landscapes, barricades and safety tape that makes this once-proud plant look like a crime scene."[69] Like uranium miners and Hanford workers, many at Pantex contracted cancer. In 2015, health issues were central during a thirty-nine-day strike. A handmade sign beside the road to the plant read, "1356, Sick, Dead, or Dying."[70] In the previous fifteen years, the Department of Labor's Energy Employees Occupational Illness Compensation Program had paid more than $170 million to former Pantex employees. Given cancer's latency period of twenty years, many more are expected to die. In 2016, the National Nuclear Security Administration evaluated Pantex's performance, and in three of six categories it received scores of under 60 percent. Six smart bombs had been assembled incorrectly.[71]

The novel *Storm Season* takes place in Amarillo, seen through the eyes of a railroad worker who helps transport nuclear devices and parts to and from Pantex.[72] He is also a tornado chaser, with a lively interest in devastation, which is shared by local fundamentalists who believe the apocalypse is at hand. A disaster does arrive: a tornado rips through the Pantex factory and the town, whose ruins suggest the aftermath of Hiroshima. A more lasting disaster emerges in the cancer that afflicts many workers, while those who remain healthy are haunted. The novel testifies to the illness and the anguish caused by working for the nuclear industry.[73]

The AEC and the Defense Department made the same mistakes at uranium mines, ore processing plants, Hanford, and Pantex. Often, legal liability was unclear, diffused among state, federal, tribal, and local governments, while much of the work was contracted out to private corporations. Not only was no clear liability established at the start, but also the dangers of radioactive materials were poorly understood, and safety precautions were inadequate. When health risks were discovered, federal officials usually downplayed them or kept them secret. Regular monitoring was arbitrarily limited to some employees. Workers' health was sacrificed to production goals and profits. Waste materials were repeatedly handled carelessly, and radioactive waste was only contained after decades of neglect. Local residents were needlessly exposed to radiation, and thousands contracted cancer and other illnesses. The federal government repeatedly responded decades too late, spent billions of dollars on cleanup, and paid billions more in worker compensation. Nevertheless, some areas still remain uninhabitable anti-landscapes.

Most of the bombs assembled at Pantex were never used. But some were exploded at the Nevada Test Site (NTS), an hour north of Las Vegas and less than a day's drive from the Grand Canyon. President Truman confiscated most of that land from the Western Shoshone in 1951.[74] Their land was desecrated by 126 open-air atomic tests, each one larger than either of the bombs dropped on Japan to end World War II. Aboveground blasts ended after the USSR and the United States signed a test ban treaty in 1963. Later tests—more than eight hundred—were moved underground, leaving the land pockmarked with subsidence craters. The mushroom clouds from open-air tests were carried by the prevailing winds to the east, and high concentrations of the radioactive dust fell on "downwinders" including ranchers and small Mormon towns, as well as on the Grand Canyon and reservations of the Navajo, Hopi, Shoshone, Piute, Hualapai, and Havasupai. Sometimes the winds blew west. In October 1958, the NTS exploded twenty atomic bombs, and in just two weeks the people of Los Angeles received the maximum annual radiation dosage permitted for a defense worker. The winds spread radioactive elements worldwide from more than four hundred open-air blasts conducted by Britain, the United States, France, and Russia. By 1970 the body of every human being and animal on earth contained strontium-90 or cesium-137, and each received an annual radiation dose of four to five millrems.[75] These isotopes have a half-life of thirty years.

The Atomic Energy Commission repeatedly told Americans that fallout from atomic testing was not dangerous.[76] In 1955, it issued a pamphlet to downwinders that declared "no person in the nearby region has ever been exposed to hazardous amounts of radiation," and insisted that "no crops or water supplies have been made hazardous to health."[77] But downwinders learned not to trust official statements. They had a disproportionate number of children with birth defects, which they called "sacrifice babies."[78] They were exposed to high levels of strontium-90 and iodine-131, which briefly rose to unacceptably high levels even as far away as New York City. Like uranium miners and workers in Hanford and at Pantex, downwinders suffered high rates of cancer, diabetes, and leukemia.[79] Yet for years they were told that these birth defects and illnesses were not related to the atomic testing program. In May 1953, the town of St. George, Utah, received more radiation in a single day than miners were permitted to receive in an entire year. More than four hundred sheep died mysteriously, but the AEC fought off a court case brought by ranchers.[80] A quarter century later, a federal court ruled that the AEC had deliberately withheld damning information.[81] In 1957, the AEC distributed pamphlets that advised "people who live near the Nevada Test Site" that "your best action is not to be worried about the fallout."[82]

The military's mistaken belief that radiation was not dangerous was starkly demonstrated at open-air bomb tests.[83] American soldiers were routinely ordered to observe them, so that they would become accustomed to atomic warfare and know that they could survive it. A quarter million servicemen witnessed the blasts, initially from seven miles away, at the same remove as the press corps[84] (figure 8.4.). But during later tests, soldiers were ordered to endure the blasts in trenches just 2,000 yards from ground zero. Even with their eyes closed and looking away, these men could see the bones in their own hands.[85] Afterward, "the men were usually expected to charge closer, rifles and bayonets raised," wearing ordinary uniforms. "Protective clothing was rare; often they were simply told to shower and change."[86] The soldiers were urged to enjoy the test as the most powerful technological display ever created. Tourists also gathered on nearby mountains to watch early blasts, as did some downwinders. This entertainment lost its attraction, however, once they understood its dangers.

Fortunately, the Cold War ended without nuclear conflict. Yet in limited wars, "depleted uranium" was used in bullets and bombs, because it is a heavier metal than lead and can penetrate protective armor and walls. In the 1991 Gulf War, "American troops fired weapons containing 340 tons of depleted uranium."[87] Yet "depleted" uranium is still 60 percent as radioactive as newly refined uranium, and anyone exposed—soldiers, nurses, doctors, or civilians—risked cancer, renal collapse, infertility, and

Figure 8.4 *Frenchman's Flat, Nevada, Members of 11th Air Bourne Division kneel as they watch mushroom cloud of atomic bomb test, 1951.* Source: Library of Congress.

genetic damage. The wars were short, the aftereffects long. The half-life of depleted uranium is 4.5 billion years, and hundreds of tons of this radioactive substance lies scattered in fragments across Afghanistan, Bosnia, Kuwait, Serbia, Somalia, and Iraq. Likewise, inside the United States the mining, refining, and use of uranium left a deadly trail, on Navajo lands, at Hanford, and in Amarillo. Moreover, a majority of all Americans lived downwind of the open-air atomic tests.

At the Nuclear Test Site the protective fences and security systems had an ironic effect. Its flora and fauna were little disturbed by human beings and in some areas less affected by radioactivity than wilderness sites to the east that were repeatedly showered with fallout. An archaeologist studied the NTS in 1965, after open-air testing ended. He found "hundreds of [species of] birds, snakes, insects, rodents, and charismatic megafauna like big horn sheep, antelope, wild horses, and burros," and even mountain lions. On the mountainsides, were Methuselah trees, a bristlecone pine more than four thousand years old.[88] They had been growing there before Columbus arrived in the Caribbean, before Caesar conquered Gaul, before Alexander conquered what was then the known world.

Handling nuclear waste demands an even longer perspective. The plutonium (PU-239) used in weapons has a half-life of 24,100 years. It will remain deadly far longer than any civilization or language has ever existed. As the cartoonist Herblock ironically reflected, only the cold part of the Cold War was over (figure 8.5). The federal government built a massive underground facility to contain radioactive materials inside Yucca Mountain, Nevada. But it remains empty, because Nevada refused to be the nuclear dump for the rest of the country. Instead, at scattered sites nuclear waste is stored "temporarily," including 40,000 tons of spent nuclear fuel in aboveground tanks in Utah on the Goshute tribe's reservation.[89] Other nuclear waste has been embedded in a thick layer of salt at the Waste Isolation Pilot Plant (WIPP) near Carlsbad, New Mexico, in man-made caverns 2,150 feet underground. What began in uranium mines ends as the reverse of mining, in a labyrinth of man-made caves, each as long as a football field and one third as wide. These chambers cover three square miles[90] and they can hold 850,000 barrels of nuclear waste. The barrels, which come from many places, are numbered but do not have bar codes and need to be X-rayed to determine their contents.[91]

Figure 8.5 Herblock, "I Hear the Cold Part of the Cold War Is Over" cartoon, 1990. *Source:* Library of Congress.

Entombing these materials has proven more difficult than anticipated. In February 2014, drum #68,660 overheated, burst open, burned, and spewed smoke into the underground facility.[92] It had been improperly packed in Los Alamos, where the staff had used an organic kitty litter rather than the inorganic zeolite clay kitty litter they were directed to use. This mistake resulted in "thermal runaway: the buildup of heat and pressure . . . due to exothermic reactions between its nitrate salt waste contents and the wheat-based kitty litter." The *Los Angeles Times* estimated that cleaning up after this seemingly small mistake ultimately cost about $2 billion, or as much as the cost of building the entire facility. (One could install a great many windmills and solar arrays for $2 billion, and they would pay for themselves.) An anthropologist studied the accident and concluded it was not an isolated error but the result of the "Quick to WIPP" campaign that accelerated shipment of wastes to Carlsbad from Los Alamos. "This campaign, marked by sped-up waste shipment tempos, hands-off oversight, and schedule-driven workforces—was what primarily set the stage for the kitty litter error going unnoticed by multiple organizations responsible."[93] There were "many oversight lapses, frenzies of collaborative enthusiasm, pressures to speedily ship waste, hiring of scientifically inexperienced schedule-driven supervisors," and a corporate culture that discouraged workers from questioning supervisors, some of whom lacked the scientific knowledge to make informed decisions. It is possible that among the tens of thousands of waste drums, another one is not safely packed and is slowly heating up. The same pattern emerges at every point in the history of uranium mining, concentration, use, cleanup, and waste storage. Repeatedly, government has outsourced work to private companies and emphasized "efficiency," leading to mistakes, contamination, illness, and enormous costs. It has not always learned from errors. The Department of Energy's internal investigation of WIPP's fire failed to mention the systemic errors built into the speed-up that made such an accident likely.

When waste shipments are packed into the WIPP salt formation until every cranny is full, its entrance will be closed and covered with earth. The facility is to last for ten thousand years, but the materials entombed will decline in radioactivity for 240,000 years.[94] Twenty-ton granite markers, a bit smaller than the vertical stones at Stonehenge, will warn away future generations in seven languages. Long before the site is safe, however, these languages will be incomprehensible to all but a few linguists

Figure 8.6 *Prayer Vigil against Nuclear Testing, Nevada, August 6, 1957*. Photographer not identified. *Source:* Library of Congress.

and historians, so there will also be warnings in pictographs. Will these be more intelligible in the year 12,020 than the Southwest's enigmatic petroglyphs? The warnings will be necessary because WIPP is located above oil and gas deposits. A 2020 government report noted an "increase in oil and gas-related drilling around the WIPP site" and estimated that there would be "4,102 boreholes within the Land Withdrawal Boundary during the 10,000-year performance period."[95] This atomic legacy will likely be a problem for more than a hundred human generations.

In the 1950s, religious protesters held prayer vigils against nuclear testing in Nevada (figure 8.6). Future protesters may seek out radioactive anti-landscapes, just as some already visit Chernobyl. What will WIPP represent? The antithesis of wilderness? A monument to colonialism? The military's mistreatment of nature? A dystopia of deadly waste? A character in Don DeLillo's novel *Underworld*, a UCLA professor of waste management, speculates, "The more dangerous the waste, the more heroic it will become. Irradiated ground. The way the Indians venerate this terrain now, we'll come to see it as sacred in the next century. Plutonium National Park. The last haunt of the White gods. Tourists wearing respirator masks and protective suits."[96] Rebecca Solnit provided a possible epitaph: "It didn't matter if the Arms Race ground to a halt, if a bomb was never used on a foreign country again, for the US government had begun a war against the people and the land here long ago and was going to lay siege to them until the half-life of the longest-lived radioactive elements was multiplied many times over."[97]

9

GRAND CANYON SINCE 1945: EPHEMERAL ANTHROPOCENE

After World War II, even as uranium mining intensified and open air atomic testing continued in the Southwest, tourists flocked to the Grand Canyon.[1] One million visitors came in 1956, and its popularity grew during the next sixty years. It surpassed Yellowstone in annual visitors occasionally between 1971 and 1984, and decisively moved ahead in 1986, when three million came to the canyon compared to 2.4 million to Yellowstone. The tide of visitors reached 4.5 million in the 1990s and almost 6 million in 2016, not counting those who flew overhead in small planes, or viewed it from one of the Native American reservations. The Grand Canyon is one of the few places that a majority of the 320 million Americans may visit during their lives.

Yet the canyon was not quite sacrosanct. During World War II the Bureau of Reclamation proposed building two dams inside it, and these were still on the Congressional agenda in 1949. The bureau felt so confidant of approval that without permission from the National Park Service or the Navajo tribe it constructed a cable tramway down to Marble Canyon.[2] Such arrogance partly explained defeat of the legislation. In 1958, the State of Arizona decided to build the two dams as state projects. It negotiated with the Hualapai for one, agreeing to compensate the tribe with more than $25 million in annual payments for the life of the dam. In contrast, Arizona told the Navajo that it already had the right to build the second dam on their land, and therefore did not need to compensate them. This tactical blunder pushed the Navajo to support a grandiose federal scheme that included California and would have diverted part of the Columbia River to the Southwest. Again, the Bureau of Reclamation began to prepare to build dams, again without formal permission. However, Senator Henry Jackson and legislators from the State of Washington opposed this scheme, as did the Hualapai who would lose their lucrative contract with Arizona and therefore threatened to build one dam by themselves. Many

Navajo and environmentalists were still angry over the Glen Canyon Dam and the betrayal of Rainbow Bridge. The Sierra Club generated nationwide publicity with a symposium held on the rim of the Grand Canyon. By 1967, the many-sided negotiations had fallen apart.[3]

If dams inside Grand Canyon National Park were defeated, however, it proved more difficult to stop uranium mining, which was considered vital to national security during the Cold War. By 2009, there were 3,500 uranium mining claims in the Grand Canyon area, when the Obama administration imposed a moratorium on new ones. As the *New York Times* noted, mining could pollute the aquifer and the Colorado River, "the source of drinking water for roughly 27 million people"[4] (figure 9.1). Few visitors seemed to know that extensive uranium mining went on near the Grand Canyon, or that it received nuclear fallout from open-air atomic tests. The canyon's rising popularity itself created other problems, however. In 1949, fewer than one hundred people had ever gone down the Colorado River in boats, and as late as 1964 fewer than one thousand had. Then river rafting became fashionable. In 1972, 16,400 took the trip, taxing the arid ecology and creating problems of waste disposal and fires. That year 132 river

Figure 9.1   Bill Gillette, *Waste at Union Carbide Uranium Processing Plant, on a tributary of the Colorado River, 1972*. Source: National Archives.

runners got dysentery because of poor sanitation. The NPS then established an annual limit of 14,000, and required them to carry out all their waste, including used toilet paper. Within a few years there was a nine-year waiting list.[5] Nevertheless, the narrow riverbanks remained crowded with campers, and investigators found that "human debris (food particles, plastic, pop tops, etc.) is being incorporated into the sand/silt deposits at rates that exceed purging capacities by natural means, causing beaches to look and smell like sandboxes in heavily used public parks."[6] Standards were more strictly enforced, but the number of visitors also increased. In 2006, the NPS permitted 985 boaters per day in the upper canyon, and 600 in the lower canyon, from Diamond Creek to Lake Mead.[7] Waste, debris, and pollution remained a problem, but boaters could not smell the radioactivity that scientists detected there in the 1980s, washed down from uranium mines.[8] Up on the rim, the Grand Canyon had traffic jams, overbooked hotels, parking problems, lines for concessions, crowds on Bright Angel Trail, and airplanes and helicopters overhead. The possible experiences continue to multiply beyond hiking and mule riding, and by 2018 included the Hualapai's steel-wire ziplines. After tourists were strapped in and released, gravity accelerated their fall to fifty miles per hour over the canyon.[9]

In its first decades, the Park Service provided accommodations and services for all visitors. But faced with millions of annual visitors, it limited hotel rooms inside the Grand Canyon National Park and restricted backpacking to 16,000 annual overnight permits. Hang gliding was prohibited as too dangerous. Guided snowmobile trips were permitted only on the North Rim, otherwise closed in winter, and camping areas were established near both rims and inside the gorge. Yet even as the Park Service tried to control tourism, Grand Canyon airport was enlarged to handle commercial jets, and motels and services expanded outside its gates. By the 1990s, *Time Magazine* reported, national parks were "plagued by much of the urban frenzy from which people try to flee in the first place." In response, the Park Service "decided to cut back sharply on visitors' access and creature comforts as a necessary cost of protecting the oasis for future generations."[10] Those who got a hotel room were urged not to take showers and to use as little water as possible, because local supplies were inadequate. On the rim there are no springs or streams, and water either had to be pumped up from Indian Gardens thousands of feet below or hauled in by truck or railroad. Waste and garbage also had to be carted away, since it clearly would not do to turn part of the canyon into a dump.

Water and refuse are but two of the problems. In the peak season, ten thousand or more vehicles daily compete for parking places. Flights over the Grand Canyon doubled in the decade after 1987. A plane or helicopter flew over some part of the canyon every ninety seconds, and some restrictions were imposed there as well. If a tourist retreated to a restaurant, there might be a two-hour wait. In October 1995, a "Guided Tour of the Park" on the Internet advised, "The whole stretch of rim trail between the El Tovar [hotel] and the head of Bright Angel Trail will be a seething mass of people during the prime tourist season. . . . The biggest part of the masses tend to congregate right outside the Bright Angel Lodge gift shop. . . . It's sad to think that this is the only view of the Canyon that some people ever get to see."[11]

Nineteenth-century tourists were not necessarily more fortunate. In the 1850s, crowds overran Niagara Falls, and they spent more time enjoying popular amusements than looking at the cataracts. One visitor complained: "Hawkers shouted on every corner. For a fee, guides offered to escort tourists down the treacherous gorge on foot trails to the base of the falls, and then collected an extra fee to lead them back up. Toll booths mushroomed, charging fees for access to areas along the overlooks walled from view by high board fences."[12] Another traveler noted that "A brisk trade in Indian ornaments and curiosities is carried on at Niagara," and many complained about the carnival atmosphere.[13] The "seething mass" of people at the Grand Canyon often spend only a few hours there; few descend below the rim and less than one in a hundred is allowed to stay overnight at the bottom (figure 9.2). They may have expected to experience magnificence in tranquility, but there is little time for ecstatic contemplation. They visit as many outlooks as they can, snap photographs, buy souvenirs, and later recollect and reprocess their experience.

There are four major ways that the public understands the canyon, and they occur for most visitors in a sequence. First is the sense of awe. John Muir early noted this reaction, and John C. Van Dyke described the typical scene in 1920, when most visitors arrived by train. They would "hurry up the steps from the station, pass along the front of the hotel, and go out at once to the Rim for a first view. You are impatient of delay in seeing this marvel of the world. Almost before you know it you are at the

Figure 9.2 Brian George, *Lipan Point Lookout, Grand Canyon, South Rim, 1994.*
Source: Library of Congress.

edge. The great abyss, without hint or warning, opens before your feet. For the moment, the earth seems cleft in twain and you are left standing at the brink. As you pause there momentarily the rock platforms down below seem to heave, the buttes sway; even the opposite Rim of the Canyon undulates slightly. The depth yawns to engulf you. Instinctively you shrink back."[14] This confrontation with the absolutely great disrupts normal perceptions and the moment seems outside the normal flow of time.

After the immediate sense of wonder or awe comes an effort to make sense of the experience and to master the details of the scene. The power of the sublime encounter may be similar for most people, but the interpretation they attach to it varies. Visitors to the Grand Canyon typically learn the names of the most striking rock formations. In almost no cases are the names derived from Native American traditions. Muir declared: "Throughout this vast extent of wild architecture—nature's own capital city—there seem to be no ordinary dwellings."[15] Since the 1870s, the canyon has been described in terms of temples, domes, minarets, towers, walls, pillars, ruins, and the like. Learning the names is a sufficient form of interpretation for some. Many names are exotic architectural metaphors invented by the White explorers, such as Isis Temple, Shiva Temple, or Vishnu Temple. As Krutch observed, "These 'temples' are much larger and much more ancient than any historical names can suggest."[16]

Next, most visitors become intrigued with how water and wind erosion carved the vast canyon. To learn more, merely looking is not sufficient. The tourist must read a guidebook or hear a short lecture. This task is made easier by the fact that each sedimentary layer has a distinctive color: 800 feet of light gray limestone at the rim, then 300 feet of darker gray sandstone. The next layers are 1,100 feet of red shales and red sandstone, and then a 500-foot wall of limestone stained a different shade of red by the sedimentary beds above it. Even if visitors do not long remember the composition of each layer (Kaibab limestone, Coconino sandstone, Hermit shale, Bright Angel shale, almost forty in all), they grasp the basic idea of the upper canyon: sedimentary layers undergoing erosion. Further down, the geology becomes more complex, including more sedimentary layers, igneous rocks, and metamorphic formations. The stone at the bottom is two billion years old. The Grand Canyon is an open book of nature, exposing the evolutionary history of the earth. Henry Ford's friend, the naturalist John Burroughs, popularized this view, and he is still cited in canyon hiking guides: "Time, geologic time, looks out at us from the rocks as from no other objects in the landscape. Geological time! How the striking of the great clock, whose hours are millions of years, reverberates out of the abyss of the past!"[17] The tourist can glean additional facts from maps, trail markers, pamphlets, campfire talks, and guidebooks. In 2010, the "trail of time" opened along the South Rim, creating a line of geological exhibits and explanations. Combining such information with views of the canyon, tourists understand the site as a record of the origins of life. The view from the rim visualizes the sweep of billions of years. Layer after sedimentary layer stretching down into the abyss express the almost unimaginable span of eternity.

As Krutch put it in his classic book on the Grand Canyon: "I am small and alone in the middle of these great distances, vertical as well as horizontal. But the gulf of time over which I am poised is inconceivably more vast and much more dizzying to peer into."[18] The visitor on the rim, even without understanding the details of the scientific argument, gazes toward the origins of the earth. The photograph of the canyon from the rim represents more than the Kantian vastness of space. The upward gaze toward sublime mountains had expressed what Kant called the "mathematical sublime," but the gaze down into the canyon epitomized the sublime of eternity. A photograph's inevitable failure to capture the Grand Canyon's plenitude of different views becomes not a defect but a confirmation of its meaning and a proof of human insignificance. The canyon becomes the spatial correlative of infinite time, and the photographic view from the rim, not from the bottom of the gorge or looking upward from a side canyon, best expresses this correlation.

Not all visitors accept geological explanations. Americans cherish the Grand Canyon, but they disagree about what it means. In the 1920s, the Park Service employed staff to explain the canyon's geology to tourists. These scientifically trained men and women presented the canyon as an "outstanding example of the work of the erosive forces of Nature, namely the cutting action of running water, of frost, wind and rain, abetted by chemical action, faulting, gravity, and growing vegetation." However, the superintendent of the park recalled in 1929 that such explanations were often "disputed by fundamentalists who accept their Bible literally and contend that the world is but six thousand years old and that it was made in six days, as per the account in the book of Genesis." Rejecting evolutionary explanations, fundamentalists "accused the rangers of being sacrilegious infidels" and on more than one occasion preferred "charges at the park headquarters."[19]

In the 1960s, well over half of Missouri-Synod Lutherans and Southern Baptists were creationists, and more than 90 percent of Seventh-Day Adventists. Since then, creationism has become even more common.[20] Today, 36 percent of Americans accept the Book of Genesis as the description of the earth's origin, and another third cannot decide if it is true or not.[21] Many Arizonans are fundamentalists who read scripture literally. In 1989, the Arizona Republican Party Convention declared the United States to be "a republic based on the absolute laws of the Bible, not a democracy."[22] Creationists understand the Grand Canyon as the product of the flood waters that carried Noah's Ark. Like some early visitors to Virginia's Natural Bridge, they see impressive landscapes as testimony to God's omnipotence. The initial sublime response of amazement may be similar for all visitors, but subsequent interpretations vary. The NPS maintains the scientific explanation, but fundamentalist Christians believe in the "young earth" theory and promote it on the Internet and in YouTube videos. The *Atlantic* explained, "Where geologists see billions of years of rock layers carved out by a persistent flow of water, young earth creationists see sediments laid down in Noah's flood. As the flood receded, they believe, water became trapped behind natural dams, until it finally broke through in a 'catastrophic erosion' that carved the Grand Canyon."[23] Fundamentalist Christians can take a river raft journey with Canyon Ministries, or they can buy an illustrated book explaining the young earth theory. A version of the catastrophe theory that Jefferson considered plausible in the 1770s lives on. Christian "young earth" researchers successfully sued the NPS after it denied their request to gather rocks inside the Grand Canyon. Although peer reviewers found their science deeply flawed, they eventually gained access.[24]

Some Native Americans have adopted another form of creationism, based on literal belief in their origin stories. In 2008, Heather Pringle explained in a blog sponsored by the Archaeological Institute of America, "Handed down by generations of elders, these stories are rich in metaphor and poetry. But lately I have heard educated young Native Americans take a surprisingly hard line on them, describing their elders' stories as reliable accounts of the beginning of the world and insisting that their ancestors were 'always' here in North America." This view rejects the "archaeological, linguistic and DNA evidence showing that the first Native Americans were Asian migrants who trekked on foot across the vast grasslands of Beringia or paddled in boats along the northern Pacific rim more than 13,000 years ago."[25] The students may have been reading Vine Deloria, a Sioux lawyer, activist, and professor at the University of Colorado. In 1998, he espoused creationist ideas in *Red Earth, White Lies: Native Americans and the Myth of Scientific Fact*. Deloria doubted the veracity of evolutionary theory, argued that Native Americans were "here at the beginning," asserted that dinosaurs were still alive in human history, and concluded that Noah's Flood was a worldwide event recorded in Native American texts.[26]

Whatever the interpretation of the Grand Canyon, the fact that millions journey to see it, and that they often return, underscores its special place in American culture. As Bill Clinton declared standing on the rim in 1996, "if you look at the Grand Canyon behind me, it seems impossible to think that anyone would want to touch it. But in the past, there have been those who wanted to build on the Canyon, to blast it, to dam it.

Fortunately, these plans were stopped by far-sighted Americans who saw that the Grand Canyon was a national treasure, a gift from God that could not be improved upon." Clinton closed his remarks with the words of President Theodore Roosevelt from 1903: "Leave the Grand Canyon as it is. You cannot improve upon it. What you can do is keep it for your children, your children's children, all who come after you."[27]

Ideally, the visitor needs days or even weeks to engage the complexities of the canyon. In 1917, when the crowds had not yet arrived, Reverend Charles W. Gilkey from Chicago gave the following advice:

> I have been sincerely sorry ever since coming away for those unfortunate visitors who have to run in and out on the next train. The Canyon refuses to yield its inner secrets to any sudden assault. You cannot take it by storm. You have to live with it, for the lights and shadows, the combinations of color are changing with every passing hour. At sunrise, high noon and sunset it changes with the changing sky and it alters its mood with yours, and you must see it at all hours; you must see it in all conditions in order really to have it impress upon you this mysterious spell. . . . You must stay awhile in order to appreciate that the other mysterious fact about the canyon is its silence. It is not only that you are silent in its presence, but that it is silent in yours; and that hush of eternity that broods over it day and night is one of the most mysterious and one of the most powerful things with which I personally have ever come into contact.[28]

Few visitors have time for this immersive experience. The immensity of the site, the pressure of the crowds, the high cost of remaining, and the difficulty of finding accommodations all encourage a search for shortcuts, notably films that conveniently compress Grand Canyon experiences. Many see the canyon for a few hours, acquire a basic understanding of the site, and later consolidate these impressions by watching a DVD or the film shown at the IMAX theater outside the park's south entrance at the National Geographic Visitor Center. This facility is as high tech as that used on the Ford River Rouge factory tour, including 12,000 watts of surround sound. The sixty-foot-high IMAX screen is eminently suited to a subject as large as the Grand Canyon. To tourists facing Arizona's summer heat, inadequate parking, long lines, overbooked accommodations, a nine-year waiting period to take a river-raft trip, and the high cost of a flight over the canyon, the air-conditioned theater seems decidedly attractive. It seats 495 people, with twelve showings every day, or potentially 40,000 viewers a week. It promises that during its thirty-four-minute film patrons will "literally experience the Grand Canyon, throughout time, as if they were actually there. Fly like an Eagle—soar over the rim of the canyon and dive into the depths of the craggy canyons. Take a whitewater rafting trip down the Colorado River and sense the raging currents thundering around you. Experience the history of the Grand Canyon and marvel at the amazing scenery while sitting comfortably in the theater."[29]

While many tourists enjoy this cinematic packaging of experience, others want sustained contact with a natural environment in pristine condition. The unhappy discovery that Grand Canyon is overrun is often combined with anger that the powerful river that carved the canyon has been dammed and siphoned off for irrigation. Its rhythms are determined not by rainfall but by the demands of air conditioners in Las Vegas and Phoenix. Industrial civilization has touched and transformed the canyon in myriad ways, and the more one looks the greater the technological intrusion appears. In the nineteenth century, nature seemed the wellspring of American national identity. Even as late as 1960 Wallace Stegner could call the canyon lands "a lovely and terrible wilderness, such a wilderness as Christ and the prophets went out into; harsh and beautifully colored, broken and worn until its bones are exposed, its great sky without a smudge or taint from Technocracy."[30]

Today the Grand Canyon can hardly be described in these terms. Parts of it may be classified as wilderness, but it faces the same environmental problems as the rest of the world. One might imagine it as vast empty space, but it never has been. Native Americans have lived there for millennia, and the Hualapai, the Navajo, and the Havasupai remain in the canyon and along its rim. Their small population suggests how many people the Grand Canyon's ecology can support through fishing, hunting, and patches of irrigated farming. But six million tourists a year require NPS employees, hotel workers, and other service providers. The canyon has gas stations, a gift shop, a general store, a small hospital, an airport, and a fire department. If the Grand Canyon of the imagination is wild, in reality it is a major tourist destination struggling with ecological limits.

The tourists who admire Hoover Dam the day after they visit the Grand Canyon appear to shift easily from the natural to the technological sublime. Great dams, skyscrapers, and other massive engineering works inspire quite different thoughts: not human weakness but mastery; not humility but pride; not the immeasurable past but an exalted future. The technological sublime is the triumphant conclusion of a second creation narrative. The experience of the natural sublime, in contrast, is not about transforming nature. Yet commercialism and the quest for strong sensory experiences obscure these differences.

Native Americans have been tempted by commercial possibilities. On the western side of the South Rim, in 2007, the Hualapai tribe opened a curved skywalk cantilevered out over the canyon. Its transparent flooring affords a giddy view straight down into the abyss. Together with other attractions on the reservation, they drew a million visitors a year before adding ziplines in 2018, which further increased attendance. At the other end of the park, sometimes called the "East Rim," the Navajo are tempted to establish additional attractions. In 2014, the tribe was divided over a tramway proposed to run from the rim 3,000 feet down to the near junction of the Little Colorado River and the Colorado River, near a site that the tribe considers sacred. The line was part of a $1 billion-dollar proposed Grand Canyon Escalade development. On the rim, it would include "a complex of restaurants, boutique hotels, stores and a trailer park." From there, the tramline "would whisk visitors down to a restaurant, an Indian cultural center and an elevated river walk on a part of the canyon floor."[31] Another commercial development was proposed in the town of Tusayan just outside the park. It would increase Tusayan's population from 600 to 5,000, with a housing estate of 2,200 homes and a shopping center. There is no water supply near the surface, however, and drilling for water might diminish the springs inside the Grand Canyon that are an essential part of its ecology. Should such a development be built, there would also be the problems of sewage and garbage.[32]

Even if no more projects are built and tourists reduce their footprint on the Grand Canyon, it cannot return to a previous "natural condition." Between 1906 and 1930 the federal government killed most of the predators in the canyon, including 816 mountain lions, 863 bobcats, and more than seven thousand coyotes.[33] Today, thousands of wild burros, a European invasive species, compete for the scarce vegetation with native animals. Bison, brought to the North Rim a century ago, have multiplied, damaged vegetation, and contaminated the water supply. To reduce their numbers from 600 to below 300, in 2017 the NPS recruited volunteer hunters to cull the herd.[34] Once there were eight species of fish in the Colorado River, and six of them could be found nowhere else. Today's survivors include the humpback chub, razorback sucker, bluehead sucker, flannelmouth sucker, and speckled dace, but the Colorado pike minnow, roundtail chub, and bonytail are extinct. The fish native to the canyon suffer because the water has been dammed upstream and is now colder and carries less sediment than before. They also must compete with brown trout and rainbow trout introduced a century ago. The Park Service has determined that the endangered species have a better chance of survival in side canyons, where conditions have changed less than in the main channel. It is therefore preventing trout from entering or spawning in Bright Angel Creek.[35]

Plant life has also changed. There are now almost two hundred nonnative plants in the canyon and they have spread rapidly and altered about half of the Grand Canyon.[36] Consider, for example, the tamarisk, also known as the salt cedar. Introduced into the American West in the nineteenth century as a hardy tree that could control erosion, it spread rapidly and made its way into the Grand Canyon during the 1920s. The salt cedar increases soil salinity and drives out native plants. Growing in dense thickets, they become a monoculture, and increase the danger of fire. The tamarisk became so dominant along the Colorado River that for years the Park Service gave up trying to eradicate it along the main channel. Instead, they focused on saving the side canyons. By 2011, more than 275,000 salt cedars had been removed. Elsewhere in the American West, the salt cedar leaf beetle was imported from Kazakhstan. When these beetles appeared in Grand Canyon in 2001, they changed its ecology again. They eradicated the tamarisk so rapidly that native species needed to be transplanted to take their place. Otherwise, endangered birds would have no habitat.[37] As these examples suggest, human beings have altered the animal, plant, and aquatic ecologies to the detriment of native species, which need help to survive. Such problems are common in most national parks. For example, due to global warming glaciers are melting and the tree line is moving toward higher elevations, endangering tundra plants, marmots, and mountain goats.[38]

Americans have used a wide range of technologies to change the Grand Canyon, including electrical generation plants, dams, airplanes, boats, automobiles, and much more. For decades, across Stegner's sky "without a smudge" smog blew in from the enormous coal-burning Four Corners Power Plant to the east and the Navajo Generating Station in the town of Page, Arizona. Both are recently closed. They burned coal strip-mined from the Navajo and Hopi reservations. The Peabody mine at Black Mesa covered 100 square miles, and it annihilated "burial and sacred sites, religious structures, and Anasazi ruins."[39] The Four Corners Power Plant spewed into the atmosphere more than 375 tons of fly ash and 1,000 tons of sulfur dioxide every day.[40] The air became so hazy that the canyon's opposite rim was indistinct. The plant's closure in 2019 has partially cleared the air, but daily, thousands of tons of Navajo coal are washed through a slurry pipeline for 270 miles to be burned in a Nevada power plant whose emissions often blow toward the canyon. That slurry line annually requires 1.3 billion gallons of water sucked from the aquifer beneath the desert.[41] It has dried up some springs and caused the water level in wells to fall as much as 100 feet.

Water supplies are also affected by the Glen Canyon Dam. Less water flows through the Grand Canyon, and it is no longer warm and red, but cold and green. With sediment impounded behind the dam, sand banks are not replenished. Because the gorge is no longer scoured out by high water each spring, the debris swept down by flash floods from side canyons is not spread out or washed away. The tame river's ecological system is monitored and managed. As the title of Philip Fradkin's classic work put it, the Colorado is *A River No More*.[42] Government agencies control it from one end to the other. The experience of the Grand Canyon begins to resemble the visit to a theme park, regulated by bureaucrats concerned with game management, waste disposal, firefighting, the logistics of transportation, crowd control, environmental protection, medical emergencies, electrical generation, preservation of biological diversity, maintaining the water supply, and air quality control.

Within this framework of regulation, the Grand Canyon is offered for consumption as an aerial view, as a series of a landscape tableaux, as an educational lecture at an evening camp fire, as a natural history lesson, as a series of books for sale at the gift shops near the rim, as DVDs, as an IMAX cinematic experience and even as the amusement park ride, "Grand Slam Canyon" in Las Vegas. The canyon is also recreated on the Internet. Google offers a virtual canyon experience, while another company advertises a tour with "over 75 interactive 360-degree panoramic views of more than 400 miles of rim and below-the-rim trails and the Colorado River corridor! Includes 3D trail maps, interpretive text, zoom links, glossary items, and bonus features."[43] Such products provide the chance to wonder at both the natural site and its technological replication. Virtual reality eliminates fellow tourists along with smog, airplanes, helicopters, poor weather, rattlesnakes, insects, sunstroke, dehydration, and the inconvenience of night. The virtual canyon is perfect and perpetually available.

Leaving the real canyon behind would mean leaving the body behind as well, abandoning the kinetic experience of the landscape and the synesthesia of its aromas, textures, sounds, and vistas. Virtual reality may mark the death of the "tourist" in the nineteenth century sense of the term. This is another way of saying that the traditional tourist landscape may be disappearing.[44] This process was underway by the 1990s, when tourist expectations had been inflected by television. In a *Far Side* cartoon a couple stands at a canyon lookout. The husband says: "I dunno. We're just so far up, I think this'd be better on the tube."[45] Sony used a similar idea in a 1992 television commercial, which showed a large television set perched near the rim. A small boy ran to it, fascinated by the canyon on TV more than the actual landscape. In the same year, General Electric used the Grand Canyon in an advertisement for the vibrant colors of its commercial lighting system. Many advertisers have been denied permission to use the park, which has rejected proposals to show people throwing wallets, hitting golf balls, and driving cars over the rim. Some of those rebuffed make footage at nearby Native American reservations.[46]

Tourists gaze down at what they expect to be absolute nature, only to find that the Grand Canyon has been a social construction from the moment its features were named, described, sketched, and photographed by explorers and artists, and later shaped by the mechanisms of mass tourism. The physical space itself is controlled by the NPS, the Environmental Protection Agency, and hydraulic engineers. The electricity generated is sold to private companies, and the water is allocated and transported to cotton fields, Phoenix, Tucson, Las Vegas, and Los Angeles. Tourists who come to see nature writ large instead find themselves within another, familiar but unwelcome experience of technologies being used to depict, to modify, to manage, and finally to replace nature. The canyon has been increasingly de-realized, beginning with the nineteenth-century paintings and photographs that made it a popular icon. The tourist has been offered ever more powerful technologies of space-time compression to assimilate the site, including railroads, automobiles, airplanes, snowmobiles, film, the IMAX theater, ziplines, pages on the Internet, and the virtual canyon.

The site that once symbolized American nature threatens to become a post-landscape that provides little therapeutic renewal. The tourist seems fated to become an interactive browser in cyberspace, a wanderer in virtual reality, seeking there the perfection and variety once pursued in the three-dimensional world.

Yet there is something missing from this argument, which carries with it a sense that simulation inevitably will replace the real. Are human beings caught within a cultural juggernaut that controls their perceptions of landscape so completely that the sublime experience of nature will prove to have been a temporary episode, a form of experience that lasted only a few centuries? Were the theories of Immanuel Kant and Edmund Burke expressions of a particular historical moment, ephemeral objectifications of a growing middle-class enthusiasm for mountains and wilderness? Or should the edifice of tourism that recycles images of the Grand Canyon be seen as an obstacle to be overcome in order to experience the site? The nineteenth century witnessed the growth of the egotistical sublime, in which an individual's exaggerated expectations of magnificence outran actual experience. As early as 1882, Clarence Dutton noted that many a visitor came "with a picture of it created by his own imagination. He reaches the spot, the conjured picture vanishes in an instant, and the place of it must be filled anew."[47] The replacement of annihilated preconceptions may take days, however, which is longer than most tourists remain.

Despite the recirculation of tourist images and the IMAX theater's best efforts to replace the site with simulacra, the power of the three-dimensional Grand Canyon persists. In the second week of December 1993, I arrived there in the late afternoon. Shadows had begun to swallow up the canyon, but I had time for several magnificent views from the lookouts before I checked in at the El Tovar hotel. A light snow fell during the night. The next morning at dawn, I walked along the rim for about a mile, without seeing or hearing another person, making the first footprints in the new-fallen snow. The dusting of white along the rim contrasted brilliantly with the red sandstone below. The mists rising from the abyss were soft, splintered rainbows. Enveloped in the canyon's vast silence, I realized that it will outlast human beings.

The Grand Canyon undermines one of the central conceits of post-structuralism, as argued by Roland Barthes.[48] In his view, every photograph ultimately is about time and loss, and an image always announces the eventual "death of the subject." But what if the subject is much older than humanity? The canyon overwhelms the categories of post-structuralism. It reminds visitors of extinct life forms preserved as fossils in its sedimentary beds. Beneath them is the billion-year-old granite of the inner canyon. Human beings have existed for less than one inch of the sedimentary layers in the Grand Canyon's one mile of eroded depth. Compared to human time, it is eternal; on the scale of geological time it announces the death and utter disappearance of whoever held the camera standing on the thin strata of rock that millions of years from now will identify the Anthropocene. No photograph of the Grand Canyon announces its death; rather, every photograph of the canyon is a reminder of how brief a period in the earth's history human beings and their artefacts have existed. As Loren Eisley once put it, "In a fortnight, as eons are measured, we may lie silent in a bed of stone."[49]

One of the messages of Mark Klett and Byron Wolfe in *Reconstructing the View* is that there can be no innocent eye when looking at the canyon. The book contains sixty-four color plates made between 2008 and 2011.[50] In each case, Klett and Wolfe first meticulously rediscovered the vantage points used to take historical photographs, and then made a panoramic photograph. Next, they inserted historical images inside this wider frame. The resulting collage reveals how fragmentary the earlier images were and contrasts the visual culture and tourism of past and present. A three-page foldout panorama illustrates the technique. It was taken from "the foot of Toroweap to the 'Devil's Anvil' overhang with an upstream view of the Colorado River." Into it are inserted four black-and-white images taken by William Bell in 1872. The rock formations are little changed after 136 years, but the sensibility is far different. Although the Colorado River was clearly visible from this vantage point, Bell purposely omitted it. He also omitted the foreground and evoked a sense of contact with an austere, untouched landscape in the distance. Early photographers on the rim framed only small segments of the scene, which Klett and Wolfe insert within their panoramic views. The resulting assemblage emphasizes the selectivity and artificiality of representation. Their precise topological measurements rediscover earlier vantage points. They show how Thomas Moran scarcely held up a mirror to nature, but rather selected, rearranged, and compressed thirteen different sketches made at Dutton Point into one painting. His canvas deleted much of the actual landscape, to create a celebrated image of sublimity. Klett and Wolfe recreate the context of that sublime but deflate it.

Their chief method of deflation is to juxtapose images from contemporary popular culture with famous Grand Canyon photographs made by Bell, Timothy O'Sullivan, Ansel Adams, and Frederick Sommer. One juxtaposition shows a woman standing on her head near the rim of the canyon, inserted next to an image taken by Alvin Langdon Coburn in 1911, depicting an unknown male photographer. The contrast between her irreverent naked legs pointing skyward and the fully clothed, gray figure holding a large camera and hovering reverently over the abyss epitomizes the contrast between the casual exhibitionism of a modern tourist and the high moral seriousness of the Victorians. On the facing page, casually clad tourists pose for photographs near Lookout Studio. In contrast, next to them is Emory Kolb's *Portrait of an Indian Man* from a century earlier. The Native American is silhouetted against a distant cliff in soft focus. He stands on a wall and holds a rifle, a pose and treatment that derives from Edward Curtis.[51] This impressionistic black-and-white photograph omits most of the vast surroundings. Next to him, in sharper focus and a century later, stand modern tourists in strong colors. Another collage depicts the popular Hopi Point lookout and employs the same kind of visual play. On the left, in color, are the legs and sandal-shod feet of modern tourists behind a fence that prevents them from falling into the canyon; beyond the fence, in black and white, wearing a dark suit and straw hat is Arthur Wesley Dow, camera in hand, perched at the outlook's upmost extremity, gazing straight down. The contrast suggests that, compared to Dow, modern tourists are mere consumers who are not engaged with the Grand Canyon's dangerous sublimity.

The complexity of the contemporary relationship to the Grand Canyon is further suggested by Mark Tansey's 1990 canvas *Constructing the Grand Canyon*[52] (figure 9.3). At first glance it appears to be a canyon in the Southwest, but on closer inspection it clearly is an excavation, where men and women are removing sedimentary rock from the bottom of the nearly precipitous walls of a red canyon. Further inspection reveals that the rubble is not rock but textual fragments. A few words are legible, but no sentences or meaningful phrases can be read. By replacing erosion with (de)construction, the image playfully answers the often-repeated questions by naive visitors at the Grand Canyon: "How was it built? What tools did they

Figure 9.3 Mark Tansey (1949–), *Constructing the Grand Canyon*, 1990, oil on canvas, dimensions 85 × 126½ inches unframed; 88¼ × 127¾ × 2⅛ in framed. *Source:* Walker Art Center.

use?" A railroad line is being constructed down the center of the Tansey's canvas, where small railway cars are being loaded with broken words to be carted away. The figures amid these disintegrated texts turn out to be poststructuralist theorists.[53] On the left, half-way up the canyon wall and gazing down at the scene is Michel Foucault. In the middle of the image, "The Yale School" is busy deploying surveying apparatus. In contrast to this group, Paul de Man, Jacques Derrida, Harold Boom, and Geoffrey Hartman are observers, not directors of the activities around them. Tansey not only depicted deconstruction as construction, but also committed the "sin" of realistic portraiture, albeit in an impossible landscape. The sedimentary rocks have been replaced by words, the raging Colorado River has been replaced by a pathetically small railroad, and muscle power is completely inadequate to excavate anything on the scale of the Grand Canyon. If the declivity depicted were set down in the actual canyon, it would disappear completely into a side canyon, a footnote. Significantly, Tansey's canyon of deracination is shorn of vegetation, as the ecosystem disappears.

Tansey suggests that the valley of deconstruction is an arbitrary construction. In his playful inversion, men excavate a canyon while nature stands outside, above even Foucault's gaze, and observes. Buffalo on the rim gaze down at deconstructionists in their self-created abyss. The buffalo are nature's tourists, reminders of another world that lies beyond the rim. The buffalo were nearly extinct by the early twentieth century. After being almost literally absent, they have come back, just as meaning comes back if one escapes the enclosed world of deconstruction. Postmodernist theorists can dig deeper into the sediments of culture and cart away the smashed results of their work. But their line has no place to go. There is no exit from their constructed abyss. This mental engineering eliminates all that does not fit within its system, notably the complexities of landscape and geological time. Mistaking the world for a text leads to a cul-de-sac. The actual landscape is a living ecology, not a lifeless zone awaiting deconstruction.

The Grand Canyon's complexity escapes depiction. It is more than sublime, more than postmodern, and more than merely ancient. It does not announce the death of the subject but suggests that humanity's triumph over the rest of nature can only be temporary. It exceeds the categories of utilitarian land development, wilderness preservation, pastoralism, and anti-landscape. The Grand Canyon measures the brevity of human time.

10

CONFLICTED LANDSCAPES

Americans are more divided today in their understanding of nature than they ever have been, and their six irreconcilable views imply different conceptions of history. First, to the Native Americans, nature and culture have always been inseparable, and the identity and the history of a tribe is thoroughly interwoven with specific places, such as Rainbow Bridge or the San Francisco Peaks. In contrast, many White Americans embrace wilderness, defined as nature that is free of human presence, with no roads, telephone lines, or electricity. The wilderness is eternal and pre-cultural, and that is why Native Americans were evicted from Yosemite, Yellowstone and many other national parks. This conception of nature as a preserved remnant of the prehuman world is at odds with both Native Americans and a third view, the utilitarian concept of nature that is dominant in American society. It treats nature as a stockpile of resources awaiting exploitation and development. National identity is created by subduing and transforming nature into bridges, dams, railroads, skylines, electrified cities, and communication networks. Its ideal is the technological sublime. Utilitarians want to exploit Grand Canyon tourism or construct a hydroelectric dam inside it. Tourists imbued with this ethic look for the road or the cable car to the bottom, and they complain that the canyon is not lighted up at night. In contrast, pastoralism tries to reconcile the wilderness ethic and utilitarianism, balancing development with preservation. In this tradition, buildings on the rim of the Grand Canyon must be limited in number and blend into the site. Pastoralism celebrates the merging of culture and nature, in contrast to wilderness, which is conceived as an everlasting realm outside of human time, while utilitarianism focuses on exploited natural resources for future rewards. Unifying these concepts has become more difficult in recent decades, due to a fifth conception of nature visible in the actions of mining interests and the military. They have at times adopted an extreme level of exploitation, treating some sites as sacrifice zones, transforming them into anti-landscapes that cannot support human life. In the Southwest, the sacrifice zones include enormous missile ranges, the atomic testing site in Nevada, and the WIPP radioactive waste facility. A sacrifice zone is the polar opposite of wilderness. Finally, creationists hold a sixth conception of nature, conceived in biblical terms. For them, God called the earth into existence only ten thousand years ago, and its natural resources are still being created. These six conceptions of nature entail six radically different understandings of history. Does nature represent eternity, ancestors, science, the present, the future, or a young earth? Is it to be revered, conserved, exploited, or sacrificed? A nation that identifies itself with nature begins to fall apart when it no longer can agree on what nature is. Moreover, some of these differences are internalized in the views of every American. Just as Henry Ford built both Greenfield Village and the River Rouge plant, so too John Wesley Powell and Theodore Roosevelt advocated both irrigation and preservation. Likewise, in 1910 residents of the new skyscraper city escaped on railroad Pullman sleeping cars to national parks. An American typically has embraced several, but not all six, conceptions of nature.

Since World War II the relationships between these conceptions have shifted dramatically. The once-dominant utilitarianism is now contested. Increasingly, Americans worry about global warming, species extinction, and pollution, and they question highway projects, new pipelines, strip mining, reliance on fossil fuels, and the location of waste disposal sites. At the same time, creationists have become more numerous, particularly in the Southwest. Their biblical sense of history explains the United States in terms of Manifest Destiny and American exceptionalism. When President Ronald Reagan ran for reelection in 1984, his campaign slogan declared "It's Morning in America." It suggested that the United States was just beginning, and that most of its second creation lay ahead. This message appealed to his creationist supporters, as did Reagan's declaration that both evolution and creation theory ought to be taught in the public schools.[1] America's second creation acquired greater resonance if human history began only a few thousand years ago. From the 1930s to the 1970s, the Bureau of Reclamation's projects, such as Glen Canyon Dam, had been justified by the utilitarian benefits of hydropower, flood prevention, irrigation, and recreational boating. But some creationists saw these projects as the unfolding of American destiny.

Even as creationism became more common, support for wilderness also grew. The wilderness movement relied on a scientific approach to landscape that called attention to all plants, birds, insects, and animals, rather than presenting human beings as a non-evolutionary special creation of God. Scientific investigation showed the complexity of landscape, documented the rising rate of species extinction, and gathered evidence of global warming. The evidence undermined the possibility of wilderness itself. As the German sociologist Ulrich Beck concluded, "Anyone who continues to speak of nature as non-society is speaking in terms from a different century, which no longer capture our reality. In nature, we are concerned today with a highly synthetic product everywhere, an artificial 'nature.' Not a hair or a crumb of it is still 'natural,' if 'natural' means nature being left to itself."[2] Historians, literary critics, and anthropologists reached similar conclusions.[3] If wilderness lacked credibility, however, to environmentalists, a designated wilderness was clearly preferable to subjecting any site to uranium mining, oil extraction, or nuclear tests.

The clash of creationism with science had philosophical implications and political consequences. Consider the philosophical implications first. Diametrically opposed views could be attached to the natural sublime, depending upon whether one believed in creationism or evolutionary science. Since Jefferson's era, some Americans have seen natural bridges and other natural wonders as proof of the existence of God, and many viewed the national parks and wilderness areas in this way. A scientific understanding of the same spectacular landscapes did not detract from their sublimity but saw in them the proof of geological theory, the immensity of time, and the insignificance of human history. Creationists and evolutionists agreed that these sites were sublime, but their understandings of them were incompatible. Nor was this the only problem. Both the technological and the natural sublime were based on a dichotomy between nature and culture, and both exalted a small number of exemplary sites. Both narratives imagined nature as raw material that awaited either human improvement or preservation. They pointed toward either an impossible escape from history into pure nature or an impossible escape from nature into purely technical constructions such as the modernist city or virtual reality. But the environmental sciences showed that pure nature did not exist, and that mankind was inextricably part of nature.[4]

Politically, tensions between different conceptions of the land sharpened conflicts over dams, irrigation, tourism, mining, atomic testing, waste storage, and wilderness. White Americans had long shifted between three customary (and contradictory) ideologies of nature: utilitarianism, pastoralism, and primitivism (wilderness). Theodore Roosevelt called for the preservation of the Grand Canyon and Rainbow Bridge, yet he vigorously supported irrigation. An Arizona dam was named after him. Sixty years later Arizona senator and presidential candidate Barry Goldwater celebrated the same two sites. Neither Roosevelt nor Goldwater opposed commercial development. Both shifted easily between contradictory ideas. For generations, Americans alternated among several land ethics, depending upon audience and occasion. Every president celebrated the utilitarian development of natural resources. Every president also praised the creation of public parks and other pastoral landscapes. And after 1964 every president designated wilderness areas. Lyndon Johnson and his successor, Richard Nixon, each set aside millions of acres to remain unspoiled in perpetuity, and the presidents after them added more.[5] Politicians had an appropriate rhetoric for each situation. Visiting a factory or mine called for the utilitarian narrative of economic growth and a brighter tomorrow. In 1977, Jimmy Carter visited West Virginia to promote coal. He declared, "One inevitable major shift in the years ahead is away from oil and natural gas and toward coal. We want to be sure that when this shift is made that a continuing substantial major portion of the coal to be used comes from the Appalachian region."[6]

In contrast, when Carter established the William O. Douglas Arctic Wildlife Range in Alaska's Brooks Mountains as a wilderness area, it was preserved so that future generations could experience a remnant of virgin land as a foil to civilization. Carter quoted the late Supreme Court Justice Douglas: "The Arctic has a call that is compelling. The distant mountains make one want to go on and on over the next ridge and over the one beyond. The call is that of a wilderness known only to a few. . . . This last American wilderness must remain sacrosanct." Carter noted that Douglas "staunchly asserted the right of all living things to be born, grow and die in a state of natural freedom. He cared for the moose and caribou of the arctic range as he cared for all those whose life and liberty were threatened by forces larger than themselves. Justice Douglas insisted that the present generation must protect environmental and human rights. . . . He took strength from the refuge that nature and wilderness give the human soul." The wildlife range "offers the solitude and grandeur of vast arctic spaces as well as the vitality of a breeding ground for thousands of birds and for one of the largest remaining caribou herds on earth."[7] Wilderness was not divided by a grid, which immediately implied private ownership, development, and history. Wilderness was a pre-narrative condition in undisturbed nature. It offered escape from the continual transformations of second creation.

During the Cold War, Americans maintained a political consensus that simultaneously they could have wilderness, pastoral retreats, and industrial development, including atomic power plants and nuclear weapons. This consensus united both Republicans (Goldwater, Nixon, and Reagan) and Democrats (Johnson, Carter, and Clinton). By the 1990s, however, this balancing act between development and preservation had become precarious. Some mining and oil interests had always opposed setting aside national monuments and wilderness areas. Likewise, many residents of western states, where national parks, monuments, and wilderness areas predominate, thought the second creation story should apply to Utah and Colorado as much as it did to New Jersey and Georgia. At the same time, creationism spread, and a 2008 Gallup poll found that 60 percent of all Republicans thought "humans were created in their present form by God 10,000 years ago," a belief shared by 40 percent of Independents and 38 percent of Democrats.[8]

The gap between the two parties on environmental issues widened during the 2000 presidential election. The former oil executive George W. Bush championed utilitarian resource extraction and second creation. His "energy plan called for drilling for oil in the Arctic National Wildlife Area, boosting federal funding and support of research and development in coal technology, and relaxing regulation on coal-fired plants."[9] (In 2018, President Trump had similar policies.) Bush did not consider global warning a serious problem, and placed a higher priority on stimulating the economy.[10] Both he and Vice President Dick Cheney argued that mining companies and petrochemical industries were entitled to national resources, a view shared by most corporations and chambers of commerce. When campaigning, Bush called CO_2 a pollutant, but after taking office, he redefined it as merely an emission.[11]

Bush's opponent, Al Gore, held opposed positions. In *Earth in the Balance*, he argued that resources were limited and that the environment was in peril. He wanted to mandate greater automobile fuel efficiency and to impose a carbon tax on industry in order to mitigate global warming. Gore gave a voice to environmentalists, indigenous peoples, workers, and injured biotic communities, including Mormon towns downwind of atomic testing, Navajo and Hopi reservations, and the ecologies of damaged sites such as Glen Canyon. He wanted to clean up and restore polluted areas. His politics extended Gifford Pinchot's work on forest restoration, New Deal conservation programs, and the Environmental Protection Agency's restitution of Superfund sites such as the River Rouge and abandoned uranium mines. As late as 2008, a few Republicans also saw global warming as a problem, including John McCain who led the party in that year's election campaign. Afterward, the two parties completed the polarization that had begun in the 1990s.[12]

In 2002, Mike Pence, who would later become Trump's vice president, gave a speech in Congress that embraced Intelligent Design, the idea that evolution took more than ten thousand years but was guided by "the Lord." He declared, "Every signer of the Declaration of Independence believed that men and women were created and were endowed by that same Creator with certain unalienable rights. The Bible tells us that God created man in his own image, male and female. He created them. And I believe that, Mr. Speaker. I believe that God created the known universe, the Earth and everything in it, including man. And I also believe that someday scientists will come to see that only the theory of intelligent design provides even a remotely rational explanation for the known universe."[13] In subsequent elections, many Republican candidates for president, including Michele Bachmann, Rick Perry, Mitt Romney, and Rick Santorum, declared that they too believed in Intelligent Design. When the well-qualified Republican candidate John Huntsman said he believed in evolution, Santorum rebuked him: "If Governor Huntsman wants to believe that he is the descendant of a monkey, then he has the right to believe that—but I disagree with him on this and the many other liberal beliefs he shares with Democrats."[14]

Two generations ago mainstream Republican and Democratic leaders embraced both science and the Declaration of Independence, both national parks and interstate highways, both wilderness and development, both the natural and the technological sublime. But Democrats increasingly became the party of environmentalists, while Republicans increasingly adopted an uncompromising utilitarianism at odds with Teddy Roosevelt's conservation policies. The national government was also internally divided. The Departments of Commerce and Agriculture maintained the utilitarian land ethic, while ecological concerns were more salient at the Environmental Protection Agency and at some (but not all) divisions of the Department of the Interior. The Department of Energy spent most of its funds on the nuclear industry, yet it also promoted wind and solar power. Moreover, every department of government was pressured to adjust its priorities when control of the White House changed.

The opposition between utilitarianism, infused with creationist zeal, and environmentalism, bolstered by scientific research, often dominates the headlines, but it does not fully express the variety of American conceptions of nature, which also include pastoralism, Native American religions, and fears of the anti-landscape. All of these conceptions of nature were articulated in relation to the grid system of land division that Americans imposed even before they wrote their Constitution (figure 10.1). The history of Detroit's River Rouge exemplifies how the grid was projected on to one local landscape. Americans erased most traces of the Mound Builders and of the French settlement, redefined the land as a commodity, and overlaid it with a grid of property rights. The subsequent transformation of the River Rouge was a utilitarian triumph that culminated in the world's largest factory complex. Yet it created such severe pollution that in the 1990s the river was designated a Superfund site. The Rouge also included three pastoral landscapes—a large city park, the Henry Ford estate, and Greenfield Village. In other regions the dominant utilitarian-pastoral system gave way to appreciation of "unimproved" nature, such as natural bridges. Most White Americans have viewed such unusual formations as sublime, even if they disagreed on whether to interpret them according to uniformitarian geology or creationism. In contrast, Native Americans often regard striking rock formations as living, sacred places. Utilitarian ideas were used to justify second creation projects along the Colorado, such as road building, mining, and irrigation, but these projects often violated the rights of Native Americans and defaced sublime natural sites, suggesting the need for national parks, national monuments, and wilderness protection. Americans at first had difficulty making sense of the Grand Canyon, which was spectacular in an entirely different way from traditional sublime landscapes such as the Alps or Yosemite. To convert a

Figure 10.1 Kent Fairbanks, "Grid Pattern of Land Division, Spring City, Sanpete County, Utah, 1968. Aerial view from Southwest." In 2010, *Forbes* magazine called Spring City one of the prettiest towns in America." Source: Library of Congress.

vast abyss into the spatial representation of eternity required new geological theories, a lengthened sense of evolutionary time, and the interpretive skill of photographers and painters. During Grand Canyon's transformation from a "profitless locality" to America's most popular national park, it had to contend with hundreds of mining claims inside its boundaries, with entrepreneurs cashing in on tourism, and with the growing hosts of visitors themselves.

The popularity of national parks increased as the nation became more urban. The railroads, the largest industries of the late nineteenth century, transported the food, building materials, and people that made parks accessible and large cities possible. Railroads advertised the sublimity of Yellowstone, Glacier National Park, the Grand Canyon, and Rocky Mountain

National Park. Railroads also exemplified the apotheosis of utilitarianism, or the technological sublime, with their high speed, enormous extent, vast stations, and steel bridges. Adoption of steel also made possible skyscrapers and the new city skyline. The dramatic vista from the summit of a skyscraper materialized the second creation narrative. The apparent triumph over nature, however, also created fatal environments like Love Canal, Picher, and other anti-landscapes of industrialization. More than fifty thousand sites suffered chemical pollution, hundreds of abandoned uranium mines polluted their surroundings, and the nuclear power industry and atomic weapons program produced tons of radioactive waste. Many polluted sites were located on Native American reservations or near the Grand Canyon, exposing them to radiation. The canyon also suffered the intentional extermination of its predators, the introduction of nonnative fish, plants, birds, and animals, and a rapid increase of tourism. Experiencing the site became so shortened, disrupted, and commercialized that substitutes became popular via the Internet, DVDs, and IMAX theaters. Yet the immensity and complexity of the Grand Canyon resist reductionist interpretations and challenge visitors who stay for more than a few hours to recognize the brevity of human time. They realize that human products such as plastic, artificial rubber, lost coins, radioactive debris, and fragments of equipment, will become part of a few inches of sediment that records the Anthropocene, sitting on top of more than a mile of rock from the several billion years before human beings existed.

The Grand Canyon underscores how myopic utilitarianism is, but in American politics and business most land is still considered raw material to be sold as real estate that owners may transform as they wish in pursuit of profit, pleasure, or personal whim. This utilitarianism is expressed in technological creation stories that provide a widely accepted roadmap of American history. They describe the movement of Europeans into an empty grid of lands that they transformed from forest to field, from prairie to farm, from trail to canal to railway, from log cabin to metropolis, from desert to irrigated garden. In this vision, nature is an inexhaustible cornucopia, and the United States is unfinished space that Americans have a duty to improve. It is a colonizing story that assumes North America was scarcely touched until Europeans arrived and made improvements that were latent in the land. The clearing in the forest, the mill in the valley, the canal and the railroad running west, the dam across the canyon, or the irrigation ditch in the desert were each understood to be in harmony with nature. As James Fenimore Cooper expressed it, "There is a pleasure in diving into a virgin forest and commencing the labors of civilization, that has no exact parallel in any other human occupation. . . . [It] approaches nearer to the feeling of creating."[15] Such thinking became the dominant ideology during Cooper's lifetime, when it seemed to be morning in America, and every road, dam, windmill, or other improvement seemed to be for the greatest good of the greatest number.

In practice, however, utilitarian development often meant short-sighted exploitation, pollution, and a throwaway culture of consumption, and in the worst cases it resulted in waste dumps, radioactive zones, and other anti-landscapes. In 1963, then then Secretary of the Interior Stewart Udall declared, "More and more Americans see that in this increasingly commercial civilization there must be sanctuaries where commercialism is barred, where . . . all forms of economic use are completely and permanently prohibited, where every man may enjoy the spiritual exhilaration of the wilderness."[16] Yet, decades later wilderness seemed more mythic than real. One did not need to read scholarly essays to discover the problems. The General Accounting Office (today, renamed the Government Accountability Office) found that wildernesses often were compromised in practice.[17] Their borders were breached by thousands of enthusiastic hikers, invasive species, air pollution, and atomic fallout. By the 1990s, so many people visited wilderness areas that their lakes often contained human bacteria. Visitors were warned to boil drinking water for ten minutes, and most of the firewood had been stripped from terrain near official "wilderness campsites."[18] As Kerwin Klein noted in an essay on tourism in the Southwest, "The fictive assertion that the parks, monuments, and wilderness areas preserved inviolate a natural state of Edenic grace not only denied the function of these landscapes as consumer commodities, but also implicitly legitimated the imperialist Turnerian vision of the western landscape as 'free' land," erasing the fact that it had been taken from Native Americans and Hispanics."[19]

When a Diné (Navajo) child is born, the family buries the umbilical cord beside the home, underscoring the child's link to that particular place. "This ensures that throughout life, she or he will always return home, that the child will always take care of his or her parents and that the child will not wander aimlessly as an adult."[20] This is a more intimate relationship with the land than mere real estate ownership. As the Navajo Roberta Blackgoat explained, "If there is a beautiful old tree, and you dig it up and move it, do you think it will continue to live? Even if you do everything you can to prepare new ground for it, do you think that old tree will live? No, it won't live. And it is the same way with us. When they move us away, we will die."[21]

Yet many Navajo have been forced to move because their homes became part of conflicted landscapes. In the 1960s, the Bureau of Reclamation had expected to build additional dams inside the Grand Canyon, which would provide the electrical power necessary to pump billions of gallons of Colorado River water to Phoenix and Tucson. When these dams were blocked by a coalition of environmentalists and Native Americans, the government successfully argued for a massive coal mine to serve one of the largest power stations in the United States. Coal mining proved deeply troubling to the Navajo. The coal-fired power plant at Page provided well-paid jobs and payments into the tribe's coffers. But the tribe members, who had always enjoyed clean air and blue skies, confronted "a brown sky smelling of burning dirty clothes and old tires. The smoke," which contained sulfur dioxide, lead, and mercury, rolled "up the hill, over the poisoned lake and the chemical-coated grass," and billowed into the skies around the Grand Canyon. To the tribe, the worst desecration was "a giant coal mining dragline" that tore up their ancestors' graves, as it heaved coal out of the earth (figure 10.2).[22] Roberta Blackgoat commented: "No compassion is left for the motherland. We've become her enemy. Money does this. This is what I say. Our prayers lose their meanings when the land becomes an industry. Highways through the canyons and the valleys are blistered like scar tissue. . . . The names on the land are the lives lived before me. They are still here."[23] After mining, where were her ancestors?

Another Navajo activist declared to the Civil Rights Commission in 1974: "To the Navajo people it seems as if these Europeans hate everything in nature—the grass, the birds, the beasts, the water, the soil, and the air."[24] The utilitarian ideology, expressed in Supreme Court decisions and land-use policies, rejects Native American perspectives, and this rejection was often intertwined with the ideology of the technological sublime. As Rob Nixon has observed, oil and mining corporations have "long sought to exploit the romance of the technological sublime—imagining the unimaginable, venturing into the unknown."[25] Highways have been bulldozed,

Figure 10.2   Lyntha Scott Eiler, *Strip Mining Coal on Navajo Burial Grounds, 1972*, Environmental Protection Agency. *Source:* National Archives.

rivers dammed, and mines carved out of the mesas. Sacred places such as the Black Hills of South Dakota are mined, and Rainbow Bridge is appropriated and developed as a tourist site. A telling exchange during a Senate hearing in 2002 revealed explicitly how the Department of the Interior repeatedly has ignored Native American requests to protect their sacred sites. The senator from Colorado, Ben Nighthorse Campbell, asked Christopher Kearney from the Department of the Interior, "Can you give the committee a couple of instances in which tribal complaints have stopped a big development, say a mine development?" Kearney admitted, "In my direct experience, nothing immediately comes to mind. Senator Campbell then noted, that Native Americans had "never been able to stop one [mine]. I mean, there might be some consultation, but the bottom line is it gets done."[26]

This exchange occurred during an investigation into why the Bush administration approved an application to mine gold on Quechan tribal lands near Yuma. In the 1990s, a Canadian company wanted to mine 150 million tons of ore and leach it with acid, leaving behind more than three hundred million tons of waste. The mine was to run day and night and to pump up from beneath the desert 1,250 acre feet of ground water per year. The tribe vehemently objected, and President Clinton's Department of the Interior concluded the mine would destroy one of the most endangered Native American sacred sites. It also would pollute the adjacent Indian Pass Wilderness Area (created in 1994) and its three natural bridges, and it would be deleterious for endangered species. After five years of hearings and investigations the Department of the Interior declared: "The proposed project would destroy portions of the Trail of Dreams, other trails, and related ceremonial areas providing a spiritual pathway between Pilot Knob, 25 miles from the site, and Newberry Mountain, 115 miles away." The Quechan and the other tribes would not be able "to travel, both physically and spiritually, along the Trail of Dreams; to make ceremonial use of the prayer circles, rock alignments, and other cultural features in the project area; to gain protection from metaphysical dangers; and to continue to use the project area for vision quests and teaching tribal youths about their culture."[27] Many shrines had been built along this trail, and the area also included "an extensive assemblage of Native American scratched petroglyphs."[28]

The Bush administration ignored these conclusions, snubbed the Quechan tribe, met with the Canadian company, and approved the lease. Senator Barbara Boxer from California was outraged. The three open-pit mines, each up to 850 feet deep, would poison the land with chemicals and leave behind gaping craters and mountains of waste. A company representative testified: "It's not cost-effective to fill in the last hole when you're done mining."[29] Senator Boxer cited the President's Advisory Council on Historic Preservation's conclusion that the mine would "destroy the tribe's ability to practice and transmit to future generations the ceremonies and values that sustain their cultural existence." The excavations would "rip the heart out of the tribe's religious center."[30] The tribe's president declared, "Without Indian Pass, we can't carry on our culture, our tradition, our religious beliefs. They will be gone forever should this land mine be permitted to proceed."[31] But as that hearing made clear, they did not control their land.[32] It appeared to be a lost cause, until California passed a law requiring mining corporations to fill in disused open pits, a requirement that made the gold mine uneconomical. The company sued, but lost, and the Quechan lands were saved.[33]

As in this case, the battles are between Republicans and Democrats, state and federal governments, Native Americans and the BIA, and environmentalists and mining corporations. All of these actors again came into conflict after President Clinton declared Grand Staircase-Escalante a national monument in 1996. The site includes "many arches and natural bridges, including the 130-foot-high Escalante Natural Bridge, with a 100-foot span, and Grosvenor Arch, a rare 'double arch.' The upper Escalante Canyons, in the northeastern reaches of the monument, are distinctive: in addition to several major arches and natural bridges, vivid geological features are laid bare in narrow, serpentine canyons, where erosion has exposed sandstone and shale deposits in shades of red, maroon, chocolate, tan, gray, and white."[34] Clinton tried to assuage fears that this monument would stifle the local economy. At its dedication, he argued, "Mining jobs are good jobs, and mining is important to our national economy and to our national security. But we can't have mines everywhere, and we shouldn't have mines that threaten our national treasures. That is why I am so pleased that PacifiCorp has followed the example set by Crown Butte New World Mine in Yellowstone. PacifiCorp has agreed to trade its lease to mine coal on these lands for better, more appropriate sites outside the monument area."[35] But this land exchange did not placate local interests. The "residents of Kanab, Utah, heard those words and released fifty black balloons into the blue desert sky, as a warning to other states that this kind of 'federal dictatorship' could happen to you." The community felt that it had lost 900 jobs at the proposed mine, that 1.7 million acres had "been 'locked up,' and that the county's economic future was 'locked out.'" Sensitive to these local rumblings, the senator from Utah Orrin Hatch called Grand Staircase-Escalante National Monument "the mother of all land grabs."[36] Similar protests in Wyoming had greeted Franklin D. Roosevelt when he created the Grand Teton National Monument, which later became a national park. The local population eventually accepted this decision, because the increased tourism proved a permanent source of income, unlike mining that provided short-term jobs and ruined the landscape with roads, craters, tailings, and pollution.

The conflict over Grand Staircase-Escalante intensified after 1996, as uranium mining increased nearby. In 2012, the Department of the Interior barred for a period of twenty years any new uranium mines on one million acres of land near the Grand Canyon. Mining companies contested this decision, but in December 2017, the Ninth U.S. Circuit Court of Appeals upheld the ban, whose purpose, as two former superintendents of Grand Canyon National Park explained, was to "protect the Grand Canyon and the millions of people in the Colorado River Basin that depend on the river for drinking water, irrigation and other uses."[37] Further protection from mining came in 2016 when President Obama created Bears Ears National Monument. The president of the Utah Association of Counties complained that the "president misuses his power under the Antiquities Act," arguing that one man should not be able to lock up a million acres or more without the consent of Congress. Yet Obama was responding to an intertribal coalition of the Hopi, Navajo, Ute, and Pueblo Nations, who had complained that "Congress has turned their back on sites sacred to tribal nations, leaving Bears Ears at risk to the continued threats of grave robbing and vandalism, while destructive uranium, oil, and gas and potash mining projects are being proposed."[38] Bears Ears is a classic example of a conflicted landscape.

Together, Grand Staircase-Escalante and Bears Ears National Monuments not only saved a unique area from exploitation but also provided endangered species with an essential land bridge between the Grand Canyon and Zion National Parks. As Williams summarizes: "National parks are ecological islands. They are natural [wildlife] refuges surrounded by a sea of human disturbance. . . . Local extinctions occur because, even at a million acres, the size of the island may still be too small to sustain viable populations."[39] Each park can suffer local species extinctions; connecting them increases survival rates. Presidents Clinton and Obama were not only preserving biological diversity, protecting archeological sites, and preventing mining. These monuments could also help human beings rediscover their place in the natural world. As Williams concluded, Clinton "signed a bill of health for all of us, human and nonhuman like. It swings the doors of our imagination wide open."[40] However, many residents of Utah's San Juan County did not share this view. They rallied in Salt Lake City against Bears Ears National Monument, holding signs that read "No Monument," "Seriously, a Monument Would Suck," and "Don't Keep Us Out." Residents feared exclusion, administrative complexity, and federal interference.

A national monument is seldom a homogeneous territory where a single set of regulations determines land use. On Bears Ears can be found thousands of Native American petroglyphs, artefacts, and ruins, many of which have suffered looting and vandalism (figure 10.3). The petroglyphs carved

Figure 10.3 David E. Nye, "Defaced Petroglyph, Grand Staircase-Escalante," 2017.

in many parts of Utah stretch back eight thousand years, with a decisive shift in style after the adoption of agriculture. In recent decades, these art works have been under attack, often shot to pieces by visitors with guns. The Bureau of Land Management has at times done a worse job of preservation than private land trusts. Bears Ears is a large site that is difficult to protect, with many stakeholders. About fifteen thousand acres are privately owned, and these resident ranchers and farmers need access to their property. The new national monument recognized their preexisting easements and rights of way, allowing them to move livestock and vehicles to and from their land. Similarly, when Grand Staircase-Escalante became a national monument, it contained 68 mining claims on 2,700 acres, 85 oil and gas leases encompassing 136,000 acres, and 18 coal leases on 52,800 acres. These leases remained valid if owners could prove that they had discovered a valuable deposit before September 18, 1996.[41] In addition, the Bureau of Land Management recognized permits for grazing and for guides and outfitters operating inside the monument. The Utah Schools and Lands Exchange Act of 1998 conveyed 24,000 acres to Grand Staircase-Escalante, but it also acknowledged existing water rights, grazing permits, and mining leases.[42] In short, while hiking through Grand Staircase-Escalante one might cross from public to private land, from wilderness to mining claims, from grazing areas to oil fields, often without obvious demarcation lines. In practice, a national monument may be a patchwork of farming, mining, drilling, grazing, ruins, and wilderness.

Given these complexities, some local residents saw new monuments as roadblocks to prosperity. Republicans not only sided with them, but began to push back against setting aside lands in perpetuity. In 2017, Secretary of the Interior Ryan Zinke recommended reducing or eliminating twenty-seven national monuments. Immediately, President Trump rescinded 80 percent of Bears Ears and 45 percent of Grand Staircase-Escalante, which reopened one million acres to oil, gas, coal, and uranium extraction. In response, 5,000 protestors came to the Utah State Capitol. Some of their signs read: "A Monumental Mistake," "What Would Teddy Do?," and "Sacred Places, Just Like a Temple." Meanwhile, the EPA was still spending hundreds of millions of dollars removing radioactive waste from abandoned mines.[43]

On first encounter, both Grand Staircase Escalante and Bears Ears appear to be harsh deserts full of unusual rock formations, visually interesting but hostile environments. However, 1500 years ago, this region had more rainfall and supported thousands of people. They built granaries and homes in the shallow caves of its cliffs, and they carved its walls extensively with petroglyphs. Native Americans see it as an ancient homeland where their ancestors lived, and they revere many locations. For the Hopi, Bears Ears is "the natural setting of their ancestors" where they are able "to walk among the centuries-old homes where generations lived" and "to sit upon the towering buttes and recognize landscapes that are recalled from prayer." Archeologists, environmentalists, and Native Americans want these national monuments. But mining companies and the Trump administration regarded the area as untapped resources awaiting exploitation. In 2018, the BLM leased mining rights for 43 sites near Bears Ears for $1.5 million. An area of 51,000 acres was turned over to mining, fracking, and drilling that was certain to cause small earthquakes and landslides. Their heavy trucks require new roads that scar the land. Mining pollutes the air and ground water and leaves behind empty pits and mounds of waste. A cleanup, if attempted, will cost more than the $1.5 million received for the leases. This sale was only a warm-up for more extensive auctions, like that planned for September 2020, to lease sites close to Bears Ears and three national parks, Canyonlands, Arches, and Capitol Reef, as well as several sites being considered for wilderness designation.[44]

The conflicting plans for Grand Staircase Escalante and Bears Ears underline the tensions at work. One side calls for conservation of resources, preservation of wilderness, protection of archeological sites, and conversion to wind and solar energy. The other side calls for development of resources, mining on public lands, minimal protection of archeological sites, and continued reliance on fossil fuels. It reiterates the utilitarian conception of nature as raw material, and disparages the Antiquities Act that permits national monument designation.[45] As with earlier uranium mining on the Navajo reservation or lead mining on Cherokee lands in Picher, Oklahoma, the focus is on immediate profits not sustainability. In such debates, Americans can no longer plausibly shift among their three traditional conceptions of nature, the wild, the pastoral, and the utilitarian. There is no shared vision. A country that for centuries identified itself with nature is divided against itself. The partially filled Glen Canyon reservoir, covering tons of radioactive waste, suggests where such intransigence can lead.

Americans remain caught in debates much like those that Jefferson knew between uniformitarianism and catastrophe theory. Opposing evolutionary science, millions of Americans on the religious right embrace "flood geology." They believe the world is only a few thousand years old, and they see the Grand Canyon, natural bridges, and other spectacular sites as sublime proof of the existence of God. The creationist thinks divine intelligence guides human history, which includes sudden changes and even miracles in a story that leads inevitably to the Last Judgment. In contrast, most scientists and environmentalists understand history as lasting billions of years. The wonders of nature are far older than humanity, shaped by (and proof of) the uniformitarian effects of erosion, gravity, and natural laws. Human beings only emerged from Africa near the end of this story to became a global force during the Anthropocene. There is nothing inevitable in this scientific story. Human beings can destroy each other or not; they can improve or degrade their environment; they can limit their numbers or increase until the earth cannot support them. In the scientific view, no divine intelligence shapes history, and human intelligence only struggles to do so.

These quite different ideas find expression when people visit an impressive site like the Grand Canyon. To the Native Americans who live there, this landscape is imbued with their origin and identity. Creationists view the same site as a product of the biblical flood. Mining corporations have regarded the canyon as a potential source of wealth, and hydroelectric engineers have sought to build dams on the Colorado River. A tourist interprets the canyon in terms of the natural sublime, which requires little knowledge of the place and treats landscape as an abstraction. The tourist seldom knows its history or ecology and appears superficial to those intimately acquainted with the place. In contrast, a biologist who gazes at distant tamarisk thickets growing along the Colorado River knows that it is an invasive species, that the river before being dammed was reddish brown, not blue, and that the park management has eradicated wolves and other predators. The powerful emotions felt at Grand Canyon are framed so variously that they no longer unify Americans.

Nor can the technological sublime play a unifying role. Americans once shifted back and forth, with little sense of contradiction, between the technological and the natural sublimes. After the atomic bomb, the Anthropocene, and global warming, however, such easy alternation has been replaced by polarized intransigence. The nation's history and politics cannot plausibly be based on second creation stories, nor can they be based on the mythology of virgin land and wilderness. Many are caught between visions of progress through resource exploitation and visions of redemption through immersion in wild nature. Both are hallucinations. Instead, Americans need to recognize the complexity of living within nature. The feeling of the sublime will not disappear, but it requires better interpretive frameworks. New structures of feeling and new narratives are urgently needed because the six American ideologies of nature have led to political conflict, policy gridlock, and landscape destruction.

Inconsistent concepts of nature have greater consequences in 2020 than they did two generations ago. Few were concerned with climate change in 1964, when the eminent cultural geographer J. B. Jackson observed that "the human landscape is changing by a series of violent and unpredictable mutations, and no one is foolhardy enough to foresee what it will look like a generation hence."[46] The uncertainty is greater in 2020, given the pace of technological innovation, population growth, pollution, species extinction, climate change, the melting of the polar ice caps and, exacerbating all of these problems, the fixation on economic growth as the measure of progress. The conflict between American conceptions of nature has intensified since 1964, even as the landscape itself has changed in disturbing and unpredictable ways. It is not morning in America, it is the Anthropocene.

11

PRAGMATIC SOLUTIONS

The six conflicting American interpretations of nature differ so much that there is little common ground, and it is tempting to tell a story that begins with unspoiled nature and ends with anti-landscapes. Such a dystopian narrative would be about humanity's exploitation and destruction of the natural world, and it would attack the philosophies or practices that seemed most culpable, notably utilitarianism, creationism, imperialism, capitalism, liberalism, consumerism, or all of the above. That is not the narrative of this book, however. It argues that culture is a part of nature; that pollution, species extinction, and other forms of the destruction are neither inevitable mistakes nor inherent to industrialization, but rather stem from failures of imagination; and that these failures are expressed in conflicted landscapes. This story is not a jeremiad that calls for a return to the values of the past. Rather, it emphasizes that existing alternatives make possible a better future.

Americans have incompatible ideas about nature that cannot be reconciled in the short term, but there are pragmatic solutions for particular problems. Democracy has always demanded discussion and political compromise. But discussions of lands and environment can no longer rely on the troika of wilderness, pastoralism, and utilitarianism. They also must include creationists, Native Americans, and the military, and they must recognize the historical moment, which includes rising global temperatures, species extinctions, and pollution. Inability to agree philosophically need not prevent cross-fertilization of ideas and creation of solutions. This exchange can lead to more nuanced mutual understanding. The environmentalist David Suzuki appreciated that he had gained from aboriginal people "an insight into a profoundly different way of seeing the world. Aboriginal people do not believe that they end at their skin or their fingertips. The earth as mother is real to them, and their history, culture, and purpose are embodied in the land."[1] And yet, Suzuki also knew that Native

Americans did not provide a model that the rest of society could simply copy. Similarly, Terry Tempest Williams realized that she could not "emulate . . . the Navajo. . . . Their traditional stories won't work for us. It's like drinking another man's medicine. Their stories hold meaning for us only as examples. They can teach us what is possible. We must create and find our own stories, our own myths, with symbols that will bind us to the world."[2]

The old story of America as second creation in a virgin land is already being rewritten. New stories and symbols can help to shape the foundations of possible compromise. Some prominent recent novels locate human beings within nature rather than outside it. Leslie Marmon Silko's *Gardens in the Dunes*, set in the late nineteenth-century Southwest, depicts how Native Americans live within a familiar nature, unlike Europeans who classify and systematize it. In the novel, a White scientist and his wife teach a Native girl and learn from her in return. Annie Proulx's *Barkskins* traces deforestation from the French settlement of Canada to the present, following characters in two extended families. It begins in trackless forests so vast it seems they could never all be cut down and ends with recovery projects that try to understand the interwoven species ecology needed to recreate a healthy forest. Louise Erdrich's *Tracks* dramatizes the destruction of the forest that underpins a tribe's culture in the upper Middle West. Richard Powers's *The Overstory* describes nine individuals who, in quite different ways, become sensitive to how trees cooperate and communicate with each other. The characters redouble their efforts to save remaining patches of old-growth forests, but logging continues as their protests are defeated, silenced, or marginalized.[3] These and many other recent novels contest the second creation stories and wilderness fantasies that have dominated American self-understanding. They reject the idea that it is "Morning in America," and show the value of intimacy with particular landscapes. Like earlier narratives that explained the geology of the Grand Canyon, these are informed by current scientific work. Powers has read widely in science, and *The Overstory* is partly based on such works as Peter Wohlleben's *The Hidden Life of Trees*, which makes the case that a forest is a social network.[4] Powers and other contemporary novelists reconceive American history as an environmental story that while fraught with destruction is not an inevitable declension.

There is also an emerging Christian environmentalism among those Protestants and Catholics who realize that culture and nature cannot be separated into a dualism. Umbrella organizations such as the North American Coalition for Christianity and Ecology, Interfaith Power and Light, and the Evangelical Environment Network emphasize mankind's role as the stewards of God's creation. Target Earth, based in Tempe Arizona, declares that it is "motivated by the Biblical call to be faithful stewards of everything God created." The Partnership for Earth Spirituality in Albuquerque promotes "a better understanding of the interdependence of ecology and spirituality . . . through retreats, forums, seasonal rituals, wilderness experiences, programs for children, hands-on projects and education for sound environmental policies."[5] Nevertheless, only a minority of Christians are engaged environmentalists. A statistical study found "very little evidence to support the idea that rank-and-file Christians are as green as non-Christians or nonreligious individuals."[6] However, this generalization does not extend to intensely religious believers, who often take environmental problems quite seriously, including their leadership.[7] The Green Seminary Initiative advocates that Christians, led by the ministry, have a "calling to turn back human-caused environmental destruction and to participate in bringing all of creation into health and wholeness."[8]

A pragmatic alliance of such religious groups, environmentalists, and Native Americans could help resolve the crisis of conflicted landscapes by reconceiving pastoralism as something different from a compromise between wilderness and utilitarian second creation. A new pastoralism could build upon Jackson's definition of landscape as the infrastructure that human beings live within. Like Wendell Berry, Americans could replace second creation narratives with stories about long-term stewardship of land. Berry found much to praise in traditional Papago and Hopi agriculture which has survived for centuries in contrast to some irrigated fields near Phoenix and Tucson that quickly became infertile due to salination. Far better to learn from the permaculture of acequia farmers in Northern New Mexico, who combine native practices with the classical advice of Alonso de Herrera.[9] The point is not to live like the Hopi but to learn from them in order to rethink land use for the long term. Many improvements are ready for adoption. Human beings have been clever enough to find alternatives to fossil fuels, to produce electric cars, to build zero energy houses, and to design products not only for use but also for efficient recycling.

A new pastoralism might learn from how other nations deal with landscape preservation. Canada once experimented with a laissez-faire approach that allowed landscapes to evolve and even die. Vegetation colonized and stabilized a famous area of shifting sand; a lake gradually shrank and disappeared; and biodiversity declined as a consequence. This hands-off policy assumed that nature would be self-regulating. However, Canadians have now recognized that in the Anthropocene human beings have always already intervened.[10] The Canadians therefore adopted a policy similar to that of the British. As Norman Henderson has pointed out, "British conservation thought is characterized by an enthusiasm for environmental intervention and manipulation. The British concept of the conservation ideal is a steady state of human intervention designed to maintain a given habitat at a particular successional stage in perpetuity."[11] Freezing a landscape at a particular stage can be problematic, as it halts natural processes. However, Britain's Nature Conservancy Council decided intervention was justifiable in order "to ensure that the national heritage of wild flora and fauna and geological and physiographic features remains as large and diverse as possible."[12] The British preserve diversity, which for them takes precedence over purity or natural succession. In practice, the American NPS has also intervened in its landscapes, though not always with the same goals. At the Grand Canyon, for example, it checked the spread of tamarisk trees and protected endangered species of fish, but it also eradicated large predators and introduced the buffalo where it had not been before. It fought off proposals to build dams inside the park but it could not prevent uranium mining. Pastoralism need not be defined as a compromise between wilderness and unbridled development. It can also be understood as principled intervention based on scientific knowledge in order to enhance biodiversity and landscape variety. The landscape can be understood as the infrastructure that human beings live within, and not as either a wild reserve or raw material to be exploited.

Wild enclaves can seldom be self-regulating, as the Dutch discovered when they tried to recreate a wilderness. In 1933, they completed a dike that cut off the Zuiderzee from the ocean.[13] For decades, they drained it and created more than sixteen hundred square kilometers of new land. Eventually, they decided to retain part of the sea as a sizeable lake and to allow some new land to revert to wilderness, which they called the Oostvaardersplassen. They introduced some plants and animals but left much of the transformation to natural processes. Many birds and small animals found their way to the site as it rewilded. The wetlands areas of Oostvaardersplassen sheltered a wide range of bird species, including endangered predators. However, there were no predators on the deer, horses, and wild cattle, which procreated beyond the land's carrying capacity. Oostvaardersplassen soon had a problem similar to that the Grand Canyon had with buffalo on the North Rim, as the herds of wild deer, cattle, and horses burgeoned to 5,000 animals. Thousands of them died during the winter of 2017–2018, and their suffering outraged the public, many of whom risked fines to throw hay over the fences to feed them.[14] Authorities then intervened in the rewilding process and culled the herd. Wilderness is an attractive idea, but in small territories it requires occasional interventions, and the land becomes less a wilderness than a new kind of pastoral landscape.

In the United States, during the 1980s some environmentalists formed the Great Plains Restoration Council. Its goal was "to re-establish and re-connect prairie wildland reserves and ecological corridors large enough for bison and all other native prairie wildlife to survive and roam freely, over great, connected distances, while simultaneously restoring the health and sustainability of our communities wherever possible so that both land and people may prosper for a very long time."[15] This rewilded land would be not wilderness but a "buffalo commons." Existing communities would remain and benefit from the thick cover of grass protecting the soil in the surrounding commons. In short, to intervene in the landscape does not necessarily mean to control areas in the British fashion; it also can include some form of rewilding, albeit with monitoring and intervention. Other forms of intervention rehabilitate Superfund sites or develop new forms of industrial recycling.[16] Planners have also designed conservation programs for cities, not only because their dense populations make smaller per-capita resource demands than sprawling suburban and rural communities of single-family homes, but also because cities become more self-sufficient when planned and built as ecologies.[17]

Wilderness and second creation are outmoded ideas, but the sublimity and complexity of nature remain. Americans might resolve some of their differences by developing a new pastoralism based on the realization that they are inescapably part of nature. They might minimize their environmental impact and revise their understanding of development to include new kinds of hybrid space, such as ranches on national monuments or rewilding interspersed with agriculture or farming in the city.[18] They might regard landscape not as something to consume but as living heritage. Admission prices to national parks might be reduced for ecologically minded tourists who engage in active stewardship of places they visit. Americans might respect Native Americans and better protect their sacred sites. They might respect ranchers and recognize that absolutist visions of wilderness do not jibe with their reality. Companies engaged in mining might be held to a higher standard that prohibits piles of radioactive waste, tons of asbestos dust, abandoned craters, and groundwater laced with cyanide. Mining pollution can be more tightly regulated, demand for metals can be reduced through recycling, and coal consumption can be curtailed by adopting alternative energies. Likewise, rather than truck tons of hazardous substances thousands of miles across the nation, Americans need a comprehensive hazardous waste program, to replace "temporary storage" of toxic chemicals and radioactive materials.

Many practices can become part of a new pastoralism, and a few examples suggest what is possible. Families might use less water, notably in Phoenix where in 2018 the price of water was artificially low, due to federal support, and cost half as much as in Chicago.[19] In agriculture, drip line irrigation (rather than spraying) gives farmers control of salinity, reduces labor, and cuts water use by half to grow alfalfa, vegetables, and other crops. Farmers can also plant pollinator habitat around their fields to increase the population of bees, butterflies, beetles, and ants.[20] Likewise, planting hedgerows reduces wind and water erosion and provides shelter and sustenance for birds, insects, and small animals, enhancing biodiversity. Consumers can eat more nuts, fruits, and vegetables and less meat, shifting to fish and fowl, which are less environmentally costly to produce. Urban farming, common before the industrial revolution, is coming back, shortening the supply chain for some produce. In 2015, nine million American households grew some of their own food, and some urban farmers in Phoenix produced half of what they ate.[21] Whether one believes in creationism or evolution, it is desirable for cities to use zoning and tax incentives to encourage hedgerows, urban farming, community gardens, recycling, green roofs, bicycling, mass transit, and electric cars.

Demand for energy has been a major reason for building a series of dams on the Colorado River and for uranium mining, and energy is another area of vast potential improvement. After California changed its policies during the 1970s, per-capita electricity use leveled off for three decades while it doubled for the United States as a whole.[22] By 2002, the average

Californian annually used just over six thousand kilowatt hours of electricity, compared to more than fourteen thousand used by Texans and almost thirteen thousand by Floridians. Those with extravagant energy use remain trapped in the second creation narrative. They still see the land as raw material that exists primarily for them to mine, drill, farm, bulldoze, and build on, as though they lived on virgin land at the beginning of history. By 2015, however, the falling cost of alternative energies made them cheaper than coal or nuclear energy, and Americans were profitably shifting to solar and wind-generated electricity, which causes less environmental damage. *Scientific American* reported that two-thirds of U.S. electricity might be supplied from solar installations in just Arizona and New Mexico.[23] Indeed, in 2017 management decided to close the enormous coal-burning Navajo Generating Station twenty-five years earlier than planned, because the alternatives were cheaper.[24] The Navajo shut down the coal-burning Mohave Power Plant in 2006. To replace it, they developed large-scale solar projects, and in 2018 the tribe opened the Kayenta solar array that supplies electricity to 13,000 homes (figure 11.1). With a twenty-eight megawatt expansion underway and even larger

Figure 11.1 "Kayenta Solar Power Array, Navajo Reservation, the first of several utility-scale alternative energy developments," 2018. *Source:* Salt River Project.

developments planned, they are transitioning from fossil fuels to alternative energy.[25] This is part of a larger trend. The Salt River Project, the largest utility in the Phoenix area, has committed to develop 1,000 megawatts of solar power.

U.S. coal powerplant capacity fell by one third between 2010 and 2018, and decommissioned plants were being replaced with alternative energies.[26] The Pew Charitable Trust found in 2016 that more than 83 percent of Americans supported building more solar panel arrays and wind turbine farms, twice as many as wanted more offshore oil drilling, coal mines, or new nuclear power stations.[27] A majority of Americans agree that wind and solar power are pragmatic solutions, and they want to speed the transition to alternative energy. The technologies already exist to reduce carbon emissions, increase energy efficiency, shorten supply chains for many foods, and reduce pollution. Even as the Trump administration attempted to prop up the coal industry, many states set deadlines for elimination of fossil fuels. They will not only reduce oil, gas, and coal extraction but also create new jobs in alternative energy, ensure cleaner air, enhance visibility, reduce respiratory illnesses, increase life expectancy, and improve the quality of produce from farms and gardens once downwind of coal-fired plants.

A new pastoralism can also be based on improvements of the built environment. Efficient houses already exist that are 100 percent energy self-sufficient, and new designs are displayed at the Department of Energy's biannual Solar Decathlons (see figure 11.2). Their cost, including heating bills during the life of a mortgage, is competitive with the poorly insulated houses of the past. Most Americans, whatever their conceptions of nature might be, would prefer more self-sufficiency, lower energy bills, and cleaner air. The *Wall Street Journal* reported in 2013 that green housing is increasing rapidly. By early 2014 Phoenix was generating thirty-two megawatts of power from solar panels on public buildings and fifteen megawatts more from installations on parking lots and other structures. It also had legislated that all new buildings ought to be zero-net energy consumers, an admirable goal but one that doesn't become mandatory for the private sector until 2050.[28] Tucson was more ambitious in 2008, when it required that all new buildings include an acceptable method for later installation of both solar hot water and photovoltaic cells.[29] In 2018, a net-zero energy apartment building in Salt Lake City cost no more than

Pragmatic Solutions 199

Figure 11.2 Dennis Schroeder, "Winning entry. House designed in Switzerland for the Solar Decathlon," Denver, 2017. *Source:* U.S. Department of Energy.

a conventional, polluting building.[30] New skyscrapers use less energy than modernist glass boxes, and may include rooftop wind turbines, water recycling, gardens, superb insulation, and green roofs. Norman Foster's Hearst Tower at Columbus Circle was the first of New York's green skyscrapers. Were New York City a state, it would have the nation's lowest per-capita energy use. It produces only one third as much CO_2 per capita as the average American city.[31] On a larger scale, the state of California's 2008 Energy Efficiency Strategic Plan set a goal of zero net energy for all new buildings by 2020.

Advances in recycling are also being realized, but unevenly. U.S. cities on average recycle one third of their waste, but the average hides enormous differences. In 2007, Salt Lake City area managed only an abysmal 2.7 percent, while San Francisco was increasing its total and a decade later reached 80 percent and aspired to do even better.[32] Likewise, some factories are adopting greener manufacturing practices. General Motors saves $1 billion annually by recycling steel, scraps, paint, cardboard, and much more, achieving a 90 percent rate of reuse.[33] Other factories have a green roof, like the Ford River Rouge plant where migrating birds now nest. The drainage systems in its parking lots channel water through nearby wetlands. Lake Mead could also become a hybrid space, partially covered by floating solar panels. Placing solar panels on reservoirs reduces evaporation, inhibits algae growth, and cools the panels. A Japanese utility has deployed 50,000 floating panels on a reservoir that supplies 5,000 homes.[34] Through dialogue, innovation, and learning from such successes, Americans could radically reduce energy consumption and move from landscape exploitation to self-sustaining hybrid spaces.[35]

Developments might be evaluated by how they affect the landscape as a whole rather than being judged in terms of short-term profits. Stockbrokers seldom think much beyond the year-end bonus, corporations beyond the next product cycle, or politicians beyond the next election. The environment is not a short-term matter, however. The Iroquois look seven generations ahead.[36] The United Nations also have taken the long view and set seventeen goals for sustainable development.[37] Adopting new goals is difficult but not impossible in the polarized United States. What is not politically attainable in Washington is being accomplished by some corporations (such as Cisco and Celgene)[38] and some cities (such as Seattle and Boston).[39] Fourteen states have formed a U.S. Climate Alliance dedicated to meeting the climate goals set in Paris. This alliance was founded by California, New York, and Washington State, and then added Colorado, Connecticut, Delaware, Hawaii, Massachusetts, Minnesota, Oregon, Rhode Island, Vermont, Virginia, and North Carolina. They produce 40 percent of the U.S. domestic product, and their environmental policies have not weakened their economies, which are growing faster than the rest of the nation.[40]

For too long, Americans celebrated the technological sublime without recognizing that it was part of a self-defeating conquest of nature. At the same time, they celebrated wilderness in terms of the natural sublime, which denied the presence of Native Americans and assumed a complete split between nature and culture. Instead, Americans need to embrace an ecological sublime and learn a new way of being in the world that is based on a perception of the almost infinitely complex relations between living organisms. Already, many have learned to see that nature is not a realm that is separate from culture and to see that human beings are a companion species immersed in the nonhuman. By adopting that perspective, Americans can learn, as Finis Dunaway put it, "to find awe and wonder in natural processes, to respect the integrity and otherness of nature without denying the connections between human society and the natural world."[41] The emergence of a new pastoralism and an ecological sublime can replace the six incompatible ideas of nature that do battle in American culture. This jumble of concepts has abetted pollution, waste, injustice, racism, misuse of resources, species extinction, and unsustainable development. This era of discord need not continue, for the United States has the new energy technologies, the necessary recycling systems, the green architecture, the new narratives, and the perspectives needed to evolve beyond conflicted landscapes.

NOTES

1 THE PROBLEM

1. Jackson, *Discovering the Vernacular Landscape*, 8. See also Campbell, "Critical Regionalism," 59–62.

2. See Meinig, *Southwest*; Kluckhohn and Strodtbeck, *Variations in Value Orientations*.

3. Works on American conceptions of nature include Marx, *Machine in the Garden*; Nash, *Wilderness and the American Mind*; Novak, *Nature and Culture*; Sears, *Sacred Places*; Cronon, ed., *Uncommon Ground*; Steinberg, *Down to Earth*.

4. From c. 1880 to 1970, planners described the city in organic terms, with a life cycle of growth, maturity, climax, and decline. Like gardens, cities had to be weeded (demolition) and replanted (urban renewal). Light, *The Nature of Cities*, 69–70, 162–167.

5. Huth, *Nature and the American*, 165–212.

6. Runte, *National Parks*.

7. Marx, "American Ideology of Space," 62–72.

8. Cary Funk, "Republicans' Views on Evolution," *Factank: News in the Numbers*, Pew Research Center, January 3, 2014, https://www.pewresearch.org/fact-tank/2014/01/03/republican-views-on-evolution-tracking-how-its-changed/.

9. Numbers, *The Creationists*, 77, 96.

10. Montgomery, "Evolution of Creationism," 8.

11. M. Ruse, *Stanford Encyclopedia of Philosophy*, https://plato.stanford.edu/entries/creationism/.

12. Frank Newport, "Republicans, Democrats Differ on Creationism," *Gallup*, June 20, 2008, https://news.gallup.com/poll/108226/republicans-democrats-differ-creationism.aspx.

13. Numbers, *The Creationists*, 323.

14. Calloway, *One Vast Winter Count*, 267–269.

15. Deloria, *Playing Indian*, 1–9, 154–180, and passim. On the difficulties of photographing Native Americans, see Gidley, *Edward S. Curtis*.

16. No book can cover everything. To do justice to Chicano/a culture, one would need to discuss Spanish colonial landscapes, Mexican land development before 1848, the U.S. imposition of the national grid, the romanticization of the region, and the scholarship that recovered Chicano/a identity and redefined the frontier as a zone of creolization and cultural exchange. See Chavez, *Lost Land*; Peña, *Mexican Americans and the Environment*; Blea, *Researching Chicano Communities*. Ideally, one might also analyze the Mormons and each Native American tribe.

17. Hughes and Swan, "How Much of the Earth Is Sacred Space?," 247.

18. Cited in Suzuki, *Sacred Balance*, 189.

19. Neihardt, ed., *Black Elk Speaks*; Erdrich, *Books and Islands in Ojibwe Country*, 40, 45, 48, 50, and passim.

20. Quoted in LaDuke, *All Our Relations*, 2.

21. Cited in Calloway, *One Vast Winter Count*, 7.

22. Lane, *Landscapes of the Sacred*, 76.

23. Erdrich, "The Theft Outright," 115–116.

24. LaDuke, *All Our Relations*, 1.

25. Ed Keheley and Associates, Inc., "History of the Picher Mining Field."

26. Findlay and Hevly, *Atomic Frontier Days*, 14–73.

27. Sanders, *Paradise of Bombs*, 12.

2 THE ONCE-DOMINANT AMERICAN DISCOURSE ON NATURE

1. Rothman, "Tourism as Colonial Economy"; Rothman, *Devil's Bargains*.

2. Botton, *The Art of Travel*, 15; Muir, *Steep Trails*, 249.

3. Nye, *American Technological Sublime*, chap. 1.

4. Hough, *The Way to the West*.

5. Sears, *Sacred Places*, 12–30, 56–64.

6. Cole, "Essay on American Scenery," 8.

7. Nixon, "Message to the Congress Proposing Establishment of New National Wilderness Areas," June 13, 1974.

8. Chase, *Playing God in Yellowstone*, 101–102.

9. Cited in Chase, 102.

10. Kelly and Prasciunas, "Did the Ancestors of Native Americans Cause Animal Extinctions," 95–121. Calloway summarizes this debate in *One Vast Winter Count*, 33–35.

11. S. W. Miller, *An Environmental History of Latin America*, 17–18.

12. Spence, *Dispossessing the Wilderness*, 43.

13. Chase, *Playing God in Yellowstone*, 106–107.

14. Hughes and Swan, "How Much of the Earth Is Sacred Space?," 253.

15. Thoreau, "Walking."

16. Cronon, "The Trouble with Wilderness," 69.

17. Slotkin, *Regeneration through Violence*.

18. Cronon, "The Trouble with Wilderness," 79.

19. U.S. General Accounting Office (GAO), *Wilderness Preservation*, 4, 60.

20. GAO, 4, 61, and passim.

21. GAO, 69–70.

22. Locke cited in Marx, "American Ideology of Space," 65.

23. Cosgrove, "The Measures of America," 8–9.

24. Marx, "American Ideology of Space," 64.

25. Cited in Graham, *With Poor Immigrants to America*, 139.

26. Nye, *America as Second Creation*, 1–70, 109–116, 153–157, 206–211, 284–292.

27. Newell, *Irrigation in the United States*, 393–394.

28. Smyth, *The Conquest of Arid America*, 329.

29. Marx, "American Ideology of Space," 76.

30. U.S. Census 2015, State Population, table 1; U.S. Census 1900, State Population.

31. Tocqueville, *Democracy in America*, 144–145.

32. Mona Chalabi, "How Many Times Does the Average Person Move?," January 29, 2015, https://fivethirtyeight.com/features/how-many-times-the-average-person-moves/.

33. "Europeans Only Move Four Times in Their Lives," REMAX, accessed June 10, 2020, http://www.at-home-in-europe.eu/home-life/europe/europeans-only-move-four-times-in-their-lives; Lane, *Landscapes of the Sacred*, 219.

34. Bryce, *The American Commonwealth*, vol. 2, 880–881.

35. Nye, *American Technological Sublime*.

36. See Nye, *America as Second Creation*, 21–39.

37. Powell, *Report on the Lands of the Arid Region of the United States*.

38. Dawson, "Reassessing Henry Carey," 465–485.

39. Nye, *America as Second Creation*, 40–43, 59–67, 109–115, 200–203, 270–277.

40. Novak, *Nature and Culture*, 33–44, 149–151.

41. Downing, *The Architecture of Country Houses*.

42. Sears, *Sacred Places*, 99–111.

43. Thomas Cole, *View from Mount Holyoke, Northampton, Massachusetts, after a Thunderstorm—The Oxbow*, 1836, Metropolitan Museum of Art, New York.

44. Sayre, "Oxymoron of American Pastoralism," 10.

45. Cole, "Essay on American Scenery," 12.

46. Rybczynski, *A Clearing in the Distance*, 236.

47. Rybczynski, 236–237, 257.

48. Hyde, *An American Vision*, 256–274.

49. Wilderness Act of 1964, Public Law 88–577 (16 U.S.C. 1131–1136), 88th Congress, 2nd Session, September 3, 1964.

50. Reagan, "Remarks on Signing Four Bills Designating Wilderness Areas," June 19, 1984, http://www.reagan.utexas.edu/resource/speeches/1984/61984d.htm.

51. Nash, *Wilderness and the American Mind*, 23–28.

52. Buell, *The Environmental Imagination*, 31–32.

53. Buell, 63–65.

54. Harvey, *A Symbol of Wilderness*, xiv.

55. Nye, *America as Second Creation*, 117–146, 175–203.

56. Runte, *National Parks*, 17–22.

57. Nabokov, *Where the Lightning Strikes*, 140–141.

58. Nabokov, 142. See also Kelley and Francis, *Navajo Sacred Places*, 170.

59. Benally, "San Francisco Peaks," 88.

60. Meinig, "The Southwest, a Definition," 3–6.

61. Jackson, *Discovering the Vernacular Landscape*, 8. See also Campbell, "Critical Regionalism," 59–62.

62. Alonso de Herrera, *Agricultura General*; Price, *Orphaned Land*, 288–289.

63. Kirk, *Doom Towns*, xi–xviii.

3 DETROIT'S RIVER ROUGE

1. Tocqueville, "A Fortnight in the Wilds," 329.

2. Massey, *For Space*, 9.

3. Nye, *America as Second Creation*, 9–14.

4. Nye, 105–109.

5. Birmingham and Eisenberg, *Indian Mounds of Wisconsin*, 3.

6. Scherzer, "Geological Report on Wayne County," 8.

7. Nabokov, *Where the Lightning Strikes*, 39.

8. Eliade, *The Sacred and the Profane*.

9. R. Nye, *Michigan*, 118.

10. R. Nye, 66.

11. Teasdale, "Old Friends and New Foes," 36–37.

12. Meinig, *Continental America*, 70.

13. Meinig, 72.

14. Teasdale, "Old Friends and New Foes," 41, 53.

15. Michigan Writers Project, *Michigan, A Guide to the Wolverine State*, 213.

16. Ford, "The Old Moravian Mission," 110.

17. Nye, *America as Second Creation*, 21–42.

18. Teasdale, "Old Friends and New Foes," 37.

19. Pierson, *Tocqueville in America*, 238–239.

20. Teasdale, "Old Friends and New Foes," 54.

21. Munger, *Detroit Today*, 25.

22. Stilgoe, *Common Landscape of America*, 132–133.

23. Hubbard, *Memorials of Half a Century*, 228.

24. Hubbard, 234.

25. Conot, *American Odyssey*, 94–95.

26. Catlin, *The Story of Detroit*, 650.

27. Watts, *The People's Tycoon*, 280–281.

28. Ford Motor Company, "From the Rouge to the Road," 1935, 8.

29. Nye, *Henry Ford: Ignorant Idealist*, 20, 82–83, 106–107.

30. Shannon Wianecki, "When America's Titans of Industry and Innovation Went Road-Tripping Together," January 26, 2016, https://www.smithsonianmag.com/history/when-americas-titans-industry-and-innovation-went-road-tripping-together-180957924/.

31. "John Burroughs Statue, 'Summit of the Years,' in 'Burroughs' Grotto' at Fair Lane, circa 1933," https://www.thehenryford.org/collections-and-research/digital-collections/artifact/282391.

32. Nye, *America's Assembly Line*, 13–38.

33. McCraw, *Prophet of Innovation*, 6–7, 256–257, 351–352.

34. US Army Corps of Engineers, "Rouge River, MI," accessed June 12, 2020, http://www.lre.usace.army.mil/Missions/Operations/Rouge-River-MI/.

35. Reisner, *Cadillac Desert*, 118–124; Maass, *Muddy Waters*, 20–54.

36. Hughes, *Networks of Power*, 329–331.

37. Hughes, 353–363.

38. Bryan, *Rouge: Pictured in Its Prime*, 25.

39. McCarthy, "Henry Ford, Industrial Ecologist or Industrial Conservationist?," 57.

40. Hawkins, *Legacy of Albert Kahn*, 23.

41. Misa, *Leonardo to the Internet*, 167.

42. Verner, personal notebook, n.p.

43. Harvey, *Condition of Postmodernity*, 232.

44. L. Miller, *Reminiscences*.

45. Nye, *America's Assembly Line*, 249–250.

46. Nevins, *Expansion*, 209–212.

47. Littmann, "Production of Goodwill," 77.

48. D. Lewis, *Public Image of Henry Ford*, 161.

49. Casey, *The Model T*, 33.

50. Lucic, *Charles Sheeler and the Cult of the Machine*, 92.

51. Corwin, "Picturing Efficiency," 156.

52. Sears, *Sacred Places*, 116–121.

53. Burton, *History of Wayne County and the City of Detroit*, 1153.

54. Michigan Writers Project, *Michigan, A Guide to the Wolverine State*, 282.

55. Upward, *A Home for Our Heritage*, 26–37.

56. Clinton, "Remarks at the Labor Unification Legislative Conference," 1.

57. "Great Ford Plant Is Cross-Section of Industrial Might of Rearming America," *Life*, August 19, 1940, 37–48. On page 75 (at the back of this issue), Herbert Gehr is credited with the photographs, which dominate the story, which is a photo essay.

58. "Battle of Detroit," *Time*, March 23, 1942, 10–21.

59. Howell, "Powering 'Progress,'" 964.

60. Daniel Goure, *The Southwest Defense Complex*, April 2016, http://www.lexingtoninstitute.org/wp-content/uploads/2016/05/Southwest-Defense-Complex.pdf.

Notes 209

61. Michigan Writers Project, *Michigan, A Guide to the Wolverine State*, 221.

62. Rotunda & Plant Visitors Attendance Statistics, 1924–1964, accession 1222, Achives, The Henry Ford.

63. Clemens, *Punching Out*, 141.

64. Nye, *America as Second Creation*, 294.

65. U.S. General Accounting Office, *Water Pollution*, 1.

66. *River Rouge Remedial Action Plan, Annual Report*, 3.

67. *River Rouge Remedial Action Plan*, 31–32.

68. *River Rouge Remedial Action Plan*, 9–11.

69. Kinkead, "Detroit's Emerging Innovation in Urban Infrastructure," 201.

70. Naughton, "Growing a Green Plant," 58–60.

71. Muller and Tarr, "The Interaction of Natural and Built Environments in the Pittsburgh Landscape," 35–40.

72. William McDonough and Michael Braungart, "Restoring the Industrial Landscape," accessed July 10, 2020, https://www.greenatworkmag.com/gwsubaccess/02sepoct/eco.html.

73. McDonough and Braungart, *Cradle to Cradle*, 164–165.

74. McDonough and Braungart, 162.

75. Michael, "Labor on Display," 151.

76. Nye, *America's Assembly Line*, 218–222.

77. Nye, 215.

78. Snelling, "The Recent Origin," 44.

79. Petr, "Creationism versus Evolutionism in Economics," 479–480.

80. Crutzen and Stoermer, "The 'Anthropocene,'" 18.

4 NATURAL BRIDGES

1. Janssen, "Nature's Bridges," 210–219.

2. Nash, *Wilderness and the American Mind*, 17.

3. Grimm, "Sacred Lands and the Establishment Clause," 10.

4. Bonham, "Devils Tower, Rainbow Bridge, and the Uphill Battle," 157–202.

5. Padover, ed., *The Complete Jefferson*, 579–582.

6. Gilmer, "On the Geological Formation of the Natural Bridge of Virginia," 187–192.

7. Oard, "Many Arches and Natural Bridges Likely from the Flood," 115–118.

8. Miller, *Jefferson and Nature*, 104.

9. Nye, *American Technological Sublime*, 21–23.

10. Padover, ed., *The Complete Jefferson*, 582.

11. Chastellux, *Voyages de M. le Marquis de Chastellux dans l'Amérique Septentrionale*. The topographical drawing is reproduced at http://explore.lib.virginia.edu/exhibits/show/nature/early-encounters/visitors.

12. Miller, *Jefferson and Nature*, 105.

13. "Natural Bridge," *Thomas Jefferson / Monticello*, accessed June 14, 2020, https://www.monticello.org/site/research-and-collections/natural-bridge.

14. "Natural Bridge," *Virginia Places*, accessed June 14, 2020, http://www.virginiaplaces.org/geology/naturalbridge.html.

15. Sears, *Sacred Places*, 4.

16. Sanford, *Quest for Paradise*, 138, 145.

17. Tompkins and Davis, *The Natural Bridge and Its Historical Surroundings*, 43.

18. Tompkins and Davis, 154.

19. Tompkins and Davis, 139.

20. Johnson, *Highways and Byways of the South*, 225–227.

21. Davis, "First Climber of the Natural Bridge," 277–290.

22. Burritt, "The Ambitious Youth," 73–76.

23. Melville, *Moby Dick*, 539.

24. Oard, "Many Arches and Natural Bridges Likely from the Flood."

25. Bernheimer, *Rainbow Bridge*, 78.

26. Nabokov, *Where the Lightning Strikes*, 201–220; Kelley and Francis, *Navajo Sacred Space*, 2, 39–61.

27. Nabokov, 74–81.

28. Hassell, *Rainbow Bridge*, 28, 30; "Interview with Jonah Yellowman (Diné)," 11; Alton and McPherson, *River Flowing from the Sunrise*, 39.

29. See Rothman, "Tourism as Colonial Economy."

30. Nabokov, *Where the Lightning Strikes*, 102–103.

31. Cited in Brady, "'Land Is Itself a Sacred, Living Being,'" 182.

32. Alton and McPherson, *River Flowing from the Sunrise*, 39–40.

33. Kolb, *Through the Grand Canyon from Wyoming to Mexico*.

34. Rothman, *America's National Monuments*, 46–47.

35. Rothman, 233–234.

36. Farmer, *Glen Canyon Dammed*, 94.

37. Birney, "To the Foot of the Rainbow," 90.

38. Cited in Farmer, *Glen Canyon Dammed*, 90.

39. Kelley and Francis, *Navajo Sacred Space*, 143.

40. Cited in Brady, "'Land Is Itself a Sacred, Living Being," 182.

41. Hassell, *Rainbow Bridge*, 120–129; Woodbury, "Protecting Rainbow Bridge," 519–528.

42. Alton and McPherson, *River Flowing from the Sunrise*, 132.

43. Fradkin, *A River No More*, 196–197.

44. Bsumek, "Imagining Indians and Revisiting Reclamation Debates," 34.

45. Deloria, *Playing Indian*, 166–167.

46. Deloria, 92–93.

47. "Nonnezoshe," in Babbitt, *Rainbow Trails*, 27.

48. Roosevelt observed: "It is surely one of the wonders of the world. It is a triumphal arch rather than a bridge." Babbitt, *Rainbow Trails*, 46.

49. Babbitt, 34.

50. Grey, *Riders of the Purple Sage*, 109.

51. Farmer, *Glen Canyon Dammed*, 167; Reisner, *Cadillac Desert*, 257.

52. Halliday, "Protection of Rainbow Bridge," 1579.

53. Committee on Resources, "Joint Hearing on the Sierra Club's Proposal to Drain Lake Powell," 21–22.

54. On the fluctuations of Lake Powell, see "Glen Canyon Dam," Bureau of Reclamation, accessed June 14, 2020, https://www.usbr.gov/uc/water/crsp/cs/gcd.html.

55. Lustgarten, "Unplugging the Colorado River."

56. Halliday, "Protection of Rainbow Bridge," 1575.

57. Thompson, "The 26,000 Tons of Radioactive Waste under Lake Powell."

58. Catherine Cullinane Thomas and Christopher Huber, "2014 National Park Visitor Spending Effects: Economic Contributions to Local Communities, States, and the Nation," accessed June 14, 2020, https://pubs.er.usgs.gov/publication/70148496.

59. Goin and Friederici, *New Form of Beauty*.

60. *Annual Report of the Director, National Park Service to the Secretary of the Interior*, June 30, 1949, 339.

5 DISCOVERING THE COLORADO RIVER

1. See Nye, "Die Niagara-Falls, der Grand Canyon und das Erhabene," 7–20; Nye, "De-Realizing the Grand Canyon," 75–94.

2. "America's Magnificent Seven," *U.S. News and World Report*, 56–57.

3. Harrison, "How a 1930s Water War between California and Arizona Delayed Parker Dam."

4. Worster, *Rivers of Empire*, 209–210.

5. Hughes, *In the House of Stone and Light*, 28.

6. Ives, *Report upon the Colorado River of the West*, 131.

7. Ives, 109–110.

8. Ives, 123.

9. Ives, "Hydrographic Report," 1–14.

10. King, *Mining Industry*. On his survey, see Goetzmann, *New Lands, New Men*, 399–405.

11. Twain, *Roughing It*.

12. Dawdy, *George Montague Wheeler*, 2.

13. Dawdy, 7.

14. Cited in Trachtenberg, *Reading American Photographs*, 146.

15. Tillotson and Taylor, *Grand Canyon Country*, 47.

16. Cited in Dawdy, *George Montague Wheeler*, 9.

17. Smith, *Pacific Vistas*, 84.

18. Powell, *The Exploration of the Colorado River and Its Canyons*.

19. Worster, *Rivers of Empire*, 138–139.

20. Worster, "Comment," 218.

21. On Edward Everett, see Nye, *American Technological Sublime*, 62–64.

22. McPhee, *Encounters with the Archdruid*, 171.

23. Powell, *Exploration of the Colorado River of the West and Its Tributaries*, 113.

24. Nabokov, *Where the Lightning Strikes*, 137–138.

25. Nabokov, 161–167 and passim.

26. Smith, *Pacific Vistas*, 74.

27. McKinsey, *Niagara Falls*, 37–125.

28. Pyne, *Dutton's Point*, 34.

29. Kinsey, *Thomas Moran and the Surveying of the American West*, 111–116.

Notes 213

30. Higgins, *Grand Cañon of the Colorado River, Arizona*, 31.

31. Nabokov, *Where the Lightning Strikes*, 108.

32. Alton and McPherson, *River Flowing from the Sunrise*, 30.

33. Dawdy, *George Montague Wheeler*, 71.

34. Cited in Boime, *The Magisterial Gaze*, 140.

35. Cited in Boime, 141.

36. Dawdy, *George Montague Wheeler*, 42.

37. Porter, *The West*, 10.

38. Porter, 456.

39. Porter, 460.

40. Porter, 462.

41. Goetzmann, "Foreword," xviii.

42. Powell, *The Exploration of the Colorado River and Its Canyons*, 379–398. To disentangle Powell's journeys of 1869–1873 from his later description of them in 1895, it is helpful to read Dellenbaugh, *A Canyon Voyage*, concerning the second expedition.

43. Fowler, ed., *"Photographed All the Best Scenery."*

44. Fowler, 85.

45. Fowler, 87.

46. Fowler, 89.

47. Dawdy, *George Montague Wheeler*, 34.

48. Gleed, ed., *From River to Sea*.

49. Smith and Crampton, eds., *The Colorado River Survey*, 4.

50. I received this information from the late Hal Rothman.

51. Smith and Crampton, eds., *The Colorado River Survey*, 254–255.

52. Lavender, *Colorado River Country*, 148–161.

53. Cited in Dawdy, *George Montague Wheeler*, 74.

54. Specialists disagree about why it was abandoned in the mid-fourteenth century. Theories include drought, overpopulation, outside interference, and disease. See Wescoat, "Challenging the Desert," 190 and passim.

55. Ives, *Report upon the Colorado River of the West*, 101.

56. This project was the subject of two novels: Ednah Aiken, *The River*, and Harold Bell Wright, *The Winning of Barbara Worth*. Samuel Goldwyn made the latter into a silent film in 1926.

57. Quoted in U.S. Department of the Interior, *The Colorado River*.

58. Worster, *Rivers of Empire*, passim.

59. Worster, 138–139.

60. Nye, *Electrifying America*, 300.

61. U.S. Department of the Interior, *The Colorado River*, 25.

62. U.S. Department of the Interior, 25.

63. U.S. Department of the Interior, 25.

64. Cited in Worster, *Rivers of Empire*, xi.

65. Bureau of Reclamation, "Bureau of Reclamation Photography and Engineering Drawings Collections," accessed June 22, 2020, https://www.usbr.gov/history/photos.html.

66. Lindholdt, "From Sublimity to Ecopornography," 1–3. See also Lindholdt, "The Inflatable Museum."

67. "Norman Rockwell Commissioned to Paint Glen Canyon Dam," accessed November 22, 2018, https://www.usbr.gov/lc/phoenix/AZ100/1970/norman_rockwell.html.

68. Gahan and Rowley. "Artists and Representations of Reclamation," 966.

69. Petrick, *Hidden in Plain Sight*, Kindle edition, chap. 8, 4.

70. Reisner, *Cadillac Desert*, 283–296.

71. Zuniga, *Central Arizona Project*, 47, accessed July 10, 2020, https://www.usbr.gov/projects/pdf.php?id=94.

72. Ibid., 31–50.

73. Bureau of Reclamation, "Hoover Dam" [brochure], December 1993.

74. Zuniga, *Central Arizona Project*, 45–46.

75. This idea is explored in Nye, *Narratives and Spaces*, 16–20, 43.

76. Weigle and Babcock, eds., *The Great Southwest of the Fred Harvey Company and the Santa Fe Railway*.

77. Nash, *Wilderness and the American Mind*, 227–237.

78. Nye, *American Technological Sublime*, 32–76.

79. Waters, *The Colorado*, 337.

6 GRAND CANYON, 1870–1940

1. Kasdan, *Grand Canyon*.

2. The three references: (1) the answer to a question on a televised quiz show; (2) in the mechanic's monologue, discussed; (3) during the film producer's (Steve Martin) diatribe about violence in society.

3. This exchange takes place during the twenty-first minute of the film.

4. For a summary, see Watson, *Philosophy of Kant Explained*, 490–499.

5. On this argument, see Nye, *American Technological Sublime*, xi–16, 26–28, 74–75, 195–198, 237–242.

6. Hughes, *In the House of Stone and Light*, 19.

7. Nabokov, *Where the Lightning Strikes*, 131.

8. Sears, *Sacred Places*; Schuyler, "The Sanctified Landscape," 93–109.

9. Discussed also in Nye, "Constructing Nature," 13–24.

10. "America's Magnificent Seven," *U.S. News and World Report*, 56–57.

11. See Sears, *Sacred Places*, 3–30 and passim; Nye, *American Technological Sublime*, 17–26.

12. Cooper felt the Rocky Mountains "possessed many noble views" but lacked a perfect "union of art and nature." Cooper, "American and European Scenery Compared," 138–139.

13. Bryant, *Picturesque America*.

14. Bryant, iii.

15. Bryant, iii–iv.

16. Novak, *Nature and Culture*, 34–44. See also Sears, *Sacred Places*, passim.

17. Jussim and Lindquist-Cock, *Landscape as Photograph*, 56.

18. Trachtenberg, *Reading American Photographs*, 119–163.

19. Hillers, *"Photographed All the Best Scenery."*

20. Bryant, *Picturesque America*, vol. 2, 510. "The picture drawn by the artist of a pinnacle in one of the angles of the Kanab is from a photograph taken by Mr. Hillers."

21. Beadle, *The Undeveloped West*, 631–633.

22. Gleed, ed., *From River to Sea*.

23. Sears, *Sacred Places*, 6–7.

24. Novak, *Nature and Culture*, 145.

25. Hughes, *In the House of Stone and Light*, 38.

26. Muir, "The Grand Canyon," 77, 79.

27. Warner, "On the Brink of the Grand Canyon," 41.

28. Hance, ed., *Personal Impressions of the Grand Canyon*, 52.

29. Hance, 90.

30. Hance, 52.

31. Rothman, *Devil's Bargains*, 57.

32. Way, "Practical Canyon Problems," 334–335.

33. Way, 334.

34. Aldo Leopold and Don Johnston, "Grand Canyon Working Plan: Uses, Information, Recreational Development," December 1916, Aldo Leopold Papers, Folio 1, 10–11. Cited in Sutter, *Driven Wild*, 59.

35. Sheridan, *Arizona*, 237–238.

36. Moran, "American Art and American Scenery," 85–87.

37. Moran, *The Chasm of the Colorado*, 1873–1874. See also Kinsey, *Thomas Moran and the Surveying of the American West*, 111–116.

38. Cited in Kinsey, 15.

39. Hughes, *In the House of Stone and Light*, 38–40.

40. Kinsey, *Thomas Moran and the Surveying of the American West*, 117.

41. Cited in Kinsey, 111.

42. See Hillers, *The Grand Canyon: From North Side near Foot of Toroweap Valley*, reproduced by Dellenbaugh in *A Canyon Voyage*, halftone facing p. 254.

43. Hughes, *In the House of Stone and Light*, 114.

44. Dellenbaugh, *A Canyon Voyage*, 7.

45. Dellenbaugh, 58.

46. Mobility long remained limited. In c. 1906 a Detroit Publishing Company cameraman made images along the Grand View Trail using 8 × 10-inch glass negatives. Five years later, Alvin Langdon Coburn photographed the Grand Canyon with a 3¾ × 4½-inch reflex camera and hauled his equipment to the bottom on mules (Coburn, *Alvin Langdon Coburn*, 84). Library of Congress, Photographic Collections, Detroit Publishing Co. view of hanging rock: LC-D4-19252 and reproduction No. LC-D4-19252 DLC. View from in front of hotel: Call No. LC-D4-19250; Reproduction No. LC-D4-19250 DLC.

47. Trachtenberg, *Reading American Photographs*, 131.

48. Masteller, "Western Views in Eastern Parlors," 55–71.

49. Taft, *Photography and the American Scene*, 308.

50. Kinsey, *Thomas Moran and the Surveying of the American West*, 101–102.

51. Cited in Taft, *Photography and the American Scene*, 302.

52. Bossen, "A Tall Tale Retold," 98–109.

53. Taft, *Photography and the American Scene*, 302.

54. Pyne, *How the Canyon Became Grand*, 49.

55. Cited in Pyne, 48.

56. Smith, *Pacific Vistas*, 74.

57. Pyne, *Dutton's Point*, 34; Dutton, *Tertiary History of the Grand Cañon District*.

58. For example, see Jack Hillers, "Grand Cañon, Colorado River, Arizona," Records of the Geological Survey 57-PS-66, National Archives.

59. Kolb, *Through the Grand Canyon from Wyoming to Mexico*.

60. Bryant, *History of the Atchison, Topeka, and Santa Fe*, 120.

61. See Kinsey, *Thomas Moran and the Surveying of the American West*, 132–134.

62. Higgins, *Grand Cañon of Arizona*, 1902. See also Higgins, *Grand Canyon Outings*, 1922.

63. Runte, *Trains of Discovery*.

64. "Notebook Used By Edsel Ford, 1911," The Henry Ford, accessed June 24, 2020, https://www.thehenryford.org/collections-and-research/digital-collections/artifact/298039/.

65. Way, *Destination Grand Canyon*, 43–44.

66. Nye, *America's Assembly Line*, 53.

67. Sheridan, *Arizona*, 239.

68. Murphy's *Three Wonderlands of the American West* includes sixteen color reproductions from paintings by Moran, and thirty-two duogravures from photographs, as well as maps of Yellowstone, Yosemite, and the Grand Canyon. See also James, *The Grand Canyon of Arizona*.

69. *The Blue Book*, 315.

70. Hales, "American Views and the Romance of Modernization," 237–238.

71. In 1993 a photograph of the room with straight-backed chairs facing the screen hung in the Kolb Studio, opposite the canyon view, near the picture window. The film is at the University of Northern Arizona, Flagstaff.

72. Bray, ed., *Guide to the Ford Film Collection in the National Archives*, 21.

73. Wright, "Air Routes to the National Parks."

74. Warren, "Aviation at Grand Canyon," 151–152.

75. Warren, 154.

76. Macready, "Non-Stop Flight across America."

77. Hughes, *In the House of Stone and Light*, 100.

78. Warren, "Aviation at Grand Canyon," 161.

79. Grand Canyon National Park, visitor statistics, https://irma.nps.gov/STATS/SSRSReports/Park%20Specific%20Reports/Annual%20Park%20Recreation%20Visitation%20(1904%20-%20Last%20Calendar%20Year).

80. Tillotson and Taylor, *Grand Canyon Country*, 61.

81. Statistics on Grand Canyon visitors available for every year since 1919 at Grand Canyon National Park visitors.

82. Krug, *Natural Resource Problems*, 294, 339.

7 SKYSCRAPER AND SKYLINE

1. Gilkey, "The Spiritual Uplift of Scenery as Exemplified by the Grand Canyon," 138–139.

2. Excerpts from the *Annual Report of the Secretary of the Interior for the Fiscal Year Ended June 30, 1915*, 38–39.

3. Walcott, "National Parks as a Scientific Asset," 117.

4. Smith, "The Survey's Contribution to the National-Park Movements," 322.

5. Pomeroy, *In Search of the Golden West*, 58–59.

6. Steinberg, *Down to Earth*, 148–149.

7. Misa, *A Nation of Steel*, 87.

8. Misa, 88.

9. Mitchell, "The Mohawks in High Steel," 40.

10. Katzer, "The Caughnawaga Mohawks," 39. See also Rasenberger, *High Steel*, 133–134.

11. McFarland, *Proceedings of a Conference of Governors*.

12. Kouwenhoven, "What's American about America?"

13. Stein, *Everybody's Autobiography*, 174.

14. Girouard, *Cities and People*, 329.

15. James, *The American Scene*, 185.

16. On the conflict between the European and the vernacular styles, see Taylor and Bender, "Culture and Architecture."

17. Goldberger, *The Skyscraper*.

18. Terminology discussed in Nye, *American Technological Sublime*, 56–57, 81–87, 96–108, 278.

19. Nye, chap. 1–4 and passim.

20. Johns, "The Excelsior of Architecture," 3.

21. Cited in Schleier, *The Skyscraper in American Art, 1890–1931*, 77.

22. Cited in Schleier, 77.

23. Lewis, *Arrowsmith*, 287.

24. Lewis, 292.

25. McKay, "Song of New York," 15.

26. Lewis, *Arrowsmith*, 293.

27. McKay, "Song of New York," 15.

28. Taylor, "New York and the Origin of the Skyline," 234. For earlier uses of the term, see van Leeuwen, *The Skyward Trend of Thought*, 84–85.

29. Schuyler, "The Sky-Line of New York," 295.

30. Hall, *The Hudson Fulton Celebration*, 252. The mayor's comments echoed those of critics in *Scribner's*. See also Benert, "Reading the Walls."

31. Cited in Trachtenberg, *Reading American Photographs*, 213.

32. Bennett, *Those United States*, 45–46.

33. Girouard, *Cities and People*, 320–321. See also Domosh, "Symbolism of the Skyscraper," 334.

34. Lewis, *Arrowsmith*, 291–292.

35. For examples of Flatiron Building photographs, including the work of both Steichen and Stieglitz, see Kreitler, *Flatiron*.

36. Marchand, *Advertising the American Dream*, 240, 242.

37. Lewis, *Arrowsmith*, 292.

38. Saltus, "New York from the Flatiron," 382–383. A widely distributed Underwood and Underwood stereograph made the same point. Reproduced in Kreitler, *Flatiron*, 47.

39. Sandburg, *Poetry*, 244.

40. Henry, "Psyche and the Pskyscraper," 3

41. "Panorama Viewed from 85th Story," 7.

42. "Sky Boys Who 'Rode the Ball' on Empire State," 33.

43. Barthes, *Eiffel Tower and Other Mythologies*, 8.

44. Certeau, *The Practice of Everyday Life*, 92.

45. Certeau, 9.

46. Oppenheim, *The Olympian*, 416–417.

47. See Nye, *American Technological Sublime*, chap. 2 and passim.

48. Coburn, *An Autobiography*, 86. The image is reproduced on 111.

49. Wells, *The Future in America*, 48.

50. Coburn, *An Autobiography*, 86.

51. Nye, *American Illuminations*, 61–83.

52. On the illuminated skyscrapers, see Nye, *Electrifying America*, 66–67, 74, 78, 80, 84; Nye, *American Technological Sublime*, 180–181, 187–198; Nye, *American Illuminations*, 153–158.

53. Hartmann, *Valiant Knights of Daguerre*, 129.

54. Hartmann, 127.

55. Cited in Schiller and Coyle, eds., "John Sloan's Urban Encounters," 71.

8 NUCLEAR ANTI-LANDSCAPES

1. Gulkeson, *Anthropologists and the Rediscovery of America*, 49.

2. Muir, *Steep Trails*; Austin, *Land of Little Rain*; Van Dyke, *The Desert*; Cather, *Death Comes for the Archbishop*.

3. Teague, *The Southwest in American Literature and Art*, 3–4, 159–170.

4. Dedek, *Hip to the Trip*, 28–41.

5. LaDuke, *All Our Relations*, 99–100; Solnit, *Savage Dreams*, 21, 69, 163–169.

6. Lowenthal, *George Perkins Marsh*, 293.

7. Jackson, *Discovering the Vernacular Landscape*, 8.

8. Allen, *Uneasy Alchemy*; LeCain, *Mass Destruction*; Zierler, *The Invention of Ecocide*.

9. Bullard et al., *Toxic Wastes and Race*. See also Steinberg, *Down to Earth*, 256.

10. Brown, *Plutopia*, 41–43, 170.

11. Ed Keheley and Associates, Inc., "History of the Picher Mining Field."

12. Findlay and Hevly, *Atomic Frontier Days*, 14–73.

13. Marsh, *Man and Nature*, 42.

14. Ponting, *Green History of the World*, 168–170.

15. LeCain, *Mass Destruction*, 169.

16. Tichi, *Shifting Gears*, 99–170. See also Nye, *American Technological Sublime*, 125–128.

17. Tuan, *Space and Place*, 6.

18. Carson, *Silent Spring*.

19. Buell, *Writing for an Endangered World*, 30–54.

20. Newman, *Love Canal*, 68, 75.

21. Newman, 75, 88–90.

22. Colten and Skinners, *The Road to Love Canal*.

23. McNeill, *Something New Under the Sun*, 29.

Notes

24. Switzer, *CERCLA*.

25. Nieves, "Our Towns."

26. CNN, "Despite Toxic History, Residents Return to Love Canal," August 7, 1998.

27. DePalma, with Staba. "Love Canal Declared Clean."

28. "Superfund Site: Carson River Mercury Site," accessed June 27, 2020, https://cumulis.epa.gov/supercpad/SiteProfiles/index.cfm?fuseaction=second.Cleanup&id=0903020#bkground.

29. Holson, "Power, Politics and Glory Dimmed."

30. U.S. General Accountability Office, "Superfund Funding and Costs," 8–10, 13–14.

31. Johnston, Dawson, and Madsen, "Uranium Mining and Milling," 133; Price, *Orphaned Land*, 139–144, 158–159.

32. Johnston, Dawson, and Madsen, 137.

33. Voyles, *Wastelanding*, 61.

34. Grand Canyon Trust, "Active Mining Claims within the Grand Canyon Withdrawal Area," *Report to Donors 2018*, 3, https://www.grandcanyontrust.org/sites/default/files/resources/RTD_2018.pdf.

35. EPA, "Navajo Nation: Cleaning Up Abandoned Uranium Mines," accessed June 26, 2020, https://www.epa.gov/navajo-nation-uranium-cleanup/cleaning-abandoned-uranium-mines.

36. Dillingham, "Exxon, Uranium, and the Navajo Nation," 27; Barry, "Navajo and Hopi's History of Inequitable Mining Leases," 16–20.

37. Bryne and Hoffman, "A 'Necessary Sacrifice,'" 107.

38. Caufield, *Multiple Exposures*, 83.

39. Pasternak, "A Peril that Dwelt among the Navajos."

40. Eichstaedt, *If You Poison Us*, 47–94.

41. Caufield, *Multiple Exposures*, 81.

42. Byrne and Hoffman, "A 'Necessary Sacrifice,'" 107–109.

43. Samet et al., "Uranium Mining and Lung Cancer in Navajo Men," 1481–1484.

44. U.S. Congress, Radiation Exposure Compensation Act, October 15, 1990.

45. Brugge, Benally, and Yazzie-Lewis, *The Navajo People and Uranium Mining*, 141, 145.

46. Byrne and Hoffman, "A 'Necessary Sacrifice,'" 109.

47. Pasternak, *Yellow Dirt*, 125.

48. EPA, "Learn about Radiation in Your World," RadTown, accessed June 26, 2020, https://www3.epa.gov/radtown/uranium-mines-mills.html.

49. Diep, "Abandoned Uranium Mines."

50. U.S. Nuclear Regulatory Commission, "NRC Five Year Plan."

51. Melosi, *Atomic Age America*, 281.

52. Pasternak, *Yellow Dirt*, 8.

53. See https://www.energyfuels.com/white-mesa-mill.

54. See "White Mesa Uranium Mill," Grand Canyon Trust, accessed June 26, 2020, https://www.grandcanyontrust.org/white-mesa-uranium-mill; EPA, "Learn about Radiation in Your World."

55. Kaufmann, Eadie, and Russell, "Effects of Uranium Mining and Milling," 296–308.

56. Peshlakai, "Indians as Anti-Nuclearists," 27.

57. Bryne and Hoffman, "A 'Necessary Sacrifice,'" 107.

58. Pasternak, *Yellow Dirt*, 154.

59. Brugge, Benally, and Yazzie-Lewis, *The Navajo People and Uranium Mining*, 6.

60. EPA, "Navajo Nation: Cleaning Up Abandoned Uranium Mines."

61. Karpius, *Uranium Mining and Milling*.

62. Findlay and Hevly, *Atomic Frontier Days*, 22.

63. Findlay and Hevly, 58.

64. See https://ecology.wa.gov/Waste-Toxics/Nuclear-waste/Hanford-cleanup/Protecting-air-water/Groundwater-monitoring.

65. Johansen *Resource Exploitation in Native North America*, 23.

66. Findlay and Hevly, *Atomic Frontier Days*, 244.

67. Findlay and Hevly, 258.

68. Associated Press, "Biggest US Nuclear Bomb Dismantled in Texas," October 25, 2011, https://www.theguardian.com/world/2011/oct/26/biggest-nuclear-bomb-dismantled-texas.

69. The Nation, "A Near Miss Nuclear Explosion.

70. Berard, "The Perils of Pantex."

71. Davis, "Feds Give Pantex Contractor 'Scathing' Review.'"

72. Hauptman, *Storm Season*.

73. For a reading of *Storm Season*, see Beck, *Dirty Wars*, 168–175.

74. Johansen, *Resource Exploitation in Native North America*, 19. See also Grinde and Johansen, *Ecocide of Native America*.

75. Caufield, *Multiple Exposures*, 132.

76. Weart, *The Rise of Nuclear Fear*, 111–114.

77. Cited in Winkler, *Life under a Cloud*, 103.

78. Gallagher, *American Ground Zero*, 217.

79. Caufield, *Multiple Exposures*, 115.

80. Howard Ball, "Downwind from the Bomb."

81. Ball, "Downwind from the Bomb."

82. Caufield, *Multiple Exposures*, 116.

83. Kirk, *Doom Towns*, 71, 189.

84. Winkler, *Life under a Cloud*, 92.

85. Interview with Professor of Physics Frank Titus, Union College, who witnessed tests in the 1950s.

86. Winkler, *Life under a Cloud*, 92. See also Solomon, *Killing Our Own*.

87. Nixon, *Slow Violence*, 204.

88. Kirk, *Doom Towns*, xiv–xv. See also Worman, *Anatomy of the Nevada Test Site*.

89. Martinez and Poupart, "Circle of Life," 142.

90. Vanderbilt, *Survival City*, 191.

91. Barrett, "How Carlsbad Got WIPPed," 135; Price, *Orphaned Land*, 159–169.

92. Ialenti, "Waste Makes Haste," 262–275.

93. Ialenti, 264.

94. Barrett, "How Carlsbad Got WIPPed," 136.

95. Vanderbilt, *Survival City*, 191; Price, *Orphaned Land*, 160; National Academies of Sciences, Engineering, and Medicine, *Review of the Department of Energy's Plans for Disposal of Surplus Plutonium*, 137.

96. DeLillo, *Underworld*, 289.

97. Solnit, *Savage Dreams*, 86.

9 GRAND CANYON SINCE 1945

1. Visitation statistics for all parks are available at https://irma.nps.gov/Stats/SSRSReports/Park%20Specific%20Reports/Annual%20Park%20Recreation%20Visitation%20(1904%20-%20Last%20Calendar%20Year).

2. Pearson, "'We Have Almost Forgotten How to Hope,'" 299–300.

3. Pearson, 301–313.

4. "Mining and the Canyon," *New York Times*, June 29, 2011, A22.

5. Hughes, *In the House of Stone and Light*, 114.

6. Cited in Fradkin, *A River No More*, 211.

7. U.S. Department of the Interior, *Colorado River Management Plan*, 2–15, 17.

8. Byrne and Hoffman, "'A Necessary Sacrifice,'" 110.

9. "Open Now: New Zipline at Grand Canyon West," January 5, 2018, https://www.prnewswire.com/news-releases/open-now-new-zipline-at-grand-canyon-west-lets-adventurers-soar-more-than-2000-feet-amid-epic-scenery-300578235.html, accessed February 12, 2018.

10. "National Parks," *Time Magazine*; "Crunch Time at the Grand Canyon," *Time Magazine*.

11. Guided Tour of Grand Canyon National Park, accessed July 10, 2020. https://www.bobspixels.com/kaibab.org/misc/gc_visit.htm.

12. Lane, *Impressions of Niagara*, 69.

13. Dow, *Anthology and Bibliography of Niagara Falls*, 1092 and passim.

14. Van Dyke, *Grand Canyon of the Colorado*, 1.

15. Muir, "The Grand Canyon," 77.

16. Krutch, *The Grand Canyon*, 21.

17. Cited in Aitchison, *Naturalist's Guide to Hiking the Grand Canyon*, 20.

18. Krutch, *The Grand Canyon*, 35.

19. Tillotson and Taylor, *Grand Canyon Country*, 3.

20. Numbers, *The Creationists*, 300.

21. Pew Research poll, 2013.

22. Sheridan, *Arizona*, 323.

23. Zhang, "Creationist Sues the Grand Canyon."

24. Zhang, "Grand Canyon Gives In to Creationist."

25. Heather Pingle, "Native American Creationists," *Archaeology Archive*, August 22, 2008.

26. Deloria, *Red Earth, White Lies*. See also Brumble, "Vine Deloria, Jr., Creationism, and Ethnic Pseudoscience," 10–14.

27. Clinton, "Remarks Announcing the Establishment of the Grand Staircase-Escalante National Monument."

28. Gilkey, "The Spiritual Uplift of Scenery as Exemplified by the Grand Canyon," 138.

29. Grand Canyon Visitor Center, IMAX schedule, accessed February 12, 2018, https://explorethecanyon.com/imax-theater/.

30. Stegner's reflections on wilderness appeared as a letter in 1960 and then in his *The Sound of Mountain Water* (1969). The letter is reproduced at The Wilderness Society website, https://wilderness.org/bios/former-council-members/wallace-stegner.

31. Nagourney, "Where Two Rivers Meet."

32. Nash, *Grand Canyon for Sale*, 63–77.

33. Nash, 46.

34. "Hunters Wanted for Grand Canyon Bison Cull," BBC News, September 12, 2017.

35. National Park Service, "Bright Angel Creek Trout Reduction Project," https://www.nps.gov/grca/learn/nature/trout-reduction.htm.

36. Nash, *Grand Canyon for Sale*, 17.

37. National Geographic, "Grand Canyon National Park Ecosystem Threatened by Kazakhstan Beetle?," accessed February 12, 2018, https://news.nationalgeographic.com/news/2011/04/110421-national-parks-grand-canyon-water-tamarisk-flycatcher/.

38. Melnick, "Climate Change and Landscape Preservation," 37.

39. Johansen, *Resource Exploitation in Native North America*, 179.

40. Sheridan, *Arizona*, 302. On air quality, see also Nash, *Grand Canyon for Sale*, 95–113.

41. LaDuke, *Recovering the Sacred*, 38–39.

42. Fradkin, *A River No More*. See also Dolan, Howard, and Gallenson, "Man's Impact on the Colorado River in the Grand Canyon," 392–401.

43. "Grand Canyon Virtual Tour on CD-Rom: The Next Best Thing to Exploring the Canyon in Person," accessed February 12, 2018, http://www.360parks.com/grand_canyon_virtual_tour.shtml. Google's virtual tour can be seen at no cost: https://www.google.com/maps/about/behind-the-scenes/streetview/treks/grand-canyon/.

44. True, if one accepts Jackson's definition of landscape as "a concrete, three-dimensional, shared reality." Jackson, *Discovering the Vernacular Landscape*, 3–8.

45. Larson, "The Far Side."

46. Warner, "The Place to Be This Year."

47. Dutton, *Tertiary History of the Grand Cañon District*, 142.

48. Barthes, *Camera Lucida*, 96 and passim.

49. Eiseley, *The Star Thrower*, 175.

50. Senf and Pyne, *Reconstructing the View*.

51. Gidley, *Edward S. Curtis*.

52. Painting at Walker Art Museum, Minneapolis. Reproduced in Danto, *Mark Tansey*, 122–123.

53. Identifications made by Tansey, Danto, 137.

10 CONFLICTED LANDSCAPES

1. Numbers, *The Creationists*, 300.

2. Beck, *Risk Society*, 81.

3. Emmett and Nye, *Environmental Humanities*, 1–21.

4. Cronon, "The Trouble with Wilderness," 80–90.

5. Volcovici, "Trump Order Could Remove Protections for National Monuments."

6. Carter, "Remarks in a Panel Discussion and Question-and-Answer Session on Energy."

7. Carter, "Proclamation 4729."

8. Frank Newport, "Republicans, Democrats Differ on Creationism," *Gallup*, June 20, 2008, https://news.gallup.com/poll/108226/republicans-democrats-differ-creationism.aspx.

9. Prestowitz, *Rouge Nation*, 139.

10. Bush, "Remarks Prior to Discussions."

11. Draper, *Dead Certain*, 121–122.

12. Lochhead, "How GOP Became Party of Denial on Global Warming"; Davenport and Lipton, "How G.O.P. Leaders Came to View Climate Change as Fake Science"; Pielke, *Climate Fix*.

13. *Congressional Record* 148, no. 93, July 11, 2002, 107th Congress, 2nd Session, H4527.

14. "In Their Own Words: GOP Candidates and Science," National Public Radio, September 7, 2011, https://www.npr.org/2011/09/07/140071973/in-their-own-words-gop-candidates-and-science.

15. Cited in Tichi, *New Word, New Earth*, 172.

16. Udall, *The Quiet Crisis*, 137.

17. U.S. General Accounting Office, *Wilderness Preservation*, 4, 60.

18. Fradkin, *Wanderings of an Environmental Journalist*, 140.

19. Klein, "Tourism, Consumerism, and the Southwestern Public Lands," 70.

20. Tapahonso, "Ode to the Land," 97.

21. Roberta Black Goat, quoted in "The Longest Walk," *Akwesasne Notes* (Summer 1978): 6.

22. Grinde and Johansen, "The Navajos and National Sacrifice," 205.

23. Benally, ed., *Bitter Water*, 32–33.

24. Quoted in Grinde and Johansen, "The Navajos and National Sacrifice," 211.

25. Nixon, *Slow Violence*, 268.

26. *Native American Sacred Places*, part 2, 12.

27. U.S. Department of the Interior, Bureau of Land Management, El Centro Field Office, "Record of Decision for the Imperial Project Gold Mine Proposal," 3, 10.

28. Bureau of Land Management, "Imperial Project Draft Environmental Impact Statement," Section 3.6.2.1, https://archive.org/stream/imperialprojecti01unse/imperialprojectimadigan01unse_djvu.txt.

29. Nick Madigan, "Tribe Prepares for Renewed Fight Over Gold Mine," *New York Times*, September 15, 2002.

30. *Native American Sacred Places*, 4.

31. *Native American Sacred Places*, 17.

32. *Native American Sacred Places*, 13.

33. "U.S. Dodges Bullet on NAFTA Glamis Case," Earthjustice Press Room, June 8, 2009, https://earthjustice.org/news/press/2009/u-s-dodges-bullet-on-nafta-glamis-case.

34. Clinton, "Establishment of the Grand Staircase-Escalante National Monument."

35. Clinton, "Establishment of the Grand Staircase-Escalante National Monument."

36. Williams, *Red*, 99–100.

37. Robert Arnberger and Steve Martin, "Grand Canyon Is a National Treasure, Not a Place for Uranium Mining," CNN, January 9, 2018.

38. Amy Joi O'Donoghue, "A Bears Ears Primer," *Deseret News*, December 18, 2016.

39. Williams, *Red*, 102.

40. Williams, 105.

41. Hora and Merritt, "Utah Lake Rock Imagery," 124–126; Bureau of Land Management, *Grand Staircase-Escalante National Monument*, 51–52.

42. Bureau of Land Management, 53–54.

43. O'Donoghue, "Bear's Ears Primer."

44. Balenquah, "Spirit of Place," 78; William H. Doelle, *Bears Ears Archeological Experts Gathering*, 2017, accessed July 13, 2020, https://www.archaeologysouthwest.org/pdf/Bears_Ears_Report.pdf.

45. Clifton, "Who Else Is in the Koch Brothers Billionaire Donor Club?"

46. Jackson, "Goodbye to Evolution," 60.

11 PRAGMATIC SOLUTIONS

1. Suzuki, *Sacred Balance*, viii.

2. Williams, *Pieces of White Shell*, 5.

3. Proulx, *Barkskins*; Silko, *Gardens in the Dunes*; Erdrich, *Tracks*; Powers, *The Overstory*.

4. Wohlleben *The Hidden Life of Trees*, 6–18 and passim.

5. "Faith-Based Groups," Home of the Green Congregation Program, Web of Creation, accessed June 30, 2020, https://www.webofcreation.org/links-to-eco-faith-groups/faith-based-environmental-groups.

6. Clements, McCright, and Xiao, "Green Christians?," 10.

7. Clements, McCright, and Xiao, 12–13.

8. "About the Green Seminary Initiative," The Green Seminary Initiative, accessed June 30, 2020, https://greenseminaries.org/.

9. Berry, "Three Ways of Farming in the Southwest," 47–76; Price, *The Orphaned Land*, 287–290.

10. See discussion of Species at Risk Act of 2002, accessed June 30, 2020, https://www.canada.ca/en/environment-climate-change/services/environmental-enforcement/acts-regulations/about-species-at-risk-act.html; The Anthropocene Project, https://theanthropocene.org/.

11. Henderson, "Wilderness and the Nature Conservation Ideal," 397.

12. Cited in Henderson, 397.

13. "The Zuiderzee and Delta Works of the Netherlands," accessed June 30, 2020, http://www.unmuseum.org/7wonders/zunderzee.htm.

14. Barkham, "Dutch Rewilding Experiment."

15. "Buffalo Commons," Great Plains Restoration Council, accessed September 20, 2018, http://gprc.org/research/buffalo-commons/.

16. See National Park Service, "Disturbed Lands Restoration," http://www2.nature.nps.gov/grd/distland; U.S. EPA, Office of Solid Waste and Emergency

Response, *Mine Reclamation Using Biosolids*, August 2001, http://www.clu-in.org/download/remed/biosolids.pdf; "Overview of EPA's Brownfields Program," https://www.epa.gov/brownfields/overview-epas-brownfields-program.

17. See McDonald, *Conservation for Cities*; Owen, *Green Metropolis*.

18. Kinkead, "Detroit's Emerging Innovation in Urban Infrastructure," 201.

19. "The Price of Water," Circle of Blue, accessed June 30, 2020, https://www.circleofblue.org/waterpricing/.

20. Penn State Extension, "Drip Irrigation for Vegetable Production," 2016, https://extension.psu.edu/drip-irrigation-for-vegetable-production; U.S. Department of Agriculture, "Dripline Irrigation Success Story," May 2011, https://www.nrcs.usda.gov/wps/portal/nrcs/az/newsroom/stories/nrcs144p2_065125/.

21. Nye, *Consuming Power*, 96; Georgann Yara, "The Urban Farm in Phoenix Teaches People How to Grow Their Own Food," *azcentral*, January 26, 2017; "Urban Farming" search results, accessed June 30, 2020, http://vitalysthealth.org/?s=urban+farming.

22. Calvin, *Global Fever*, 207.

23. Zweibel, Mason, and Fthenakis, "A Solar Grand Plan"; U.S. Energy Administration, "What Is US Electricity Generation by Energy Source?," accessed July 10, 2020, https://www.eia.gov/tools/faqs/faq.php?id=427&t=3.

24. Jonathan Thompson, "Seven Things You Need to Know about Navajo Generating Station's 2019 Closure," *High Country News*, February 14, 2017.

25. Williams, *The Hour of Land*, 261; "Navajo Nation Solar Facility Expansion Expected to Double Power Output," August 25, 2018, http://ktar.com/story/2189238/navajo-nation-kayenta-solar-renewable-energy-expansion/.

26. "U.S. Coal Plant Retirements Near All-Time High," November 9, 2018, https://about.bnef.com/blog/u-s-coal-plant-retirements-near-all-time-high/.

27. Funk and Kennedy, "The Politics of Climate."

28. "Environmental Sustainability Goals," City of Phoenix, accessed June 30, 2020, https://www.phoenix.gov/sustainability/energy.

29. "Residential Solar Readiness Ordinance (Citywide)," Mayor & Council Communication, Tucson, Arizona, June 17, 2008, https://www.tucsonaz.gov/files/pdsd/pdfs/GreenBuilding/june17-08-311.pdf.

30. Rohwedder, "Green Goes Mainstream for New Homes"; Evans, "The Utah Group Just Proved That Net Zero Energy Buildings Don't Have to Be More Expensive."

31. "Green Buildings Could Save Our Cities," January 24, 2017, https://www.nationalgeographic.com/environment/urban-expeditions/green-buildings/benefits-of-green-buildings-human-health-economics-environment/.

32. Joseph M. Dougherty, "Recycling Grows in Utah, Utahns Say They Want It—But Vast Majority Don't Put It into Practice" *Deseret News*, February 2, 2009; Katie Brigham, CNBC, "How San Francisco Sends Less Trash to the Landfill than Any Other Major U.S. City," July 14, 2018.

33. Joann Muller, "How GM Makes $1 Billion A Year by Recycling Waste," *Forbes*, February 21, 2013.

34. Erica Goode, "New Solar Plants Generate Floating Green Power," *New York Times*, May 20, 2016.

35. Campbell, "Critical Regionalism," 74–77; Emmett and Nye, *Environmental Humanities*, 163–175; Bloomberg and Pope, *Climate of Hope*, 245–262.

36. Emmett and Nye, *Environmental Humanities*, 176.

37. The UN's goals are available at http://www.un.org/sustainabledevelopment/climate-change-2/.

38. Based on "Green Ranking," *Newsweek*, January 8, 2019.

39. Nye, "The United States and Alternative Energies since 1980," 103–125.

40. NRDC, "Climate Alliance States Show Us What Real Leadership Looks Like," *EcoWatch*, September 21, 2017, https://www.ecowatch.com/us-climate-alliance-2487955480.html.

41. Dunaway, *Natural Visions*, 196. The concept of the "ecological sublime" is further discussed in chapter 8 of my forthcoming book (2022) with the MIT Press, which considers new formations of the sublime.

BIBLIOGRAPHY

Aiken, Ednah. *The River*. Indianapolis: The Bobbs-Merrill, 1914.

Aitchison, Stewart. *A Naturalist's Guide to Hiking the Grand Canyon*. Englewood Cliffs, NJ: Prentice-Hall, 1985.

Allen, Barbara. *Uneasy Alchemy: Citizens and Experts in Louisiana's Chemical Corridor Disputes*. Cambridge, MA: MIT Press, 2003.

Alonso de Herrera, Gabriel. *Agricultura General*. Madrid: La Imprenta Real, [1513] 1819.

Alton, James M., and Robert S. McPherson. *River Flowing from the Sunrise: An Environmental History of the Lower San Juan*. Logan: Utah State University Press, 2000.

"America's Magnificent Seven." *U.S. News and World Report*, April 21, 1975.

Annual Report of the Director, National Park Service to the Secretary of the Interior. June 30, 1949. Washington, DC: U.S. Government Printing Office, 1949.

Arnold, Horace L., and Fay L. Faurote. *Ford Methods and the Ford Shops*. New York: Engineering Company, 1915.

Austin, Mary. *Land of Little Rain*. Boston: Houghton Mifflin, 1903.

Babbitt, James E. *Rainbow Trails: Early-Day Adventures in Rainbow Bridge Country*. Page, AZ: Glen Canyon Natural History Association, 1990.

Balenquah, Lyle. "Spirit of Place: Preserving the Cultural Landscape of Bears Ears." In Keeler, *Edge of Morning*, 75–80.

Ball, Howard. "Downwind from the Bomb." *New York Times Archives*, 006033, February 9, 1986. https://www.nytimes.com/1986/02/09/magazine/downwind-from-the-bomb.html.

Barclay, Hartley. W. *Ford Production Methods*. New York: Harper & Bros., 1936.

Barkham, Patrick. "Dutch Rewilding Experiment Sparks Backlash as Thousands of Animals Starve," *Guardian*, April 27, 2018.

Barnes, Djuana. *New York*. Edited by Alyce Barry. Los Angeles: Sun and Moon Press, [1913] 1989. Reprinted from the *Brooklyn Daily Eagle* series from October 12 to December 14, 1913.

Barrett, William P. "How Carlsbad Got WIPPed." *Forbes Magazine*, October 19, 1998, 135–136.

Barry, Tom. "The Navajo and Hopi's History of Inequitable Mining Leases." *American Indian Journal* 5, no. 3 (March 1979): 16–20.

Barthes, Roland. *Camera Lucida: Reflections on Photography*. New York: Hill and Wang, 1981.

Barthes, Roland. *The Eiffel Tower and Other Mythologies*, trans. Richard Howard. New York: Hill and Wang, 1979.

"Battle of Detroit." *Time*, March 23, 1942, 10–14.

Beadle, J. H. *The Undeveloped West; or Five Years in the Territories: Being a Complete History of That Vast Region between the Mississippi and the Pacific*. New York: Arno Press, [1873] 1973.

Beck, John. *Dirty Wars: Landscape, Power, and Waste in Western American Literature*. Lincoln: University of Nebraska Press, 2009.

Beck, Ulrich. *Risk Society: Towards a New Modernity*. London: Sage, 1992.

Benally, Klee. "The San Francisco Peaks and the Politics of Cultural Genocide." In Keeler, *Edge of Morning*, 87–104.

Benally, Malcolm D., trans. and ed. *Bitter Water: Diné Oral Histories of the Navajo-Hopi Land Dispute*. Tucson: University of Arizona Press, 2011.

Benert, Annette Larsen. "Reading the Walls: The Politics of Architecture in *Scribner's Magazine*, 1887–1914." *Arizona Quarterly* 47, no. 1 (Spring 1991): 49–79.

Bennett, Arnold. *Those United States*. London: Martin Secker, 1912.

Berard, Yamil. "The Perils of Pantex: Hundreds of Workers Sickened at Texas Nuclear Weapons Plant." *Fort Worth Star-Telegram*, December 12, 2015.

Bernheimer, Charles L. *Rainbow Bridge: Circling Navajo Mountain and Explorations in the "Bad Lands" of Southern Utah and Northern Arizona*. Garden City: Doubleday, 1924.

Berry, Wendell. "Three Ways of Farming in the Southwest." In *The Gift of Good Land*, 47–76. New York: North Point Press, 1981.

Biggs, Lindy. 1996. *The Rational Factory: Architecture, Technology and Work in America's Age of Mass Production*. Baltimore: Johns Hopkins University Press, 1996.

Birmingham, Robert A., and Leslie E. Eisenberg. *Indian Mounds of Wisconsin*. Madison: University of Wisconsin Press, 2000.

Birney, Hoffman. "To the Foot of the Rainbow." In Babbitt, *Rainbow Trails*, 79–90.

Blea, Irene Isabel. *Researching Chicano Communities: Social-Historical, Physical, Psychological, and Spiritual Space*. Westport: Praeger, 1995.

Bloomberg, Michael, and Carl Pope. *Climate of Hope.* New York: St. Martin's Press, 2017.

The Blue Book: A Comprehensive Official Souvenir View Book of the Panama-Pacific International Exposition at San Francisco, 1915. San Francisco: R. A. Reid, 1915.

Boime, Albert. *The Magisterial Gaze: Manifest Destiny and American Landscape Painting, 1830–1865.* Washington, DC: Smithsonian Institution Press, 1991.

Bonham, Charton H. "Devils Tower, Rainbow Bridge, and the Uphill Battle Facing Native American Religion on Public Lands." *Law and Inequality* 20 (Summer 2002): 157–202.

Bossen, Howard. "A Tall Tale Retold: The Influence of the Photographs of William Henry Jackson on the Passage of the Yellowstone Park Act of 1872." *Studies in Visual Communication* 8, no. 1 (Winter 1982): 98–109.

Botton, Alain de. *The Art of Travel.* London: Penguin Books, 2004.

Brady, Joel. "Land Is Itself a Sacred, Living Being": Native American Sacred Site Protection on Federal Public Lands amidst the Shows of Bear Lodge." *American Indian Law Review* 24, no. 1 (1999–2000): 153–186.

Bray, Mayfield, ed. *Guide to the Ford Film Collection in the National Archives.* Washington, DC: The National Archives, 1970.

Brown, Kate. *Plutopia: Nuclear Families, Atomic Cities, and the Great Soviet and American Plutonium Disasters.* New York: Oxford University Press, 2013.

Brugge, Doug, Timothy Benally, and Ester Yazzie-Lewis. *The Navajo People and Uranium Mining.* Albuquerque: University of New Mexico Press, 2006.

Brumble, H. David. "Vine Deloria, Jr., Creationism, and Ethnic Pseudoscience." *Reports of the National Center for Science Education* 18, no. 6 (1998): 10–14. https://ncse.com/library-resource/vine-deloria-jr-creationism-ethnic-pseudoscience.

Bryan, Ford R. *Rouge: Pictured in Its Prime.* Detroit: Wayne State University Press, 2003.

Bryant, Keith L. *History of the Atchison, Topeka, and Santa Fe.* New York: Macmillan, 1974.

Bryant, William Cullen. *Picturesque America; or the Land We Live In.* New York: Appleton & Co. 1872.

Bryce, James. *The American Commonwealth.* New York: Macmillan, 1919.

Bryne, John, and Steven M. Hoffman. "A 'Necessary Sacrifice'; Industrialization and American Indian Lands." In *Environmental Justice: Discourses in Political Economy,* vol. 8, Energy and Environmental Policy series, edited by John Bryne, Leigh Glover, and Cecilia Martinez, 97–118. New Brunswick: Transaction Publishers, 2002.

Bsumek, Erika. "Imagining Indians and Revisiting Reclamation Debates." *RCC Perspectives No. 1*. Eco-Images: Historical Views and Political Strategies. Munich University, Rachel Carson Center, 2013, 27–42.

Buell, Lawrence. *The Environmental Imagination: Thoreau, Nature Writing, and the Formation of American Culture*. Cambridge, MA: Harvard University Press, 1995.

Buell, Lawrence. *Writing for an Endangered World*. Cambridge, MA: Harvard University Press, 2000.

Bullard, Robert D., Paul Mohai, Robin Saha, and Beverly Wright. *Toxic Wastes and Race*. New York: United Church of Christ, Commission for Racial Justice, 1987.

Bureau of Land Management. *Grand Staircase-Escalante National Monument: Approved Management Plan*. Washington, DC: U.S. Department of the Interior, 2000.

Bureau of Land Management. "Imperial Project Draft Environmental Impact Statement." https://archive.org/stream/imperialprojecti01unse/imperialprojecti01unse_djvu.txt.

Burritt, Elihu. "The Ambitious Youth: A Tale of the Natural Bridge." *The Connecticut Common School Journal and Annals of Education* 3 (11), no. 3 (March 1856): 73–76.

Burton, Clarence Monroe. *History of Wayne County and the City of Detroit*. Chicago: S. J. Clarke Publishing Company, 1930.

Bush, George W. "Remarks Prior to Discussions with Chancellor Gerhard Schroeder of Germany and an Exchange with Reporters," March 29, 2001. http://www.presidency.ucsb.edu/ws/index.php?pid=45658&st=Bush&st1=global+warming.

Calloway, Colin G. *One Vast Winter Count: The Native American West before Lewis and Clark*. Lincoln: University of Nebraska Press, 2003.

Calvin, William. *Global Fever*. Chicago: University of Chicago Press, 2008.

Campbell, Neil. "Critical Regionalism, Thirdspace, and John Brinckerhoff Jackson's Western Cultural Landscapes." In *Postwestern Cultures: Literature, Theory Space*, edited by Susan Kollin, 59–81. Lincoln: University of Nebraska Press, 2007.

Carson, Rachel. *Silent Spring*. Boston: Houghton Mifflin, 1962.

Carter, Jimmy. "Proclamation 4729—William O. Douglas Arctic Wildlife Range, February 29, 1980." http://www.presidency.ucsb.edu/ws/index.php?pid=33001&st=wilderness&st1=Carter.

Carter, Jimmy. "Remarks in a Panel Discussion and Question-and-Answer Session on Energy, Charleston, West Virginia, March 17, 1977." http://www.presidency.ucsb.edu/ws/index.php?pid=7182&st=wilderness&st1=Carter.

Casey, Robert. *The Model T: A Centennial History*. Baltimore: Johns Hopkins University Press, 2003.

Cather, Willa. *Death Comes for the Archbishop*. New York: Alfred A. Knopf, 1927.

Catlin, George B. *The Story of Detroit*. Detroit: The Detroit News, 1923.

Caufield, Catherine. *Multiple Exposures: Chronicles of the Radiation Age*. Chicago: University of Chicago Press, 1989.

Certeau, Michel de. *The Practice of Everyday Life*. Berkeley: University of California Press, 1984.

Chandler, Alfred D. *Scale and Scope*. Harvard University Press, 1990.

Chase, Alston. *Playing God in Yellowstone: The Destruction of America's First National Park*. New York: Harcourt Brace, 1986.

Chastellux, Marquis de. *Voyages de M. le Marquis de Chastellux dans l'Amérique Septentrionale: dans les Années 1780, 1781 and 1782*. Vol. 2 of 2 vols. Paris: Chez Prault, 1786.

Chavez, John R. *The Lost Land: The Chicano Image of the Southwest*. Albuquerque: University of New Mexico Press, 1984.

Clemens, Paul. *Punching Out: One Year in a Closing Auto Plant*. New York: Doubleday, 2011.

Clements, John M., Aaron M. McCright, and Chenyang Xiao. "Green Christians? An Empirical Examination of Environmental Concern within the U.S. General Public." *Organization & Environment* 27, no. 1: 85–102.

Clifton, Eli. "Who Else Is in the Koch Brothers Billionaire Donor Club?" *The Nation*, November 3, 2014.

Clinton, William J. "Establishment of the Grand Staircase-Escalante National Monument," September 18, 1996, https://clintonwhitehouse6.archives.gov/1996/09/1996-09-18-proclamation-of-grand-staircase-national-monument.html.

Clinton, William J. "Remarks Announcing the Establishment of the Grand Staircase-Escalante National Monument at Grand Canyon National Park, Arizona," September 18, 1996.

Clinton, William J. "Remarks at the Labor Unification Legislative Conference," February 21, 1999. https://www.govinfo.gov/content/pkg/WCPD-1999-03-01/pdf/WCPD-1999-03-01-Pg268.pdf.

Coburn, Alvin Langdon, *An Autobiography*. New York: Dover, 1978.

Cole, Thomas. "Essay on American Scenery." *American Monthly Magazine* 1 (1836): 1–12.

Colten, Craig E., and Peter N. Skinners. *The Road to Love Canal*. Austin: University of Texas Press, 1996.

Comer, Krista. *Landscapes of the New West*. Chapel Hill: University of North Carolina Press, 1999.

Committee on Resources, House of Representatives. "Joint Hearing on the Sierra Club's Proposal to Drain Lake Powell or Reduce Its Water Storage Capability," 105th Congress, September 24, 1997. Washington, DC: U.S. Government Printing Office, 1998.

Conot, Robert. *American Odyssey*. New York: William Morrow, 1974.

Cooper, James Fenimore. "American and European Scenery Compared." In *Lotos-Eating: A Summer Book*, edited by George W. Curtis, 137–143. New York: Harper & Brothers, 1852.

Corner, James, and Alex S. MacLean. *Taking Measures Across the American Landscape*. New Haven: Yale University Press, 1996.

Corwin, Sharon. "Picturing Efficiency: Precisionism, Scientific Management, and the Effacement of Labor." *Representations* 84 (Autumn 2003): 139–165.

Cosgrove, Denis. "The Measures of America." In Corner and MacLean, *Taking Measures*, 3–14.

Cronon, William, ed. "The Trouble with Wilderness; or Getting Back to the Wrong Nature." In *Uncommon Ground: Rethinking the Human Place in Nature*, 69–90. New York: W. W. Norton, 1995.

"Crunch Time at the Grand Canyon." *Time Magazine*, July 3, 1995.

Crutzen, Paul, and Eugene Stoermer. "The 'Anthropocene.'" *IGBP Newsletter* 41 (May 2000): 17–18.

Danto, Arthur. *Mark Tansey*. New York: Harry N. Abrams, 1992.

Davenport, Coral, and Eric Lipton. "How G.O.P. Leaders Came to View Climate Change as Fake Science," *New York Times*, June 3, 2017.

Davis, Aaron. "Feds Give Pantex Contractor 'Scathing Review.'" *Amarillo Globe-News*, May 17, 2016.

Davis, Curtis Carroll. "The First Climber of the Natural Bridge: A Minor American Epic." *The Journal of Southern History* 16, no. 3 (August 1950): 277–290.

Dawdy, Doris Ostrander. *George Montague Wheeler: The Man and the Myth*. Athens: Swallow Press/Ohio University Press, 1993.

Dawson, Andrew. "Reassessing Henry Carey (1793–1879): The Problem of Writing Political Economy in Nineteenth Century America." *Journal of American Studies* 34 (December 2000): 465–485.

Dedek, Peter. *Hip to the Trip: A Cultural History of Route 66*. Albuquerque: University of New Mexico Press, 2007.

DeLillo, Don. *Underworld*. London: Picador, 1997.

Dellenbaugh, Frederick S. *A Canyon Voyage: The Narrative of the Second Powell Expedition*. Tucson: University of Arizona Press, [1908] 1991.

Deloria, Philip. *Playing Indian*. New Haven: Yale University Press, 1998.

Deloria, Vine. *Red Earth, White Lies: Native Americans and the Myth of Scientific Fact*. New York: Scribner, 1995.

DePalma, Anthony, with David Staba. "Love Canal Declared Clean, Ending Toxic Horror." *New York Times*, March 18, 2004.

Diep, Francie. "Abandoned Uranium Mines: An 'Overwhelming Problem' in the Navajo Nation." *Scientific American*, December 30, 2010.

Dillingham, Brint. "Exxon, Uranium, and the Navajo Nation." *American Indian Journal* 3, no. 4 (April 1977): 27.

Dolan, Robert, Alan Howard, and Arthur Gallenson. "Man's Impact on the Colorado River in the Grand Canyon." *American Scientist* 62, no. 4 (July–August 1974): 392–401.

Domosh, Mona. "The Symbolism of the Skyscraper: Case Studies of New York's First Tall Buildings." *Journal of Urban History* 14 (May 1988): 320–345.

Dow, Charles Mason. *Anthology and Bibliography of Niagara Falls*, 2 vols. Albany: State of New York, 1921.

Downing, Andrew Jackson. *The Architecture of Country Houses*. New York: Dover, 1969.

Draper, Robert. *Dead Certain: The Presidency of George W. Bush*. New York: Free Press, 2007.

Dunaway, Finis. *Natural Visions: The Power of Images in American Environmental Reform*. Chicago: University of Chicago Press, 2005.

Dutton, Clarence E. *Tertiary History of the Grand Cañon District*. Salt Lake City: Peregrine Smith Books, [1882] 1977.

Ed Keheley and Associates, Inc. "History of the Picher Mining Field." 40th Annual Meeting, the Geological Society of America, South Central Section, March 6–7, 2006.

Eichstaedt, Peter H. *If You Poison Us*. Santa Fe, NM: Red Crane Books, 1994.

Eiseley, Loren. *The Star Thrower*. New York: Times Books, 1978.

Eliade, Mircea. *The Sacred and the Profane: The Nature of Religion*. New York: Harcourt and Brace, 1959.

Emmett, Robert S., and David E. Nye. *The Environmental Humanities: A Critical Introduction*. Cambridge, MA: MIT Press, 2017.

Erdrich, Heid E. "The Theft Outright." In Keeler, *Edge of Morning*, 115–117.

Erdrich, Louise. *Books and Islands in Ojibwe Country*. New York: Harper Perennial, 2003.

Erdrich, Louise. *Tracks*. New York: Harper and Row, 1988.

Evans, Eric. "The Utah Group Just Proved That Net Zero Energy Buildings Don't Have to Be More Expensive." *Deseret News*, June 13, 2018.

Excerpts from the *Annual Report of the Secretary of the Interior for the Fiscal Year Ended June 30, 1915, Relative to the National Parks and Monuments*. National Park Service. *Hearing before the Committee on the Public Lands, House of Representatives*, 64th Congress, 1st Session, on H.R. 434 and H.R. 8668, bills to establish a National Park Service and for other purposes. April 5 and 6, 1916.

Farmer, Jared. *Glen Canyon Dammed: Inventing Lake Powell and the Canyon Country*. Tucson: University of Arizona Press, 1999.

Ferry, W. Hawkins. *The Legacy of Albert Kahn*. Detroit: Wayne State University Press, 1989.

Findlay, John M., and Bruce Hevly. *Atomic Frontier Days: Hanford and the American West*. Seattle: University of Washington Press, 2011.

Fitch, James Marston, and William Bobenhausen. *American Building: The Environmental Forces That Shape It*. New York: Oxford University Press, 1999.

Ford, Henry A. "The Old Moravian Mission." In *Historical Collections: Collections and Researches Made by the Michigan Pioneer and Historical Society*, vol. 10, edited by Henry Fralick, 107–114. Lansing, MI: State Printers, 1908.

Ford, Henry, with Samuel Crowther. *My Life and Work*. London: Heinemann, 1922.

Fowler, Don D., ed. *"Photographed All the Best Scenery": Jack Hillers's Diary of the Powell Expeditions, 1871–1875*. Salt Lake City: University of Utah Press, 1972.

Fradkin, Philip L. *A River No More: The Colorado River and the West*. Tucson: University of Arizona, 1984.

Fradkin, Philip L. *Wanderings of an Environmental Journalist*. Albuquerque: University of New Mexico Press, 1993.

Funk, Cary, and Brian Kennedy. "The Politics of Climate," Pew Research Center, October 4, 2016. https://www.pewresearch.org/internet/wp-content/uploads/sites/9/2016/10/PS_2016.10.04_Politics-of-Climate_FINAL.pdf.

Gahan, Andrew H. and William D. Rowley. "Artists and Representations of Reclamation." In United States Department of the Interior, *Reclamation: Managing Water in the West, 1945–2000*, vol. 2, 952–967. Washington, DC: Bureau of Reclamation, 2012.

Gallagher, Carole. *American Ground Zero: The Secret Nuclear War*. Cambridge, MA: MIT Press, 1993.

Gidley, Mick. *Edward S. Curtis and the North American Indian, Incorporated*. Cambridge: Cambridge University Press, 2000.

Gilkey, Charles W. "The Spiritual Uplift of Scenery as Exemplified by the Grand Canyon." In *Proceedings of the National Parks Conference*, 138–140. Washington, DC: U.S. Government Printing Office, 1917.

Gilmer, Francis William. "On the Geological Formation of the Natural Bridge of Virginia." *Transactions of the American Philosophical Society* 1 (1818): 187–192.

Gingrich, Newt. *Winning the Future: The 21st Century Contract with America*. Washington, DC: Regency Publishing, 2005.

Girouard, Mark. *Cities and People: A Social and Architectural History*. New Haven: Yale University Press, 1985.

Gleed, Chas. S., ed. *From River to Sea: A Tourists' and Miners' Guide from the Missouri River to the Pacific Ocean*. Chicago: Rand, McNally, 1882.

Goetzmann, William H. Foreword to *A Canyon Voyage: The Narrative of the Second Powell Expedition down the Green-Colorado River from Wyoming, and the Explorations on Land, in the Years 1871 and 1872*, by Frederick S. Dellenbaugh, xv–xxvi. New Haven: Yale University Press, [1908] 1962.

Goetzmann, William H. *New Lands, New Men: America and the Second Great Age of Discovery*. New York: Viking, 1986.

Goin, Peter, and Peter Friederici. *A New Form of Beauty*. Tucson: University of Arizona Press, 2016.

Goldberger, Paul. *The Skyscraper*. New York: Alfred A. Knopf, 1981.

Graham, Stephen. *With Poor Immigrants to America*. New York: Macmillan, 1914.

Gray, Wayland. "Sacred Is Sacred." In Keeler, *Edge of Morning*, 153–158.

"Great Ford Plant is Cross-Section of Industrial Might of Rearming America." *Life*, August 19, 1940, 37–48.

Grey, Zane. *Riders of the Purple Sage*. New York: Harper & Brothers, 1912.

Grimm, Lydia T. "Sacred Lands and the Establishment Clause: Indian Religious Practices on Federal Lands." *Natural Resources & Environment* 12 (1997): 19–24.

Grinde, Donald, and Bruce Johansen. "The Navajos and National Sacrifice." In Meléndez et al., *Multicultural Southwest*, 204–217.

Grinde, Donald, and Bruce Johansen. *Ecocide of Native America: Environmental Destruction of Indian Lands and People*. Santa Fe: Clear Light Publishers, 1995.

Gulkeson, John S. *Anthropologists and the Rediscovery of America, 1886–1965*. Cambridge: Cambridge University Press, 2010.

Hales, Peter Bacon. "American Views and the Romance of Modernization." In *Photography in Nineteenth-Century America*, edited by Martha A. Sandweiss, 204–257. New York: Abrams, 1991.

Hall, Edgar H. *The Hudson Fulton Celebration, 1909.* Vol. 1. Albany: State of New York, 1910.

Halliday, William R. "Protection of Rainbow Bridge." *Science* 133, no. 3464 (May 19, 1961): 1572–1583.

Hance, Captain John, ed. *Personal Impressions of the Grand Canyon of the Colorado River.* San Francisco: Whitaker and Ray, 1899.

Harrison, Scott. "How a 1930s Water War between California and Arizona Delayed Parker Dam." *Los Angeles Times*, August 30, 2015.

Hartmann, Sadakichi. *The Valiant Knights of Daguerre.* Berkeley: University of California Press, 1978.

Harvey, David. *The Condition of Postmodernity.* Oxford: Blackwell, 1989.

Harvey, Mark W. T. *A Symbol of Wilderness: Echo Park and the American Conservation Movement.* Albuquerque: University of New Mexico Press, 1994.

Hassell, Hank. *Rainbow Bridge.* Boulder: University Press of Colorado, 1999.

Hauptman, William. *Storm Season.* Austin: University of Texas Press, 2000.

Henderson, Norman. "Wilderness and the Nature Conservation Ideal: Britain, Canada, and the United States Contrasted." *Ambio* 21, no. 6 (September 1992): 394–399.

Henry, O. "Psyche and the Pskyscraper." *New York World Sunday Magazine*, January 15, 1905.

Higgins, Charles A. *Grand Cañon of the Colorado River, Arizona.* With original illustrations by Thomas Moran, H. F. Farny, and F. H. Lungren. Chicago: Passenger Department, Santa Fe Railroad, 1893.

Higgins, Charles A. *The Grand Canyon of Arizona; Being a Book of Words from Many Pens, about the Grand Canyon of the Colorado River in Arizona.* Chicago: Passenger Department, Santa Fe Railroad, 1902.

Higgins, Charles A. *Grand Canyon Outings.* Chicago: Atchison, Topeka, and Santa Fe Railroad Company, 1922.

Holson, Laura. "Power, Politics and Glory Dimmed; Pacific Gas and Electric Finds No Sympathy Among Customers or Once-Docile State Legislature." *New York Times*, February 22, 2001.

Hora, Elizabeth, and Christopher Merritt. "Utah Lake Rock Imagery: An Intersection of Public Lands, Recreational Shooting, and Cultural Resources." *Utah Historical Quarterly* 88, no. 2 (Spring 2020): 121–128.

Hough, Emerson. *The Way to the West, and the Lives of Three Early Americans, Boone, Crockett, Carson.* New York: Grosset & Dunlap, 1903.

Howell, Jordan P. "Powering 'Progress': Regulation and the Development of Michigan's Electricity Landscape." *Annals of the Association of American Geographers* 101, no. 4, Geographies of Energy (July 2011): 962–970.

Hubbard, Bela. *Memorials of Half a Century.* New York: G. P. Putnam's, 1887.

Hughes, J. Donald. *In the House of Stone and Light: A Human History of the Grand Canyon.* Flagstaff, AZ: Grand Canyon Natural History Association, 1978.

Hughes, J. Donald, and Jim Swan. "How Much of the Earth Is Sacred Space?" *Environmental Review* 10, no. 4 (1986): 247–259.

Hughes, Thomas P. *American Genesis: A Century of Invention and Technological Enthusiasm.* Harmondsworth: Penguin Books, 1989.

Hughes, Thomas P. *Networks of Power: Electrification in Western Society, 1880–1930.* Baltimore: Johns Hopkins University Press, 1983.

Hunter, Louis C., and Lynwood Bryant. *A History of Industrial Power in the United States, 1780–1930.* Cambridge, MA: MIT Press, 1991.

Huth, Hans. *Nature and the American.* 2nd edition. Lincoln: University of Nebraska Press, 1990.

Hyde, Anne Farrar. *An American Vision: Far Western Landscape and National Culture, 1820–1920.* New York: New York University Press, 1990.

Ialenti, Vincent. "Waste Makes Haste: How a Campaign to Speed Up Nuclear Waste Shipments Shut Down the WIPP Long-Term Repository." *Bulletin of the Atomic Scientists* 74, no. 4 (June 2018): 262–275.

Ives, Joseph C. *Report upon the Colorado River of the West: Explored in 1857 and 1858.* Washington, DC: U.S. Government Printing Office, 1859.

Jackson, J. B. *Discovering the Vernacular Landscape.* New Haven: Yale University Press, 1984.

Jackson, J. B. "Goodbye to Evolution." In Yates, *Essential Landscape*, 58–63.

Jackson, Kenneth. *The Crabgrass Frontier.* New York: Oxford University Press, 1985.

James, George Wharton. *The Grand Canyon of Arizona; How to See It.* Boston: Little, Brown, and Company, 1910.

James, Henry. *The American Scene.* London: Chapman and Hall, 1907.

Janssen, Raymond E. "Nature's Bridges." *The Scientific Monthly* 57, no. 3 (1943): 210–219.

Japan Forum, *Environmental History* 17, no. 2 (April 2012): 217–300.

Johansen, Bruce E. *Resource Exploitation in Native North America: A Plague upon the Peoples.* Santa Barbara, CA: Praeger, 2016.

Johns, Orrick. "The Excelsior of Architecture." *New York Times Magazine*, July 20, 1924.

Johnson, Clifton. *Highways and Byways of the South*. New York: Macmillan, 1904.

Johnston, Barbara Rose, Susan E. Dawson, and Gary E. Madsen. "Uranium Mining and Milling: Navajo Experiences in the American Southwest." In *The Energy Reader*, edited by Laura Nader, 132–146. Oxford: Wiley-Blackwell, 2010.

Jolas, Eugene. "The Industrial Mythos." *transition* 12 (November 1929).

Jussim, Estelle, and Elizabeth Lindquist-Cock. *Landscape as Photograph*. New Haven: Yale University Press, 1985.

Karpius, Peter Joseph. *Uranium Mining and Milling*. Los Alamos National Laboratory, February 2, 2017. http://permalink.lanl.gov/object/tr?what=info:lanl-repo/lareport/LA-UR-17-20809.

Kasdan, Lawrence. *Grand Canyon*, Twentieth Century Fox, 1991. Major roles: Danny Glover, Kevin Kline, Steve Martin, Mary McDonnell, Mary-Louise Parker, and Alfre Woodard.

Katzer, Bruce. "The Caughnawaga Mohawks: The Other Side of Ironwork." *Journal of Ethnic Studies* (Winter 1988): 39–55.

Kaufmann, Robert F., Gregory G. Eadie, and Charles R. Russell. "Effects of Uranium Mining and Milling on Ground Water in the Grants Mineral Belt, New Mexico." *Groundwater* 14, no. 5 (September 1976): 296–308.

Keeler, Jacqueline, ed. *The Edge of Morning: Native Voices Speak for the Bears Ears*. Salt Lake City: Torrey House Press, 2017.

Kelley, Klara Bonsack, and Harris Francis. *Navajo Sacred Places*. Bloomington: Indiana University Press, 1994.

Kelly, Robert L., and Mary Prasciunas. "Did the Ancestors of Native Americans Cause Animal Extinctions in Late-Pleistocene North America?" In *Native Americans and the Environment*, edited by Michael E. Harkin and David Rich Lewis, 95–122. Lincoln: University of Nebraska Press, 2007.

King, Clarence. *Mining Industry*. Washington, DC: U.S. Government Printing Office, 1870.

Kinkead, Dan. "Detroit's Emerging Innovation in Urban Infrastructure: How Liabilities Become Assets for Energy, Water, Industry, and Informatics." In *Why Detroit Matters*, edited by Brian Doucet, 195–207. Bristol: Bristol University Press, 2017.

Kinsey, Joni Louise. *Thomas Moran and the Surveying of the American West*. Washington, DC: Smithsonian Institution Press, 1992.

Kirk, Andrew G. *Doom Towns: The People and Landscapes of Atomic Testing*. New York: Oxford University Press, 2017.

Klein, Kerwin L. "Tourism, Consumerism, and the Southwestern Public Lands, 1890–1990, *Pacific Historical Review* 62, no. 1 (February 1993): 39–71.

Kluckhohn, Florence, and Fred Strodtbeck. *Variations in Value Orientations*. Evanston, IL: Row, Peterson, 1961.

Kolb, Ellsworth Leonardson. *Through the Grand Canyon from Wyoming to Mexico*. Foreword by Owen Wister. New York: Macmillan, 1914.

Kouwenhoven, John. "What's American about America?" *Harper's Magazine*, July 1956.

Kreitler, Philip William. *Flatiron: A Photographic History of the World's First Steel Frame Skyscraper, 1901–1990*. Washington, DC: American Institute of Architects, 1990.

Krug, J. A. *Natural Resource Problems: Annual Report of the Secretary of the Interior, 1946*. Washington, DC: U.S. Government Printing Office, 1946.

Krutch, Joseph Wood. *The Desert Year*. New York: William Sloan Associates, 1952.

Krutch, Joseph Wood. *The Grand Canyon*. Tucson: University of Arizona Press, 1989.

LaDuke, Winona. *All Our Relations*. Chicago: Haymarket Books, 2015.

LaDuke, Winona. *Recovering the Sacred: The Power of Naming and Claiming*. Cambridge, MA: South End Press, 2005.

Lane, Belden C. *Landscapes of the Sacred: Geography and Narrative in American Spirituality*. Baltimore: Johns Hopkins University Press, 2002.

Lane, Christopher W. *Impressions of Niagara: The Charles Rand Penney Collection of Prints of Niagara Falls*. Philadelphia: The Philadelphia Print Shop, Ltd., 1993.

Larson, Gary. "The Far Side." *International Herald Tribune*, October 19, 1995.

Lavender, David. *Colorado River Country*. New York: E. P. Dutton, 1982.

LeCain, Timothy. *Mass Destruction: The Men and Giant Mines That Wired America and Scarred the Planet*. New Brunswick: Rutgers University Press, 2009.

Lewis, David. *The Public Image of Henry Ford*. Detroit: Wayne State University Press, 1976.

Lewis, Robert. "Redesigning the Workplace: The North American Factory in the Interwar Period." *Technology and Culture* 42, no. 4 (October 2001): 665–684.

Lewis, Sinclair. *Arrowsmith*. New York: Harcourt, Brace and World, 1952.

Light, Jennifer S. *The Nature of Cities: Ecological Visions and the American Urban Professions, 1920–1960*. Baltimore: Johns Hopkins University Press, 2009.

Lindholdt, Paul. "From Sublimity to Ecopornography: Assessing the Bureau of Reclamation Art Collection." *Journal of Ecocriticism* 1, no. 1 (January 2009): 1–25.

Lindholdt, Paul. "The Inflatable Museum." *Southern Review* 53, no. 2 (Spring 2017): 319–331.

Littmann, William. "The Production of Goodwill: The Origins and Development of the Factory Tour in America." *Perspectives in Vernacular Architecture* 9 (2003): 71–84.

Lochhead, Carolyn. "How GOP Became Party of Denial on Global Warming," *San Francisco Chronicle*, April 28, 2013.

Lowenthal, David. *George Perkins Marsh: Prophet of Conservation*. Seattle: University of Washington Press, 2000.

Lucic, Karen. *Charles Sheeler and the Cult of the Machine*. London: Reaktion Books, 1991.

Lustgarten, Abraham. "Unplugging the Colorado River." *New York Times*, May 20, 2016.

Maass, Arthur. *Muddy Waters: The Army Engineers and the Nation's Rivers*. New York: Da Capo Press, 1974.

Macready, John A. "Non-Stop Flight across America." *National Geographic Magazine* 46 (July 1924): 62–68.

Madigan, Nick. "Tribe Prepares for Renewed Fight Over Gold Mine." *New York Times*, September 15, 2002.

Marchand, Roland. *Advertising the American Dream*. Berkeley: University of California Press, 1985.

Marsh, George Perkins. *Man and Nature*. Edited by David Lowenthal. Seattle: University of Washington Press, [1864] 2003.

Martin, Calvin Luther. *The Way of the Human Being*. New Haven: Yale University Press, 1999.

Martinez, Cecilia, and John Poupart. "The Circle of Life: Preserving American Indian Traditions and Facing the Nuclear Challenge." In *Environmental Justice: Discourses in Political Economy*, vol. 8, Energy and Environmental Policy series, edited by John Bryne, Leigh Glover, and Cecilia Martinez, 119–146. New Brunswick: Transaction Publishers, 2002.

Marx, Leo. "The American Ideology of Space." In *Denatured Visions: Landscape and Culture in the Twentieth Century*, 62–78. New York: Museum of Modern Art, 1991.

Marx, Leo. *The Machine in the Garden*. New York: Oxford University Press, 1965.

Marx, Leo. "Open Spaces, City Places, and Contrasting Versions of the American Myth." In *Open Spaces, City Places: Contemporary Writers on the Changing Southwest*, edited by Judy Nolte Temple, 31–40. Tucson: University of Arizona Press, 1994.

Massey, Doreen. *For Space*. Thousand Oaks, CA: Sage, 2005.

Masteller, Richard N. "Western Views in Eastern Parlors: The Contribution of the Stereograph Photographer to the Conquest of the West." *Prospects* 6: 55–71.

McCarthy, Tom. "Henry Ford, Industrial Ecologist or Industrial Conservationist? Waste Reduction and Recycling at the Rouge." *Michigan Historical Review* 27, no. 2 (Fall 2001): 52–88.

McCraw, Thomas K. *Prophet of Innovation: Joseph Schumpeter and Creative Destruction*. Cambridge, MA: Harvard University Press, 2007.

McDonald, Robert I. *Conservation for Cities*. Washington, DC: Island Press, 2015.

McDonough, William, and Michael Braungart. *Cradle to Cradle*. New York: North Point Press, 2002.

McFarland, J. Horace. "Address." In *Proceedings of a Conference of Governors*, 153–156. Washington, DC: U.S. Government Printing Office, 1909.

McGreevy, Patrick V. *Imagining Niagara: The Meaning and Making of Niagara Falls*. Amherst: University of Massachusetts Press, 1994.

McKay, Claude. "Song of New York." *The New Masses* 1 (May 1926): 15.

McKinsey, Elizabeth. *Niagara Falls: Icon of the American Sublime*. Cambridge: Cambridge University Press, 1985.

McNeill, J. R. *Something New Under the Sun: An Environmental History of the Twentieth-Century World*. New York: W. W. Norton, 2000.

McPhee, John. *Encounters with the Archdruid*. New York: Farrar, Straus and Giroux, 1971.

Meinig, D. W. *Continental America, 1800–1867*. Vol. 2. New Haven: Yale University Press, 1993.

Meinig, D. W. *Southwest: Three Peoples in Geographical Change*. New York: Oxford University Press, 1971.

Meinig, D. W. "The Southwest, a Definition." In Meléndez et al., *Multicultural Southwest*, 3–6.

Meléndez, A. Gabriel, et al., eds. *The Multicultural Southwest: A Reader*. Tucson: University of Arizona Press, 2001.

Melnick, Robert. "Climate Change and Landscape Preservation." *APT Bulletin: The Journal of Preservation Technology* 40, no. 3/4 (2009): 35–42.

Melosi, Martin. *Atomic Age America*. New York: Pearson Education, 2013.

Melville, Herman. *Moby Dick*. New York: Modern Library, 1950.

Michael, Wendy Lynnette. "Labor on Display: Ford Factory Tours and the Romance of Globalized Deindustrialization." Dissertation. University of Michigan, 2014.

Michigan Department of Environmental Quality. *River Rouge Remedial Action Plan, Annual Report*. Lansing, Michigan, 1992.

Michigan Writers Project. *Michigan: A Guide to the Wolverine State*. Washington, DC: Federal Writers Project Administration, 1941.

Miller, Charles A. *Jefferson and Nature: An Interpretation*. Baltimore: Johns Hopkins University Press, 1988.

Miller, Logan. *Reminiscences* [typescript]. Owen Bombard Oral History Collection, The Henry Ford.

Miller, Shawn William. *An Environmental History of Latin America*. Cambridge: Cambridge University Press, 2007.

Misa, Thomas J. *Leonardo to the Internet: Technology and Culture from the Renaissance to the Present*. 2nd edition. Baltimore: Johns Hopkins University Press, 2011.

Misa, Thomas J. *A Nation of Steel*. Baltimore: Johns Hopkins University Press, 1995.

Mitchell, Joseph. "The Mohawks in High Steel." *New Yorker*, September 17, 1949, 38–41.

Montgomery, David R. "The Evolution of Creationism." *GSA Today* 22, no. 11 (2012): 4–8.

Moran, Thomas. "American Art and American Scenery." In Higgins, *Grand Canyon of Arizona*, 85–87.

Muir, John. "The Grand Canyon." In *The Grand Canyon: Early Impressions*, edited by Paul Schullery, 77–81. Boulder: Colorado Associated University Press, 1981.

Muir, John. *Steep Trails*. San Francisco: Sierra Club Books, 1994.

Muller, Edward, and Joel Tarr. "The Interaction of Natural and Built Environments in the Pittsburgh Landscape." In *Devastation and Renewal*, edited by J. Tarr, 11–40. Pittsburgh: University of Pittsburgh Press, 2004.

Munger, Thomas. *Detroit Today*. Detroit: Detroit Board of Commerce, 1921.

Murphy, Thomas Dowler. *Three wonderlands of the American West: being the notes of a traveler, concerning the Yellowstone Park, the Yosemite National Park, and the Grand Canyon of the Colorado River, with a chapter on the other wonders of the Great American West*. Boston: L. C. Page & Co., 1912.

Nabokov, Peter. *Where the Lightning Strikes: The Lives of American Indian Sacred Places*. New York: Penguin, 2006.

Nagourney, Adam. "Where 2 Rivers Meet, Visions for Grand Canyon Clash." *New York Times*, December 3, 2014.

Nash, Roderick. *Wilderness and the American Mind*. 3rd edition. New Haven: Yale University Press, 1982.

Nash, Stephen, *Grand Canyon for Sale: Public Lands versus Private Interests in the Era of Climate Change*. Berkeley: University of California Press, 2017.

The Nation. "A Near Miss Nuclear Explosion." *The Nation*, December 18, 2006.

National Academies of Sciences, Engineering, and Medicine. *Review of the Department of Energy's Plans for Disposal of Surplus Plutonium in the Waste Isolation Pilot Plant*. Washington, DC: The National Academies Press. https://doi.org/10.17226/25593.

"National Parks." *Time Magazine*, July 25, 1994.

Native American Sacred Places: Hearing before the Committee on Indian Affairs, United States Senate, 107th Congress, 2nd Session, July 17, 2002, part 2.

Naughton, K. "Growing a Green Plant." *Newsweek*, November 13, 2000, 58–60.

Neihardt, John, ed. *Black Elk Speaks*. Lincoln: University of Nebraska Press, 2014.

Nevins, Alan. *Expansion and Challenge*. New York: Scribner, 1957.

Newell, Frederick Haynes. *Irrigation in the United States*. New York: Thomas Y. Crowell & Co, 1902.

Newman, Richard S. *Love Canal: A Toxic History, from Colonial Times to the Present*. New York: Oxford University Press, 2016.

Nieves, Evelyn. "Our Towns. Love Canal: 'Houses Sell Themselves.'" *New York Times*, July 21, 1996.

Nixon, Richard. "Message to the Congress Proposing Establishment of New National Wilderness Areas," June 13, 1974.

Nixon, Rob. *Slow Violence and the Environmentalism of the Poor*. Cambridge, MA: Harvard University Press, 2011.

Nostrand, Richard L. *Los chicanos: geografia, historica regional*. Mexico City: Sep-Setentas, 1976.

Novak, Barbara. *Nature and Culture: American Landscape and Painting, 1825–1875*. New York: Oxford University Press, 1980.

Numbers, Ronald L. *The Creationists: The Evolution of Scientific Creationism*. Berkeley: University of California Press, 1992.

Nye, David E. *America as Second Creation: Technology and Narratives of New Beginnings*. Cambridge, MA: MIT Press, 2003.

Nye, David E. *America's Assembly Line*. Cambridge, MA: MIT Press, 2013.

Nye, David E. *American Technological Sublime*. Cambridge, MA: MIT Press, 1994.

Nye, David E. *Consuming Power: A Social History of American Energies*. Cambridge, MA: MIT Press, 1998.

Nye, David E. "Constructing Nature: Niagara Falls and the Grand Canyon." In *Narratives and Spaces: Technology and the Construction of American Culture*, 13–24. New York: Columbia University Press, 1998.

Nye, David E. "De-Realizing the Grand Canyon." In *Emotion and Postmodernism*, edited by Gerhard Hoffmann and Alfred Hornung, 75–94. Heidelberg: Universitätsverlag C. Winter, 1997.

Nye, David E. "Die Niagara-Falls, der Grand Canyon und das Erhabene," *Zeitschrift für Semiotik* 19, no. 1–2 (1997): 7–20.

Nye, David E. *Electrifying America: Social Meanings of a New Technology*. Cambridge, MA: MIT Press, 1990.

Nye, David E. *Henry Ford: Ignorant Idealist*. Port Washington, NY: Kennikat Press, 1979.

Nye, David E. *Narratives and Spaces: Technology and the Construction of American Culture*. New York: Columbia University Press, 1999.

Nye, David E. *American Illuminations: Urban Lighting, 1800–1920*. Cambridge, MA: MIT Press, 2018.

Nye, David E. "The United States and Alternative Energies since 1980: Technological Fix or Regime Change?" *Theory, Culture, and Society* 31, no. 5 (2014): 103–125.

Nye, Russel B. *Michigan*. New York: Coward McCann, 1966.

Oard, Michael J. "Many Arches and Natural Bridges Likely from the Flood." *Journal of Creation* 23, no. 1 (April 2009): 115–118.

O'Donoghue, Amy Joi. "A Bears Ears Primer." *Deseret News*, December 18, 2016.

Olson, Byron, and Joseph Cabadas. *The American Auto Factory*. St. Paul: MBI Publishing, 2002.

Oppenheim, James. *The Olympian*. New York: Harper & Brothers, 1912.

Owen, David. *Green Metropolis*. New York: Riverhead Books, 2009.

Padover, Saul K. ed. *The Complete Jefferson*. Freeport, NY: Books for Libraries Press, 1969.

"Panorama Viewed from 85th Story." *New York Times*, May 2, 1931.

Pasternak, Judy. "A Peril that Dwelt among the Navajos." *Los Angeles Times*, November 19, 2007.

Pasternak, Judy. *Yellow Dirt: An American Story of a Poisoned Land and a People Betrayed*. New York: Free Press, 2010.

Pearson, Byron E. "'We Have Almost Forgotten How to Hope': The Hualapai, the Navajo, and the Fight for the Central Arizona Project, 1944–1968." *Western Historical Quarterly* 31, no. 3 (Autumn 2000): 297–316.

Pierson, George Wilson. *Tocqueville in America*. Baltimore: Johns Hopkins University Press, 1996.

Pielke, Roger, Jr. *The Climate Fix*. New York: Basic Books, 2010.

Peña, Devon G. *Mexican Americans and the Environment*. Tucson: University of Arizona Press, 2005.

Peshlakai, Elsie. "Indians as Anti-Nuclearists." *American Indian Journal* 5, no. 5 (May 1979): 27.

Petr, Jerry L. "Creationism versus Evolutionism in Economics: Societal Consequences of Economic Doctrine." *Journal of Economic Issues* 17, no. 2 (June 1983): 475–483.

Petrick, Jane Ellen. *Hidden in Plain Sight: The Other People in Norman Rockwell's America*. Miami: Informed Decisions Publishing, 2013.

Pomeroy, Earl. *In Search of the Golden West: The Tourist in Western America*. Lincoln: The University of Nebraska Press, 1957.

Ponting, Clive. *A Green History of the World*. Hammersmith: Penguin Books, 1992.

Porter, Robert P. *The West: From the Census of 1880*. Chicago: Rand, McNally, 1882.

Powell, John Wesley. *Exploration of the Colorado River of the West and Its Tributaries: Explored in 1869, 1870, 1871, and 1872*. Washington, DC: Government Printing Office, 1875.

Powell, John Wesley. *The Exploration of the Colorado River and Its Canyons*. New York: Dover Publications, [1895] 1961.

Powell, John Wesley. *Report on the Lands of the Arid Region of the United States*. 2nd edition. Edited by Wallace Stegner. Cambridge, MA: Harvard University Press, [1879] 1962.

Powers, Richard. *The Overstory*. New York: W. W. Norton, 2018.

Prestowitz, Clyde. *Rouge Nation: American Unilateralism and the Failure of Good Intentions*. New York: Basic Books, 2003.

Price, V. B. *The Orphaned Land: New Mexico's Environment since the Manhattan Project*. Albuquerque: University of New Mexico Press, 2011.

Proulx, Annie. *Barkskins*. London: HarperCollins, 2016.

Pyne, Stephen J. *Dutton's Point: An Intellectual History of the Grand Canyon*. Grand Canyon Natural History Association, Monograph Number 5, 1982.

Pyne, Stephen J. *How the Canyon Became Grand*. New York: Viking, 1998.

Rasenberger, Jim. *High Steel: The Daring Men Who Built the World's Greatest Skyline*. New York: Harper Collins, 2004.

Rauchenbush, Carl. *Fordism, Ford and the Workers, Ford and the Community.* New York: League for Industrial Democracy, 1937.

Raymond D. Gastil, *Cultural Regions of the United States.* Seattle: University of Washington Press, 1975.

Reagan, Ronald. "Remarks on Signing Four Bills Designating Wilderness Areas," June 19, 1984. http://www.reagan.utexas.edu/resource/speeches/1984/61984d.htm.

Reisner, Marc. *Cadillac Desert: The American West and Its Disappearing Water.* New York: Penguin Books, 1987.

Rohwedder, Cecelie. "Green Goes Mainstream for New Homes." *Wall Street Journal*, May 2, 2013.

Rothman, Hal. *America's National Monuments.* Urbana: University of Illinois Press, 1989.

Rothman, Hal. *Devil's Bargains: Tourism in the Twentieth-Century American West Development of Western Resources.* Lawrence: University Press of Kansas, 1998.

Rothman, Hal. "Tourism as Colonial Economy: The Distribution of Economic Power and the Significance of Place in Western Tourism," Paper 26 in the Odense American Studies International Series (OASIS), University of Southern Denmark, February 1997.

Runte, Alfred. *National Parks: The American Experience.* 2nd edition. Lincoln: University of Nebraska, 1987.

Runte, Alfred. *Trains of Discovery: Western Railroads and the National Parks.* Flagstaff, AZ: Northland Press, 1984.

Rybczynski, Witold. *A Clearing in the Distance: Frederick Law Olmsted and America in the Nineteenth Century.* New York: Simon & Schuster, 1999.

Saltus, Edgar. "New York from the Flatiron." *Munsey's Magazine* 33 (July 1905): 382–383.

Samet, Jonathan M., Daniel M. Kutvirt, Richard J. Waxweiler, and Charles R. Key. "Uranium Mining and Lung Cancer in Navajo Men." *New England Journal of Medicine* 310 (June 7, 1984): 1481–1484.

Sandburg, Carl. *Poetry.* Chicago: H. Monroe, 1912.

Sanders, Scott Russell. *The Paradise of Bombs.* Athens: University of Georgia Press, 1987.

Sanford, Charles L. *The Quest for Paradise: Europe and the American Moral Imagination.* Urbana: University of Illinois Press, 1961.

Sayre, Gordon M. "The Oxymoron of American Pastoralism," *Arizona Quarterly* 69, no. 3 (Winter 2013): 1–23.

Schiller, Joyce K., and Heather Campbell Coyle, eds. *John Sloan's New York*. Wilmington: Delaware Art Museum, 2007.

Schleier, Merrill. *The Skyscraper in American Art, 1890–1931*. New York: Da Capo, 1986.

Schuyler, David. "The Sanctified Landscape: The Hudson River Valley, 1820–1850." In *Landscape in America*, edited by George F. Thompson, 93–109. Austin: University of Texas, 1995.

Schuyler, Montgomery. "The Sky-Line of New York, 1881–1897." *Harper's Weekly*, March 20, 1897.

Sears, John. *Sacred Places: American Tourist Attractions in the Nineteenth Century*. New York: Oxford University Press, 1989.

Senf, Rebecca A., and Stephen J. Pyne. *Reconstructing the View: The Grand Canyon Photography of Mark Klett and Byron Wolfe*. Berkeley: University of California Press, 2012.

Sheridan, Thomas E. *Arizona: A History*. Tucson: University of Arizona Press, 1995.

Scherzer, W. H. "Geological Report on Wayne County." *State of Michigan Geological and Biological Survey*. Publication 12. Geological Series 9. Lansing, MI: State Printers, 1913.

Silko, Leslie Marmon. *Gardens in the Dunes*. New York: Simon and Schuster, 1999.

"Sky Boys Who 'Rode the Ball' on Empire State." *Literary Digest*, May 23, 1931.

Slotkin, Richard. *Regeneration through Violence*. Middletown: Wesleyan University Press, 1973.

Smith, Dwight L., and C. Gregory Crampton, eds. *The Colorado River Survey: Robert B. Stanton and the Denver, Colorado Canyon & Pacific Railroad*. Salt Lake City: Howe Brothers, 1987.

Smith, George Otis. Director of the United States Geological Survey. "The Survey's Contribution to the National Park Movement." In *Proceedings of the National Parks Conference*, 322. Washington, DC: U.S. Government Printing Office, 1917.

Smith, Michael. *Pacific Vistas: California Scientists and the Environment, 1850–1915*. New Haven: Yale University Press, 1987.

Smyth, William E. *The Conquest of Arid America*. New York: Macmillan, 1905.

Snelling, Andrew. "The Recent Origin of Bass Strait Oil and Gas." *Ex Nihilo* 5, no. 2 (1982): 43–46.

Solnit, Rebecca. *Savage Dreams: A Journey into the Hidden Wars of the American West*. San Francisco: Sierra Club Books, 1994.

Solomon, Norman. *Killing Our Own: The Disaster of America's Experience with Atomic Radiation*. New York: Delacorte, 1982.

Spence, Mark David. *Dispossessing the Wilderness: Indian Removal and the Making of the National Parks*. New York: Oxford University Press, 1999.

Stegner, Wallace. *The Sound of Mountain Water*. Garden City: Doubleday, 1969.

Stein, Gertrude. *Everybody's Autobiography*. London: Virago, 1985.

Steinberg, Ted. *Down to Earth: Nature's Role in American History*. New York: Oxford University Press, 2002.

Stilgoe, John R. *Common Landscape of America, 1580 to 1845*. New Haven: Yale University Press, 1982.

Sutter, Paul S. *Driven Wild*. Seattle: University of Washington, 2002.

Suzuki, David. *The Sacred Balance: Rediscovering Our Place in Nature*. Vancouver: Graystone Books, 1997.

Switzer, Carole Stern. *CERCLA—Comprehensive Environmental Response, Compensation, and Liability Act (Superfund)*. American Bar Association, 2009.

Taft, Robert. *Photography and the American Scene*. New York: Dover, [1938] 1964.

Tapahonso, Luci. "Ode to the Land." In Meléndez et al., *Multicultural Southwest*, 97–101.

Tarr, Joel. *The Search for the Ultimate Sink: Urban Pollution in Historical Perspective*. Akron, OH: University of Akron Press, 1996.

Taylor, William R. "New York and the Origin of the Skyline." *Prospects* 13 (1988): 225–248.

Taylor, William R., and Thomas Bender. "Culture and Architecture: Some Aesthetic Tensions in the Shaping of Modern New York City." In *Visions of the Modern City*, edited by William Sharpe and Leonard Wallock, 189–219. Baltimore: Johns Hopkins University Press, 1987.

Teague, David W. *The Southwest in American Literature and Art*. Tucson: University of Arizona Press, 1997.

Teasdale, Guillaume. "Old Friends and New Foes: French Settlers and Indians in the Detroit River Border Region." *Michigan Historical Review* 38, no. 2 (Fall 2012): 35–62.

Thompson, Jonathan. "The 26,000 Tons of Radioactive Waste under Lake Powell." *High Country News*, December 18, 2017.

Thoreau, Henry David. "Walking." *The Atlantic*, June 1862. https://www.theatlantic.com/magazine/archive/1862/06/walking/304674/.

Tichi, Cecelia. *New Word, New Earth: Environmental Reform in American Literature from the Puritans through Whitman*. New Haven: Yale University Press, 1979.

Tichi, Cecelia. *Shifting Gears: Technology, Literature, Culture in Modernist America*. Chapel Hill: University of North Carolina Press, 1987.

Tillotson, M. R., and Frank J. Taylor. *Grand Canyon Country*. Stanford, CA: Stanford University Press, 1935.

Tocqueville, Alexis de. *Democracy in America*. Vol. 2. New York: Vintage Books, 1945.

Tocqueville, Alexis de. "A Fortnight in the Wilds." In *Journey to America*, ed. J. P. Mayer. New Haven: Yale University Press, 1960.

Tompkins, Edmund Pendleton, and J. Lee Davis. *The Natural Bridge and Its Historical Surroundings*. Natural Bridge, VA: Natural Bridge of Virginia, Inc., 1939.

Trachtenberg, Alan. *Reading American Photographs: Images as History, Matthew Brady to Walker Evans*. New York: Hill and Wang, 1989.

Tuan, Yi-Fu. *Space and Place*. Minneapolis: University of Minnesota, 1979.

Twain, Mark. *Roughing It*. In *The Works of Mark Twain*, vol. 2, ed. Frederick Anderson and Robert H. Hirst. Berkeley: University of California Press, 1974.

Twombly, Robert C. *Frank Lloyd Wright: An Interpretive Biography*. New York: Harper & Row, 1973.

Udall, Stuart. *The Quiet Crisis*. New York: Holt, Reinhart and Winston, 1963.

Upward, Geoffrey C. *A Home for Our Heritage: The Building and Growth of Greenfield Village and Henry Ford Museum*. Dearborn, MI: Greenfield Village and Henry Ford Museum, 1979.

U.S. Department of the Interior. *The Colorado River: A Comprehensive Report on the Development of the Water Resources of the Colorado River Basin for Irrigation, Power Production, and Other Beneficial Uses in Arizona, California, Colorado, Nevada, New Mexico, Utah, and Wyoming*. Washington, DC, March 1946.

U.S. Department of the Interior. *Colorado River Management Plan, Record of Decision*. Washington, DC, February 17, 2006.

U.S. Department of the Interior, Bureau of Land Management, El Centro Field Office. "Record of Decision for the Imperial Project Gold Mine Proposal, Imperial County, California," January 17, 2001.

U.S. Energy Administration. "What Is US Electricity Generation by Energy Source?," viewed July 10, 2020, https://www.eia.gov/tools/faqs/faq.php?id=427&t=3.

U.S. General Accountability Office. "Superfund Funding and Costs." *Report to Congress*. July 18, 2008.

U.S. General Accounting Office. *Water Pollution: Efforts to Clean Up Michigan's Rouge River*. Washington, DC: General Accounting Office, 1988.

U.S. General Accounting Office. *Wilderness Preservation: Problems in Some National Forests Should Be Addressed*. Washington, DC: U.S. Government Printing Office, 1989.

U.S. Nuclear Regulatory Commission. *NRC Five Year Plan to Address Uranium Contamination in the Navajo Nation*. Washington, DC, December 2016.

Van Dyke, John C. *The Desert*. New York: C. Scribner's Sons, 1901.

Van Dyke, John C. *The Grand Canyon of the Colorado: Recurrent Studies in Impressions and Appearances*. Foreword by Peter Wild. Salt Lake City: University of Utah, 1992. Reprint of Charles Scribner's Sons, 1920.

van Leeuwen, Thomas A. P. *The Skyward Trend of Thought*. The Hague: AHA Books, 1986.

Vanderbilt, Tom. *Survival City: Adventures among the Ruins of Atomic America*. Chicago: Chicago University Press, 2002.

Verner, William F. Personal notebook, 1919 to 1920. Accession 52. Archives, The Henry Ford.

Volcovici, Valeri. "Trump Order Could Remove Protections for National Monuments," *Scientific American*, April 26, 2017. https://www.scientificamerican.com/article/trump-order-could-remove-protections-for-national-monuments/.

Voyles, Traci Brynne. *Wastelanding: Legacies of Uranium Mining in Navajo Country*. Minneapolis: University of Minnesota Press, 2015.

Walcott, Charles D. "National Parks as a Scientific Asset." In *Proceedings of the National Parks Conference*, 112–115. Washington, DC: U.S. Government Printing Office, 1917.

Warner, Charles Dudley. "On the Brink of the Grand Canyon." In *The Grand Canyon: Early Impressions*, edited by Paul Schullery, 41–46. Boulder: Colorado Associated University Press, 1981.

Warner, Fara. "The Place to Be This Year." *Brandweek*, November 30, 1992.

Warren, Ronald L. "Aviation at Grand Canyon: A 75-Year History." *Journal of Arizona History* 36, no. 2 (Summer 1995): 151–172.

Waters, Frank. *The Colorado*. New York: Holt Reinhart and Winston, 1946.

Waters, Frank. *The Man Who Killed the Deer*. Columbus: Swallow Press, [1942] 1989.

Watson, John. *The Philosophy of Kant Explained*. Glasgow: James Maclehose and Sons, 1908. Facsimile reprint, New York: Garland, 1976.

Watts, Stephen. *The People's Tycoon: Henry Ford and the American Century*. New York: Alfred A. Knopf, 2005.

Way, L. Claude. "Practical Canyon Problems." In *Proceedings of the National Parks Conference*, vol. 4. Washington, DC: U.S. Government Printing Office, 1917.

Way, Thomas E. *Destination Grand Canyon: The Story of Travel to the Grand Canyon*. Phoenix: Golden West Publishers, 1990.

Weart, Spencer. *The Rise of Nuclear Fear*. Cambridge, MA: Harvard University Press, 2012.

Weigle, Marta, and Barbara A. Babcock, eds. *The Great Southwest of the Fred Harvey Company and the Santa Fe Railway*. Phoenix: The Heard Museum, 1996.

Wells, H. G. *The Future in America*. Leipzig: Bernhard Tauchnitz, 1907.

Wescoat, James L. "Challenging the Desert." In *The Making of the American Landscape*, edited by Michael P. Conzen, 186–203. London: Routledge, 1994.

Williams, Terry Tempest. *Pieces of White Shell*. Albuquerque: University of New Mexico Press, 1987.

Williams, Terry Tempest. *The Hour of Land: A Personal Topography of America's National Parks*. New York: Farrar, Straus and Giroux, 2016.

Williams, Terry Tempest. *Red: Passion and Patience in the Desert*. New York: Pantheon, 2001.

Wilson, Richard Guy. "Architecture in the Machine Age." In *The Machine Age in America, 1918–1941*, edited by Richard Guy Wilson, Dianne H. Pilgrim, and Dickran Tashjian, 149–204. New York: Harry N. Abrams, 1986.

Winkler, Allan M. *Life under a Cloud: American Anxiety about the Atom*. New York: Oxford University Press, 1993.

Wohlleben, Peter. *The Hidden Life of Trees: What They Feel, How They Communicate*. Vancouver: Greystone Books, 2016. Translation of *Das geheime Leben der Baume*. Munich: Ludwig Verlag, 2015.

Woodbury, Angus M. "Protecting Rainbow Bridge." *Science* 132 (August 26, 1960): 519–528.

Worman, Frederick. *Anatomy of the Nevada Test Site*. Berkeley: University of California-Los Alamos Scientific Laboratory, 1965.

Worster, Donald. "Comment: A Response to 'John Wesley Powell and the Unmaking of the West,'" *Environmental History* 2, no. 2 (April 1997): 216–219.

Worster, Donald. *Rivers of Empire: Water, Aridity, and the Growth of the American West*. New York: Pantheon, 1985.

Wright, Harold Bell. *The Winning of Barbara Worth*. New York: Grosset & Dunlap, [1911] 1966.

Wright, Orville. "Air Routes to the National Parks." In *Proceedings of the National Parks Conference*, vol. 4. Washington, DC: U.S. Government Printing Office, 1917.

Yates, Steven A. ed. *The Essential Landscape: The New Mexico Photography Survey with Essays by J. B. Jackson*. Albuquerque: University of New Mexico Press, 1985.

Zhang, Sarah. "A Creationist Sues the Grand Canyon for Religious Discrimination." *The Atlantic*, May 17, 2017.

Zhang, Sarah. "Grand Canyon Gives In to Creationist Suing for Religious Discrimination." *The Atlantic*, July 3, 2017.

Zierler, David. *The Invention of Ecocide: Agent Orange, Vietnam, and the Scientists Who Changed the Way We Think about the Environment*. Athens: University of Georgia Press, 2011.

Zuniga, Jennifer. *The Central Arizona Project*. Washington, DC: Bureau of Reclamation, 2000. https://www.usbr.gov/projects/pdf.php?id=94.

Zweibel, Ken, James Mason, and Vasilis Fthenakis. "A Solar Grand Plan." *Scientific American* 298, no. 1 (January 2008): 64–73.

INDEX

Abbott, Berenice, 114, 120
Adams, Ansel, 127, 167
Adams, Henry, 70
Air Force, 13, 26, 128
Amarillo, Texas, 140, 141
Anthropocene, 22, 46, 179, 189
Anti-landscape, 126–142, 145–148, 179–180
  atomic test sites, 142–145, 148
  defined, 2, 7
  mining and, 133–140
  radioactive waste, 129–130, 134, 140, 143, 145–148, 172
  River Rouge, 42–43, 177
  Superfund sites, 30, 42–43, 63, 127, 132–134, 137–140, 176–177
  utilitarianism and, 2, 7, 127, 134, 180
Antiquities Act of 1906, 55, 58, 185, 188
Apache tribe, 73
Aqualantes, 61
Arches National Park, 55, 188
Arctic Wildlife Area, 174
Arizona
  exploration, 67, 75
  growth, 16,
  federal presence, 7, 128, 174
  irrigation, 14, 67, 68, 74, 78, 79, 82–84, 151, 174
  mining, 73, 74
  national parks and monuments, 9, 58 (*see also* Grand Canyon)
  religion in, 157, 193

solar power, 197–198
southwest and, 24, 68
uranium mining and processing, 133–139
Army Corps of Engineers, 3, 35, 64, 70
Assembly line, 34–39, 44, 102
Atomic Energy Commission (AEC), 134, 140, 141, 142, 143
Atomic testing, 7, 128, 142–145, 148, 151, 172, 174, 176
Automobiles
  fuel efficiency, 176
  manufacture, 30, 34–37, 39, 41, 43
  tourism, 101–102, 104–105
Automobile workers, 33, 34, 36, 38, 40, 42, 44
Aviation, 7, 104, 154

Barthes, Roland, 119–120, 165–166
Basso, Keith, 73
Beadle, J. H., 90–91
Beaman, E. O., 90, 98
Bears Ears National Monument, 185, 187–188
Beck, Ulrich, 173
Bennett, Arnold, 115
Bergland, Eric, 78
Berry, Wendell, 193
Bible, 48, 59, 157, 176
Biological diversity, 6, 163, 185, 194
Black Elk, 5
Blackgoat, Roberta, 181
Boxer, Barbara, 183
Bright Angel Creek, 162

Bright Angel Lodge, 100, 154
Bright Angel Trail, 92, 97, 104, 153, 154
Brower, David, 62
Bryant, William Cullen, 89–91
Bryce, Lord, 16–17
Bryce Canyon National Park, 127
Buell, Lawrence, 22, 132
Buffalo, 169, 194, 195
Buffalo, New York, 102, 109, 125
Buffalo Bill, 92
Buffalo Commons, 195
Bureau of Indian Affairs, 22, 135, 184
Bureau of Reclamation
    dam building, 35, 71, 78–82, 105, 151, 181
    irrigation, 61, 78–82
    Rainbow Bridge and, 2, 59–62
    utilitarianism of, 3, 22, 64, 71, 105, 172, 181
Burke, Edmund, 51, 112, 165
Burroughs, John, 34, 40, 156
Bush, George W., 134, 175, 182, 183

California, 67–68, 76, 78, 183, 196, 200
Cameron, James, 92–93
Campbell, Ben Nighthorse, 182
Cancer, 135–141, 142, 143
Canyonlands National Park, 188
Carson, Rachael, 132
Carson River, 133
Carter, Jimmy, 174, 175
Central Arizona Project (CAP), 82–83
Central Park (New York City), 20, 39
Certeau, Michel de, 121
Chaffey, George, 78
Chastellux, Marquis de, 51
Cherokee tribe, 188
Chicago, 107, 108, 109, 111, 124, 125
Christian environmentalism, 192
Church, Frederick Edwin, 51
Church Rock, New Mexico, 138–139

Climate change, 11, 190. *See also* Anthropocene
Clinton, William, 40, 158–159, 175, 184, 185
Coal
    alternative energies and, 196, 197, 198
    industrial uses, 30 36, 38, 41
    mining, 23, 105, 162–163, 174, 181–182, 184, 187
    Navajo and, 5, 83, 162–163, 181–182
    power plants and, 162–163, 175, 197, 198
    railroads and, 76, 108
Coburn, Alvin Langdon, 123, 167
Cold War, 41, 45, 138, 145–146, 152, 175
Cole, Thomas, 10, 18–20, 51
Colorado River, 29, 67–69. *See also* Grand Canyon
    dams, 60, 67, 70, 71, 81–85, 105, 189
    ecology of, 161–162
    exploration, 57, 67–77, 91
    fish of, 161–162
    geology and, 99–100
    irrigation and, 74, 77–81, 181, 185
    mining and, 76, 77, 92, 93, 138–139, 152, 178
    Navajo and, 57, 161
    photography of, 57, 60, 102–104, 165–167
    rafting 9, 152, 153
    railroads and, 72, 76–77, 90, 92, 100, 102–103, 108
    region, 24, 68–70, 177
    tourism, 89–92, 101–103, 159–160, 163
Colorado River Storage Project Act of 1956, 60
Comprehensive Environmental Response, Compensation and

Liability Act of 1980 (CERCLA), 133–134
Cooper, James Fenimore, 180
Creationism
    belief in, 1, 3, 50, 157–158, 172, 177, 189
    Grand Canyon and, 7, 157–158, 189
    Native Americans and, 158
    natural bridges and, 55
    number of adherents, 3–4, 157, 175
    Republican Party and, 45, 157, 172
    science and, 173
Cronon, William, 12
Cuvier, Georges, 48–49, 99

Dams, 78–84
    Colorado River and, 67, 71, 82–85
    controversies over, 1, 7, 60–62, 64, 83, 105, 151–152, 181, 189, 194
    hydroelectric, 26, 35, 61, 62, 68, 79–80, 82–85, 105, 152, 172
    irrigation and, 61, 71, 78, 81 (see also Irrigation)
    Native Americans and, 6, 57, 59, 81–82, 151–152, 181
    pollution and, 63, 138, 152
    rainbow bridge and, 60–61
    sublime and, 17, 85, 160
    utilitarianism and, 9, 26, 79–80, 127, 171, 172, 179–180
Dearborn Massacre, 40
DeLillo, Don, 149
Dellenbaugh, Frederick S., 95
Deloria, Vine, 158
Democrats
    creationism and 2, 175
    global warming and, 8, 174, 176
    Native Americans and, 183–184
    wilderness and, 175
Department of the Interior, 59, 60, 79, 177, 182–183, 184
Detroit. *See also* River Rouge
    British, 32
    founding, 31–33
    French, 31–32
    industry in, 33–42, 44
    Native Americans and, 30, 32
    pastoral, 39–40, 43
Devil's Tower National Monument, 48, 58
Diné. *See* Navajo
Dominy, Floyd, 71
Douglas, William O., 174–175
Downing, Andrew Jackson, 19
Downwinders, 137, 142–143
Dunaway, Finis, 200
Dutton, Clarence, 72, 100, 165

Economic creationism, 45
El Tovar Hotel, 92, 100, 101, 103, 154, 165
Emerson, Ralph Waldo, 19, 34, 40
Empire State Building, 109, 111, 115, 119
End-of-life-vehicle-directive, 43
Energy. *See also* Coal; Dams; Uranium
    alternative energies, 44, 147, 177, 188, 196–200
    hydroelectric, 1, 60, 62, 67, 71, 78–84, 151–152, 160, 181, 194
    mining, 23, 105, 162–163, 174, 181–182, 184, 187
    Navajo and, 5, 83, 162–163, 181–182
    power plants, 162–163, 175, 197, 198
Environmental Protection Agency, 1, 22, 133–135, 137, 139–140, 164, 176, 177, 182, 187
Erdrich, Heid E., 6
Erdrich, Louise, 5, 192
Evolution, 3, 15, 156–158, 172, 173, 176, 189

Factory tour, 38, 42, 44
Farmers, 10, 18, 24, 71, 79, 80, 83, 187, 193, 196

Flatiron Building, 101, 118
Ford, Edsel, 101
Ford, Henry
    assembly line, 34–42
    Grand Canyon and, 101
    home, 34, 39
    pastoralism and, 34, 39, 172, 177
Ford, William Clay, 43
Ford Motor Company, 34–44, 103
Forest Reserve Act of 1891, 58
Frary, Michael, 80–81
French colonialism, 31
Friends of the Earth, 3

Gallup polls, 3, 175
General Accounting Office, U.S., 12–13, 42, 180
General Motors, 42, 43, 199
Geology, 1, 48–50, 71, 72, 99–100, 155–158, 177, 189
Geometric sublime, 122
Gilbert, Karl, 99
Gilkey, Charles W., 107, 159
Glacier National Park, 64, 108, 178
Gleed, Charles, 90–91
Glen Canyon Dam, 57, 59–64, 71, 77, 81–82, 152, 163, 172
Goetzmann, William H., 75
Goin, Peter, 64
Goldwater, Barry, 9, 58, 174, 175
Google, 163
Gore, Albert, 175–176
Grand Canyon, 87–106, 151–170
    American identity and, 2, 8, 17, 67, 85, 89–90, 92, 98–99, 102, 165, 174, 189
    creationists and, 3, 8, 157–158, 189
    dams and, 82–83, 105, 151–152. 163, 181
    deconstruction and, 167–168
    exploration, 55, 68–70, 75, 88
    films of, 87, 103–104, 159–160, 163
    geology of, 99–100
    interpretations of, 10, 68–69, 72–75, 87–88, 90–93, 107, 154–159, 166, 169, 179
    mining in, 76, 77, 92–93, 178, 184–185
    National Park Service, 22, 58, 104–105, 153, 158–159, 161–162, 194
    Native Americans and, 12, 22, 73, 88, 161, 189
    paintings of, 72, 93–94, 99, 100–102, 124
    pastoralism and, 3, 19–20, 171
    photography of, 73, 75, 77, 90, 94–98, 100, 102, 103, 157, 165–167
    pollution of, 135–136, 139, 142, 151, 152, 179, 181, 184–185
    Santa Fe Railroad and, 92, 100–101, 103, 108, 178
    sublime and, 8, 10, 71–73, 77, 88–92, 101–102, 105, 107, 108, 122, 124–125, 177–178
    tourism, 5, 9, 26, 91–93, 100–105, 151–164
    utilitarianism and, 93, 105, 171, 179
    virtual, 163–164
    wilderness and, 26, 160, 164
    wildlife of, 161–162, 185
    world's fairs and, 102–103
Grand Canyon (film), 87–88
Grand Canyon Trust, 135
Grand Junction, Colorado, 76, 137
Grand Staircase Escalante National Monument, 184–188
Great Plains Restoration Council, 195
Greenfield Village, 39–40, 45, 45, 172, 177
Green housing, 198
Grey, Zane, 58, 61–62

Hanford, Washington, 129–130, 134, 140, 141, 143
Hartmann, Sadakichi, 123

Harvey, David, 37
Harvey, Mark, 22
Hayden, F. V., 98
Henderson, Norman, 194
Henry, O., 118–119
Herrera, Alonso de, 24, 26, 193
Highland Park Plant, 35
Hillers, Jack, 75, 90, 95, 102
Hitler, Adolf, 41
Hooker Chemical Company, 132
Hoover Dam, 35, 62, 68, 70, 83–85, 105, 160
Hopi
    agriculture of, 193
    Blue Lake, 55
    fallout and, 142, 176
    Grand Canyon and, 88, 101, 167
    mining and, 162–163
    sacred spaces of, 23–25, 88, 185, 188
    San Francisco Peaks, 23–24, 55
Hualapai, 68, 142, 151, 153, 160, 161
Hutton, James, 50

IMAX theater, 159–160, 163, 164, 179
Imperial Valley of California, 78
Indian Gardens, 92, 93, 153
Indian Pass Wilderness Area, 183
Industrialism. *See also* Anti-landscape; Dams; Ford Motor Company; Irrigation; River Rouge; Superfund sites; Technological sublime
    culture of, 127, 131, 191
    factories and, 30, 33–46
    farming and, 26
    nature and, 160, 175, 179
    pollution and, 18, 42–43, 160, 195
Internet, 154, 158, 160, 179
Irrigation. *See also* Dams; Grand Canyon
    Colorado River and, 61, 71, 73, 77–83, 185
    conflicts over, 78, 82, 85, 174
    economics of, 18, 61, 64, 196
    second creation and, 15, 16, 26, 71, 79–83, 177, 179–180
    utilitarianism, 15, 26, 177
Ives, Charles Christmas, 68–70, 85, 87, 89

Jackling, Daniel, 131
Jackson, Senator Henry, 151
Jackson, John B., 1, 7, 24, 128, 190, 193
Jackson, William H., 98
James, Henry, 110–111, 123
Jefferson, Thomas, 18, 48–51, 79, 85, 158, 173, 189
Johnson. Clifton, 53
Johnson, Lyndon, 9, 174, 175

Kahn, Albert, 37
Kant, Immanuel, 10, 88, 112, 122, 157, 165
Kayenta solar array, 197–198
King, Clarence, 70–71, 84
Kinsey, Joni, 94
Klett, Mark, 166–167
Kluckhohn, Clyde, 59
Kolb brothers, 57, 75, 95, 100, 102, 103
Krutch, Joseph Wood, 156

Lake Mead, 62, 63, 153, 199
Lake Powell, 57, 59, 62–64, 71
Landscape. *See also* Anthropocene; Anti-landscape; Geology; Natural sublime, Nature; Second creation; Space; and *specific sites*
    conflicted, 3–8, 31, 85, 171–190, 193, 194–195
    defined, 1–3, 24, 26–27, 163–164, 190
    deconstruction and, 167–169
    desert, 24, 26, 89–90
    grid and, 13–14, 17, 32, 46

Landscape (cont.)
  industrial, 34–46, 141 (see also Mining)
  intervention, 193–195
  nationalism and, 1, 2, 8, 51–52, 88, 89, 91, 189
  painting, 51, 71, 80–82, 93–95, 100, 165, 167–169
  pastoral, 1, 3, 8, 10, 18–22, 39–40, 169, 171, 174, 187, 193
  photography, 97–98, 100, 123, 165–167 (see also Photography)
  polluted, 42–43, 127–129, 132, 134, 145–148
  standardization of, 17, 32
  skyscraper and, 112, 115–126
  sublime, 72–73, 77, 85, 105, 165, 188 (see also Natural sublime; Technological sublime)
  utilitarian, 13–18, 23, 38, 71, 80,
  wilderness and, 10–13, 21, 70–71, 173–195
Landscape Arch, 55–56
Lane, Belden, C., 5, 16
Las Vegas, 26, 76, 82, 125–126, 160, 163, 164
LeCain, Timothy, 130
Leopold, Aldo, 92–93
Lewis, Sinclair, 112–113
Life magazine, 40–41
Little Colorado River, 105, 139, 161
Locke, John, 13
Los Angeles, 16, 38, 82, 87, 142, 164
Lost Orphan Mine, 135–136
Love Canal, 132–133, 139, 179
Lowenthal, David, 128

Magisterial gaze, 116–117, 122
Manifest Destiny, 6, 67, 77, 80, 91, 172
Marchand, Roland, 116
Marsh, George Perkins, 128–129
Marx, Leo, 13–14, 16
McCain, John, 176

McDonough, William, 43
McKay, Claude, 113, 115
Meinig, D. W., 24
Melville, Herman, 54
Methuselah trees, 145
Mexico, 32, 42, 78
Michael, Wendy Lynnette, 44
Miners, 70, 136–137, 139, 141, 143
Mining
  coal, 23, 105, 162–163, 174, 181–182, 184, 187
  copper, 23, 70, 76, 130–131
  uranium, 63, 105, 128, 133–140, 145, 152, 153, 179, 184, 185, 187
Misa, Thomas, 108–109
Mohave Power Plant, 197
Mohawk, 109
Möllhausen, Heinrich Balduin, 69
Monument Valley, 61, 127, 135, 137
Moran, Thomas, 72, 90, 93–94, 99–101, 102, 166
Mound Builders, 30, 32, 44, 46, 177
Muir, John, 10, 71, 91–92, 127, 154, 155

Nabokov, Peter, 57
Nash, Roderick, 47
National grid, 13–14, 17–18, 26, 32, 39, 45, 46, 70, 85, 110, 175, 177–179
Nationalism. *See also* Sacred places
  American West and, 54–55, 67, 76, 89–90, 108, 127
  Grand Canyon and, 2, 67, 85, 89–93, 98–99, 102
  national parks and, 2, 10–11, 17, 23, 55, 64, 88–92, 107, 109, 154–156, 159, 174–175
  natural bridges, 51–52, 65
  nature and, 1, 2, 8, 51 (see also Natural sublime)
  technological sublime and, 8, 123, 171, 189

Yellowstone, 2, 10–11, 55, 89, 90, 91
Yosemite and, 2, 10, 17, 55, 88, 89
National Land Ordinance. *See* National grid
National parks, psychological effect of, 107, 109, 154–156, 159
National Park Service (NPS), 3, 22. *See also individual parks*
   Grand Canyon and, 22, 93, 105, 151, 153, 157–158, 160, 161, 164
   natural bridges and, 50, 58, 59, 64, 194
Native Americans. *See also individual tribes*
   Bureau of Indian Affairs, 22, 47, 135, 184
   creationism and, 158
   erasure of historical presence, 12, 24, 27, 29, 31–33, 46, 177, 180, 200
   farming, 69, 78, 193
   federal government and, 22, 73, 74, 78, 135, 171, 181–182 184
   Grand Canyon and 12, 22, 73, 88, 160–161, 189
   landscape and, 8, 11, 71–73, 177, 188–189, 192
   petroglyphs, 2, 4, 77, 148, 183, 185–186, 188
   River Rouge and, 29–32
   Rainbow Bridge and, 56–57, 59
   sacred space, 1, 6, 8, 18, 23–25, 47, 55, 57, 59, 88, 139, 161, 163, 177, 182–183, 185, 196
   skyscrapers and, 109, 124
   uranium and, 129, 134–140, 179
   wilderness and, 11–12, 18, 171, 177
   world view, 4–6, 8, 18, 47–48, 127
Natural Bridge of Virginia, 21, 48–54, 85, 90, 157
Natural Bridges, 47–66, 173, 177, 183, 184, 189

Natural Bridges National Monument, 55
Natural sublime, 2, 17, 51–52, 54, 124, 126
   aesthetic of, 2, 10, 17, 119, 122, 124, 126, 161, 173, 200
   nationalism and, 8, 51–52, 88, 89, 91
   tourism and, 10, 55, 88–91, 189
Nature. *See also* Landscape; Natural sublime; Wilderness
   conflicting perceptions of, 1–27, 40, 64, 65, 71, 171–172, 174, 177–178, 188, 193, 194, 196
   creationists and, 1, 3–4, 7, 157–158
   Native Americans and, 5, 23–25, 47–48, 56–57, 88, 180–182
   pastoralism and, 1, 3, 8, 10, 18–22, 39–40, 169, 171, 174, 175, 187, 193
   sacrifice zones and, 7, 128, 171–172
   utilitarian conception of, 2–3, 13–18, 26–27, 32, 61, 64, 65, 67, 71, 74, 84, 89, 92–93, 105, 169, 174, 175, 177
   wilderness and, 2–3, 7, 10, 12–13, 145, 159, 173, 180, 185, 192, 194–195, 200
Nature Conservancy Council (Britain), 194
Navajo, 192
   atomic tests and, 142, 176
   Bears Ears and, 185
   dams and, 59–62, 81–82, 151–152
   Grand Canyon and, 88, 160, 161, 162–163
   mining and, 83, 105, 134–140, 145, 162–163, 189–181, 188
   nature and, 5, 23–25, 58–62, 88, 185
   power plants, 162–163, 181–182, 197
   radiation poisoning of, 134–140, 142
   Rainbow Bridge and, 57, 58–62
   sacred spaces of, 23–25, 58–62, 88

Nellis Air Force Base, 26, 128
Nevada
    atomic tests in, 26, 128, 142–145, 148, 172
    exploration, 67, 70
    irrigation, 79
    military sites, 26, 128
    mining, 70, 73, 74, 133, 163
    Southwest and, 16, 24
Newberry, John, 99
New Mexico
    art and literature in, 127
    exploration, 67
    federal presence, 127–128, 145
    irrigation, 24, 79, 193
    military sites, 128
    national parks, 127
    native Americans in, 24
    Southwest and, 24
    uranium mining and waste, 133, 134, 137, 138–139, 145–147
New pastoralism, 193–196, 198, 201
Newspaper Rock, 4–5
New York City
    Central Park, 20
    energy efficiency of, 199
    fallout in, 143
    lighting, 123
    paintings of, 124
    skyline, 108–109, 112–123, 126
Niagara Falls, 10, 21, 51, 88, 90, 124, 132, 154
Noble, John W., 80
Novak, Barbara, 91
Nuclear Regulatory Commission, 137
Nuclear Test Site, 142–145, 148
Nuclear weapons assembly 141–142

Obama, Barack, 152, 185
Ojibwe tribe, 5, 6
Olmsted, Frederick Law, 20
Oostvaardersplassen, 194–195

Oppenheim, James, 121–122
O'Sullivan, Timothy, 90

Page, Arizona, 135, 162, 181
Pantex weapons plant, 140–142, 143
Pastoralism. *See also* Landscape; Nature; Wilderness
    defined, 2–3, 18–22, 169, 171, 174
    Henry Ford and, 34, 39–40, 46, 85, 177
    Jefferson and 18, 85
    nationalism and, 1, 18–22, 174
    national parks and, 20, 39–40, 174, 175
    new forms of, 46, 193–201
    opposing concepts, 1–8, 19–20, 171, 177, 191
    urban, 39
    utilitarianism and, 8, 34, 44, 188
Peabody Mine, 163
Pecos Wilderness, 13
Pence, Mike, 176
Peshlakai, Elsie, 139
Petrick, Jane Allen, 81–82
Petrified National Forest, 58
Petroglyphs, 2, 4, 77, 148, 183, 185–186, 188
Phantom Ranch, 104
Phoenix, 38, 83, 128
    urban farming, 196
    utilities, 198
    water in, 78, 82–83, 164, 181, 196
Photography
    aerial, 104
    Bureau of Reclamation and, 61, 80
    Colorado River, 57, 60, 102–104, 165–167
    factory, 38–39, 41
    Grand Canyon, 73, 75, 77, 89, 90, 94–98, 100, 102, 103, 154, 157, 164–167
    landscape, 2, 26, 51, 97–98, 100, 123, 165–167

Index

mining, 93
skyscraper, 111, 112
Southwest, 127
time and, 165–166
urban, 114, 120, 123
Yellowstone, 98
Yosemite, 98
Picher, Oklahoma, 7, 129, 131, 179, 188
Plutonium. *See also* Anti-landscape; Mining; Plutonium waste; Uranium
creation, 129, 140
reactor, 7
weapons-grade, 7
Plutonium waste, 7, 145, 149
Pollution. *See also* Anti-landscape; Mining
air, 13, 137
fear of, 132–133, 172
ground, 18, 129, 132–133, 139, 179, 184, 196
Native Americans and, 6, 133, 134, 139–140
politics of, 8, 176
radioactive, 7, 27, 63, 129, 134–149, 172, 179, 180, 187, 188, 196
utilitarian view of, 18, 23, 134
water, 13, 42–43, 129, 138–139, 153, 177, 179
wilderness and, 180
Porter, Robert P., 74
Postmodern theorists, 168–169
Powell, John Wesley, 71–72, 74–75, 77, 79, 84, 85
Powers, Richard, 192
Primitivism, 2, 10, 11, 12, 174
Pringle, Heather, 158
Proulx, Annie, 192
Puerco River, 138–139
Pyne, Stephen J., 72, 99

Quechan tribe, 182–183

Radiation Exposure Compensation Act, 136–137
Railroad
industry and, 33, 37, 38–39, 76–77, 178
narratives, 15, 30, 168, 179
national parks and, 22, 72, 76, 100–103, 108, 172, 178
resource demands, 33, 78
social effects, 18, 33, 44, 108, 121–122
tourism and, 72, 89, 90, 92, 100–101
utilitarianism and, 15, 17, 23, 44, 67, 71, 171, 179
Rainbow Natural Bridge, 21, 55–62, 64
Reagan, Ronald, 21, 172, 175
Reaganomics, 45
Recycling, 8, 43–44, 193, 195, 196, 199, 201
Republicans, 3, 45, 187
creationism and 2, 175
global warming and, 8, 176
Native Americans and, 184
wilderness and, 175, 176–177
River Rouge, 29–30, 33–35, 39, 42, 44–46
River Rouge Park, 39
River Rouge Plant, 34–46
Rockwell, Norman, 81–82
Roosevelt, Franklin D., 184
Roosevelt, Theodore, 15, 57, 58, 61, 109, 159, 172, 174, 187

Sacred places. *See also* Natural sublime; Technological sublime; Wilderness
Hopi, 23–25, 55, 88, 171
national parks as, 23, 64, 89, 92, 102, 107, 109, 154–156, 159, 175
Native American, 1, 6, 8, 18, 23–25, 47–48, 139, 161, 163, 177, 185
Navajo, 23–25, 55, 57, 59, 171, 181,
Quechan, 182–183

Sacrifice zones, 7, 128, 171–172
Salt Lake City, 185, 199
Salton Sea, 78
Salt River, 78, 198
Saluskin, Margaret, 5
San Francisco, California, 103, 199
San Francisco Peaks, 23–25, 171
San Juan River, 57
Sandberg, Carl, 118
Sanford, Charles, 51–52
Santa Fe, New Mexico, 127
Santa Fe Railroad, 72, 90, 92, 100, 102–103, 108
Sapir, Edward, 127
Sayre, Gordon, 19–20
Schleier, Merrill, 112
Schumpeter, Joseph, 35
Schuyler, Montgomery, 114, 115
Scranton, Pennsylvania, 15
Sears, John, 51, 91
Second creation. *See also* Anti-landscape; Dams
  defined, 13–16, 23, 29–30, 179–180
  Detroit and, 40, 45–46
  energy and, 14, 196–197
  environmental limits, 46, 62–63, 172, 179
  extractive industries and, 64, 70, 134–135, 175
  failed narrative, 42, 62–63, 82–84, 128, 192, 193, 195
  future and, 14, 172, 190, 192
  Glen Canyon Dam and, 64, 81–82
  national parks and, 23
  skyscraper and, 17, 118–120, 179
  Southwest and, 79–80, 134–135
  technological sublime and, 15–16, 23, 161, 179
  uranium and, 134–135
  utilitarianism and, 14–15, 23, 45, 79–80, 83, 172, 174, 175, 177, 193
  wilderness and, 175, 195
Sheeler, Charles, 38–39

Sierra Club, 3, 60–62, 152
Silko, Leslie, 192
Singer Building, 115, 116, 123, 124
Skyline, 112–115, 123–126, 179
Skyscrapers, 8, 17, 108–126, 179
Sloan, John, 124
Snake River, 79
Solar Decathlon, 198–199
Solar energy, 44, 147, 177, 188, 197–200
Solnit, Rebecca, 149
Southwest. *See also* Colorado River; Grand Canyon; Irrigation; and *individual states*
  defined, 24, 127
  exploration, 67–76
  federal government and, 41, 58, 127–128,
  growth of, 16, 38
  iconic sites, 26, 127
  irrigation, 78–80, 83–84
  military and, 7, 26
  sacrifice zones in, 172
  tourism, 100–105, 151, 180
  writers and, 127
Space. *See also* Anti-landscape; Landscape; National grid; Pastoralism, Sacred places, Second creation, Wilderness
  American ideology of, 13–16, 70, 83–84, 121–123, 179
  Cartesian, 84
  compression of, 37, 164
  conflicted, 1–8, 84–85, 89, 171–190, 191
  hybrid, 195, 199, 200
  manufacturing, 37–38
  military, 6, 7, 8, 41, 127–130, 142–145, 171, 191
  Native Americans and, 18, 23–25, 30, 65, 84, 160
  secular/sacred, 23, 64, 89, 92, 102, 107, 109, 154–156, 159, 175

Index

skyscraper and, 17, 111–121
Southwest, 16, 26, 127–128
standardization of, 13–14, 16–18, 26, 32, 39, 45, 46, 70, 110, 175, 177–179
timeless, 17, 107, 124, 156, 166, 171
utilitarian, 16, 18, 23, 29, 35–37, 44, 70, 179
vast, 10, 38, 68, 84, 85, 119, 121, 131, 155–157, 160, 165, 175
Species extinction, 1, 8, 11, 22, 172, 173, 185, 190, 191, 201
Stanton, Robert Brewster, 76–77, 84, 85
Stegner, Wallace, 160
Steichen, Edward, 116
Stein, Gertrude, 110–111
Stieglitz, Alfred, 116, 124, 127
Stilgoe, John, 32
Storm Season (novel), 141
Sublime. *See* Natural sublime; Technological sublime
Superfund sites, 30, 44, 63, 127, 132–134, 137, 139, 140, 176–177
Susquehanna River, 15, 35, 90
Suzuki, David, 191–192

Taft, Howard, 58
Tansey, Mark, 167–169
Technical metabolism, 44, 45
Technological sublime
   atomic tests and, 143–144
   defined, 3, 17–18, 23, 111–112, 200
   nationalism and, 8, 123, 171, 189
   natural sublime and, 17–18, 84, 119, 124–125, 160–161, 173, 176
   second creation and, 15–16, 23, 161, 179
   tourism and, 38, 108
   transient, 125–126
   utilitarianism and, 110, 121, 124, 179, 181, 193, 200
Thoreau, Henry David, 19, 40

Tillotson, M. R., 104–105
Time
   circular, 47, 72
   compression of, 37, 97, 159–160, 164
   creationism and, 3–4, 48, 50, 99, 173, 175
   eternal, 12, 17, 88, 124, 156–157, 166 (*see also* Wilderness)
   geologic, 11, 72, 99–100, 156–158, 173, 177, 178, 189
   human, 169, 171, 173, 179, 195
   linear, 47, 73, 125, 155
   photography and, 165–166
Tocqueville, Alexis de, 16, 29, 32
Tourism. *See also* Grand Canyon; Natural Bridge of Virginia; Rainbow Natural Bridge
   aerial, 104
   atomic 143
   automotive, 39, 101–102, 105, 154
   dams and, 83–84
   IMAX film and, 159–160, 163, 164, 179
   nationalism and, 51, 52, 91
   national parks and, 80, 90–92, 99, 100, 103, 104–105, 151–165, 178–179
   Native Americans and, 12, 56–57, 59, 151, 153, 161, 171, 187
   Natural Bridge of Virginia, 48–54, 157
   Niagara Falls, 154
   photography and, 95, 98, 100, 103, 165, 167
   Plutonium National Park, 149
   railroad, 72, 75, 76, 89, 90, 92, 100–101, 124, 178
   Rainbow Bridge and, 57, 59, 61–64
   River Rouge Plant and, 38, 41, 43–44
   skyscraper, 110, 119–120
   utilitarianism and, 160, 171

Tourism (cont.)
  virtual, 164
  wilderness and, 11, 12–13, 26, 180
Toxic waste, 6, 129, 132–133, 145–148, 172
Truman, Harry, 142
Trump, Donald, 175, 187, 198
Tuan, Yi-fu, 132
Tucson, Arizona, 82, 83, 181, 193, 198
Twain, Mark, 70

Udall, Stuart, 139, 180
Uniformitarian theory, 50, 53, 55, 177, 189
Uranium. *See also* Plutonium
  Grand Canyon and, 105, 135–136, 152, 153
  mines, 7, 23, 64, 105, 128, 134–138, 176, 179, 184–185, 187, 196
  radiation from, 136–141, 143, 151
  refinement, 63, 129, 138, 140
  depleted, 143–145
Uranium waste, 64–65, 137–140, 145–147
U.S. Climate Alliance, 200
U.S. Forest Service, 22, 93
U.S. Geological Survey, 63, 107
Utah
  exploration, 74
  federal presence, 128, 184–185, 187
  growth, 16, 67, 175, 178
  irrigation and, 79
  mining and refining, 137–138
  national parks and monuments, 21, 55–56, 184, 187–188
  petroglyphs in, 4–5, 185–187
  radiation pollution, 133, 134, 137, 138, 143, 145
Ute tribe, 73, 74, 185
Utilitarianism. *See also* Mining; Skyscrapers
  anti-landscapes and, 2, 7, 127, 134, 180

Colorado River and, 29, 61, 64, 65, 67, 71, 84, 89, 172
defined, 2–3, 13–18, 26
Grand Canyon and, 92–93, 105, 169
grid and, 13–14, 17–18, 32, 177 (*see also* National grid)
Henry Ford and, 34, 38, 40, 41, 177
Native Americans and, 74, 181
opposing ideas, 2, 7–8, 11, 23, 40, 65, 71, 171, 174, 177, 188
River Rouge and, 27
second creation and, 14–15, 23, 45, 79–80, 83, 172, 174, 175, 177, 179–180, 193
sublime and, 8, 17, 110, 121, 124, 179, 181, 193, 200

Van Dyke, John C., 127, 154–155
Virginia, 11, 18, 51, 200 (*see also* Natural Bridge of Virginia)

Warner, Charles Dudley, 92
Waste Isolation Pilot Plant (WIPP), 145–148, 172
Waters, Frank, 85
Wells, H. G., 123
West Virginia, 174
Wheeler, George Montague, 70–71, 73–74, 77, 84, 90, 99
White Canyon Mill, 63
White Sands Missile Range, 128
Wilderness. *See also* Natural sublime; Nature
  areas, 174–176, 183, 188
  defined, 2–3, 8–9, 11–12, 190
  federal government and, 11, 20, 22
  Native Americans and, 18, 22, 29
  pastoralism, primitivism, and, 8, 10, 18, 20, 171, 174, 175, 187, 191
  politics of, 8, 9, 174–177
  as pre-narrative condition, 171, 175
  problems with, 7, 12–13, 145, 173, 180, 192, 195

Index   269

recreated, 194–195
representations of, 19
spirituality and, 21, 91, 107, 159, 160, 193
sublime and, 2–3, 10, 173, 200
utilitarianism and, 13, 64, 71, 177–178, 193, 194, 196
Wilderness Act, 11, 20, 62
Wildlife
   extinction, 1, 11, 46, 161–162, 173, 179, 185
   Grand Canyon, 161–162, 185
   invasive species, 12, 22, 161–162, 180, 189, 194
   Native Americans and, 5, 6
   nuclear testing and, 7, 145
   pastoralism and, 22
   sanctuaries, 11, 174, 185, 195
   wilderness, 174–175
Williams, Terry Tempest, 185, 192
Wilson, Woodrow, 23, 58
Wohlleben, Peter, 192
Wolfe, Byron, 166–167
Woolworth Building, 110, 112, 115, 116, 117
Worster, Donald, 71, 78
Wright, Orville, 39, 104

Yellowcake, 138, 140
Yellowstone National Park, 184
   compared to Grand Canyon, 12, 89, 91, 94, 99, 102, 151
   eviction of Native Americans, 12, 171
   nationalism and, 2, 10–11, 55, 89, 90, 91
   photography of, 98
   railroads and, 108, 178
Yosemite
   compared to Grand Canyon, 91, 94, 102, 177–178
   eviction of Native Americans, 12, 171
   Hetch Hetchy Valley and, 23
   landscaping of, 20
   nationalism and, 2, 10, 17, 55, 88, 89
   photography of, 98
   sublime and, 20, 51, 52, 124, 177
   tourism, 17, 20–21, 90–91, 124
   Young Earth theory and, 3
Young earth theory, 3, 158, 172
Yuma, 78, 182

Zinke, Ryan, 187
Zion National Park, 26, 185